ECONOMIC POLICY IN ANCIENT INDIA

ECONOMIC POLICY IN ANCIENT INDIA

RAVINDRA NATH

KALPAZ PUBLICATIONS

Delhi- 110052

Economic Policy in Ancient India

Rs. 690

ISBN : 81-7835-581-7

Published in 2007 in India by

Kalpaz Publications
C-30, Satyawati Nagar
Delhi-110052
email : kalpaz@hotmail.com

Laser Type Setting by: Mega Graphics, Delhi
Printed at: Salasar Imaging System, Delhi

Dedication

To

My

Parents

Contents

Preface

The economic policy of ancient India rotates around the goddess Shri, whose other and most popular name is Lakshmi, She is believed to have been holding the reign of wealth or riches as the wife of Lord Vishnu, who maintains the world after its creation by Brahmā. It is natural that he, who is entrusted by Lord Nārāyaṇa, the supreme God, for maintaining the world through out the span of Sristi, must be vested with the power of controlling the physical material by the use of which, the living beings, including the mankind, remain alive. Whether or not Goddess Lakshmi is the spouse of Lord Vishnu, may be the subject-matter of belief, but the control over the physical world which is before us must be running according to the direction of any such divine power which would be governing the same in terms of the norms or rules of the law of Sristi or the divine law.

Lord Brahmā, the creator of the universe, is also the creator of Law of Sristi and the framer of the rules thereunder. Shri Vishnu and His Māyā, the divine power, popularily known as Lakshmi, have to follow the law of Sristi and the rules framed thereunder by Him (Brahmā) for maintaining the world. He and His spouse Lakshmi have no powers to make any ammendment therein for the convenience of implementation of those rules and the divine law of economics. Knowing this aspect of divine law of economics fully well, the sages made provisions in the Shāstras for the worship and praise of Goddess Lakshmi with the chanting of hymns and muttering of prayers. It is believed that the worship and praise of Goddess Lakshmi will come out with good result and the worshipper would be benefited with economic prosperity and glory in his life time.

Our shāstras have made a clear distinction between the sacrifices performed with the desire of eternal-spiritual benefits and those performed for the accomplishment of the worldly or economic desires, the aim or object of a sacrifice which is performed for the economic gains is the pleasure in the present life. The desire of riches does not extend to the next life. Such an economic desire is viewed with the present eyes and is liked to be fulfilled before the same. This notion is fully expressed in the Vedic hymns which are chanted during the performance of such kind of sacrifice.

The Vedic spiritualism, to which our Purāṇas explains, is not aimed at the pleasure of next life only but it brings within its ambit the pleasure of the present life too. The aim of callings to the gods, at the place (Vedi) of sacrifice to accept their shares in the offerings, is the pleasure of the present life through righteous way. Whether the aim be the economic prosperity or the gain of property the principle of righteousness has always been kept in the mind by the worshipper or the sacrificer. It is this principle of which is when adopted produces good fruits and leads the path of salvation, the supreme goal of the human life.

Economic well-being is a worldly truth. It is the wealth which facilitates the performance of a sacrifice. If a king or a sage, who has no wealth in sufficient quantity, he will never be able even to think of any kind of sacrifice, whether it be aimed at prosperity or spiritual benefits. When king Yudhisthir was asked to perform horse-sacrifice by his advisers after the end of the Kurukshetra war, he expressed his declination for that, owing to lack of sufficient quantity of wealth as described in the Ashvamedhaparva of Mahābhārat. A king like Yudhishthir, who never appreciated wealth in his whole life had to submit expressly before that when the question of horse-sacrifice arose before him. He was forced by the circumstances to accept and make use of the riches brought by Arjun and his other brothers in the form of tax collected from the states which surrendered to them or defeated by them. I would not be mistaken, if I mention here that horse-sacrifice is aimed at War-economy and through that the prosperity of the sacrificer and establishing glory, through the same, of various kinds.

It is true that the Vedic philosophy is against the worldly desires and the enjoyment thereof. But at the same place the values and importance of the wealth in the worldly life have been desired. This aspect of Vedic principles is clear in the story of coming into being of Goddess Lakshmi during the course of churning of Milk-sea by the gods and the demons and her praise with the chanting of 'Shri Sukta' by the sages. If a section of sages treat Her as praiseworthy and actually do so, it is apparent from their conduct that they favour Her appearance for the well-being of the people of the world. In the practical worldly life the true value of wealth was, thus, admitted by the conduct of the sages, who engaged themselves in the performance of sacrifice with the expectation of salvation.

The emphasis given in the Shāstras on the donations and the gifts to the Brāhmaṇs in general, and at the time of performance of sacrifice in particular, goes to establish that the wealth is required even to perform the religious rites. Even a simple sacrifice is beyond the reach of a poor or an economically weak person, so the principle through which it has been propagated that 'God is true and the world is untrue' mainly concerns to the Yogis, who are engaged in the concentration of mind. It has no concern with the sages, who engaged themselves in the performance of sacrifice, such sages always recommended or advised to the kings and the individuals to carry on sacrifices according to their capacity and through that achieve prosperity as well as accretion of the wealth. Thus, in the Vedic and Puraṇic godism spiritual and worldly gains both travel simultaneously with full care to each other, provided a righteous path has been followed.

It is surprising to come across that Lord Shiva who is known for leading his life living totally in the state of nature made his seat at Mount Kailash, after completing His austerity at Mount Mandar in the east, a hilly region rich in precious stones and metals. After installing and coronating Kuber as the king of riches and wealth of the said part of middle Himalayas, Lord Shiva himself shifted to that place to make if a capital of His Kingdom and liked to be coronated as Emperor. The story pertaining to this has been incorporated in this book at the proper place. Lord Shiva, has been acknowledged by the learned class as blind donor, perhaps, because of that reason.

According to the Chapter-3 of Āshvamedhikparva of Mahābhārat King Yudhisthir managed to bring riches from that region for the performance of the horse-sacrifice. This historical fact goes to establish that the territory ruled by Lord Shiva was rich in precious stones and other valuable metals.

Further it is a bare fact of the Indian economic history that no king, whether his kingdom located on hilly tract or in the region of forest, has been described as barren one. The one of the causes of his glorious position has always been described as economically based. A description of glory of any state reflects its economic position, whether it be of heaven, Chaitrathvan, kingdom of Kuber, Hastinapur or Ayodhyā. The glory of Lanka has also its base on the gold which was found in abundance there.

On the basis of these worldly facts, the state in ancient India were always remain effortful to achieve economic prosperity within a spell of short period for which various kinds of tax on the tradable articles, lands and the agricultural products were thought proper and justified provided it was levied reasonably with in the paying capacity of the payers.

It cannot be said with certainty that Goddess Lakshmi, how far, favoured war economy as a righteous source of state prosperity or income. But it came into practice among the society of kings in India in the very beginning. When general human population took a turn into a political society, the stateism came into existence and from then big states always favoured economic war for the sake of developing their kingdom, because of the fact that it costed nothing to the subjects directly. In the present time war is considered to be an economic burden on the people the country which engages itself in the warfare.

According to a description in the Chapters-52-53 of Virātparva of the Mahābhārat the state of Hastinapur attacked over Virātnagar for the sake of taking away its cows which were in large number. To make a mention of that event here is to bring to light that the economic war was also resorted to off and on by the Indian states in the past. None of the reputed Brāhmaṇas ever expressed his views against the said action of Hastinapur which was not apparently justified from any viewpoint. It gives an indication, therefore, that during the Krishna's period an economic war became a tradional one. The learned class too became accustomed of those wars.

So in the state economy of ancient India the strict principles of righteousness were being ignored in certain circumstances, which was neither good in general, nor beneficial to the state ignoring such principles to satisfy its ego of material greediness. It was that greediness which ruined not only king Dhritrāshtra and his descendants but also so many others states of the then Asia.

The gods never favoured any such policy of economic growth. The main cause of enemity between gods and their step brothers Daityas who were in favour of uplifting their economic position by the means of war. It is also a historical fact that gods never attacked any state for the economic well-being of their own state. They never showed any interest in taking away of the properties of their step brothers' state as and when they (gods) defeated them (Daityas).

The present book has been written on the subject of policy if state economy in the form of a reference-book to facilitate the scholars, who are desirous of persuing the research on it. Stories relating to the economic growth finding place in the Puraṇas and the Hymns of Vedas on this subject have been reproduced in this book. So that the scholars may find free hand to derive conclusions according their viewpoint. The comments of the author wherever given are of general character and do not reflect his angle of vision in the citations.

It is hoped that this book will fulfil the outstanding need of the scholars for long. The subject matter of the book is so divided in the chapters that none would face any difficulty in its study. But the judgement of a writer's work is always in the hands of the readers and the scholars. They are best judge of the success or otherwise of the writer's labour and study on the subject. I had left the idea of writing any more book after completing my work on 'Arya Dharma Key Tattva'. As the fate of a person is never in the hands of concerned one, so it happened to me also. I was offered to write a reference book on this subject in the month of October last year by Dr. Bharat Jhunjhunwala, a well known economist. As I came in his contact for the first time, I accepted his offer with due respect.

Without caring the age factor and the disease which trouble me every now and then, I have done my labour best to complete the book with in a minimum possible time by the grace and blessings of Lord Chitragupta and Lord Shiva. I am thankful to Dr. Bharat Jhunjhunwala, who has taken utmost interest in the preparation of the manuscript and has given valuable suggestions wherever needed for the proper placing of the stories. The printers and publishers also deserve my thanks that took its publication with no hesitation and placed the book in the hands of readers.

Ravindra Nath

reach of cereals because he worships cereal as that of Brahma. O God (Nārad asked to Sanat Kumar) whether there is anything greater than cereal? Please tell me now that. (6/9/1-2).

Replying the above question sage Sanat Kumar tells in the tenth sub-chapter to the Chhāndogyopnishad as follows—

Water is greater than cereal. Owning to this when there is no proper rainfall, the soul gets troubled that the output of cereal will decrease and when there is sufficient rainfall then by thinking so that the production of cereal will be adequate, soul becomes glad. What this earth is, it is water in the physical form and that what the space, sun, mountain, god and man, animals and birds, grasses, vegetation, lagged (creatures), and insects and flys and the living bodies to the extent of ants, all are water in the physical form. Therefore, you worship to the water. One, who worship water as that it is Brahma achieves all the desires and gets satisfaction. So much the water reaches he reaches to that extent by will because he worships water as that It is Brahma. O God! Whether anything is greater than water? (Yes,) There is greater than water. O God, exhort me that. (6/10/1-2)

As the dialogue between Nārad and Sanat Kumar is long on the other subjects cutting short by taking the extract of the same to the extent of our need it is said that in the said two sub-chapters of chapter six, the exhorting sage has thrown light on the subject of utility of cereal and water for the existence and the activities of the body and the soul. By bringing to light the values of both the primary things of Indian economy, the sage wants to establish those things as the foundation stones of the economic world. The entire economy of the human beings or the society is standing on that foundation. Every economic progress is meaningless if the human world has no cereal and water on the earth. This is the reason why the wasteful consumption of both the things is treated as sin.

It is also clear from the above discourse that when the sages preferred to express their thoughts on the issue of water-cereal economy they kept in the mind that where water supplies energy to the self or soul, at the same place cereal supplies energy to the body. When both the things join hands with each other the body and the soul get strength for proper functioning by the right manner in the right directions. This line of thinking of the ancient Indian scholars or economists paved the way to initiate and develop an economy based on the joint footings of water and cereal.

The economy based on flesh-fish-liquor also has its root in the water-cereal economy. Where the liquor is the another form of water (juice), the flesh-fish are the naturally processed form of cereal or vegetation. So when it is said that the real economy has its root in the water and cereal, the expression is based on scientific principles. The principle of strengthening the dweller (soul or self) and dwelling (body) jointly by water and cereal, respectively, is also clear.

How the principle of our economy reached so deep as to join hands with the scientific principles is worthwhile to be examined here. The Chhāndogyopnishad throws light on this subject also. The same is like this:—

The eaten cereal is of three kinds. Its physical form becomes night soil, the middle part gets converted into flesh and the part which is too minute goes to the mind. (Likewise) the drunk water (also) gets three form. Its physical form becomes urine, the middle part gets converted into blood and that its minute part goes to the soul. (In the same way) the other things, (ghee etc. which generate heat in the body) which when turn to take there forms. Its physical part takes the form of bone, the middle part becomes lubricant and the minute part gets converted into speech. It is only by this reason that the mind is full of cereal, soul (Praṇ) is full of water and that speech is full of heat or splendour. (6/5/1 to 4).

As such the economy of ancient India is based on the deep study of the scholars on this subject in relation to the body, soul, mind and the speech. They have not caught hold of the subject in the midway for the purpose of their study. The subject of the economy is not one which be studied only in reference to the outwardly thing of human use or need. It has a link with the body, soul, mind and speech as well as the other sense organs of the man. The above discourses are the result of study of such link between them interse and that of the food material and the drinks. The economy of ancient India before coming into operation had to pass through such examinations and investigations in depth.

Fast : Its Link With Economic Stability

There is a close relation between the fast and the economic stability of the family or the state. When the members of a family observe fast one or two days in a month the cereals or the food stuffs to be consumed on those days are saved for future use. Moreover, the organs of the body which are engaged in digesting the food material get rest at least a day in a fortnight. The logic behind this is that a fast is based on the natural principle of work and rest. Many abdomen disorders or problems are solved by keeping fast without the aid of any medicine.

These matters were also the subject of discussion in the remote past among the scholars. The Nārād-Purāṇa throws light on this subject.

Nāradpurāṇa - Uttarbhāg

King Māndhātā of Ayodhyā asks from sage Vasishtha the ways and means for extinction of the effects of sins done in the life in these words:–

Kindly let me know in what ways the sins can be burnt. (1/6 I Part)

In reply sage Vasishtha says–

O great King! Listen, in what fire a sin which is wet and dry gets burnt leaving no residue. A person, who after controlling the sense organs keep a fast on the day of Ekadāshi (the eleventh day of a fortnight) and worships Lord Vishnu together with Amalaba fruits, takes bath and keeps himself awakened in the night, his sins vanish in the same way as a thief takes way the movables. (1/6 II part to 9).

O great King! Ekādashi fast is such a fire in which sins of past hundred lives burn as that of fuel. (1/10)

There is no other way for a man to extinct sins and make the body pious as that of Ekādashi fast. (1/11)

O King! Sin remains in the body of a man to the extent of the day he does not keeps fast on Ekādashi. (1/12)

Thousands of horse-sacrifice and the hundred of Rajsuya-sacrifice cannot claim equality with the sixteenth art of an Ekādashi-fast. (1/13)

O great! Whichever sins are done by the eleven sense-organs, all vanishes by keeping fast on Ekādashi. (i/14)

There is nothing vanisher of sin like that of an Ekādashi fast. Even fast kept on the day of Ekādashi deceitfully it does not allow the presence of Yama. (1/15)

The fast on Ekādashi provides heaven, salvation, state, son, wife, and keep the body disease free. (1/16)

What the Nāradpurāṇa depicts about the result of keeping fast on the day of Ekādashi in both the fortnights of a month appears imaginary having no relevancy with the economy of a family an individual or a state. But when our study goes deep in it we find that what is said in the slokas cited above mainly concern with the economic problems. If is the economic problem which generates criminal or wrongful activities in the mind to be resorted to as solutions thereof. When a man keeps fast his mind becomes fresh and the bad effect of the foodstuffs is completely washed out. The person gets rid of the bondage of ill will. Moreover, one begins to try to live on righteous method for earning his livelihood. When a person thereafter takes food by breaking the fast good sense prevails in the mind. When this fast is kept by all the family members the economic scarcity of the concerning family is solved to some extent, so is the case of a state. A statewide fast of two days in a month may bring economic stability. At the time when the reproduction of cereal at a mass scale was not in practice by way of agriculture, the principle of fast played important role in solving the economic problems. Over and above the fast provides a chance to regain the last energy by the body for further activities.

Duties of Householders Towards Society

What are the duties of a new entrant in the household affairs have been laid down the Yajyavalkyasmriti.

Yajyavalkyasmriti

Sage Yajyavalkya says thus:–

One should never wish to earn wealth either from improper place or by improper means, or from the persons who are against the self study. He should be always satisfied (from his earnings). (1/6/129)

He again says–

Getting before sunrise one should think over his own interest. According to the capacity one should not leave the performance of righteousness (Dharma), earning wealth and enjoyment or desire at the proper time. (1/115)

Education, deeds (good), age, brother and a richman are to be honoured according to the order. (1/116 - I part)

One should part with cereal and water in favour of manes and men. Make self study everyday. But do not cook food for himself only. (11/104)

Boy, good married woman, old, lady in family way, diseased (sick), girl, guest and servants should be given food, with first priority, then the spouses should take the remaining portion. (1/105)

Guests should be provided with the meal in order of class (Varna) according to the capacity. If any guest comes in the evening he should also be given honour with sweet words, place, cot and water. (1/107)

Beggars and bachelors (Brahmachārīs) should be given alms with honour. Visiting (the house) in time, the friends, relations and brethren should be provided with the meal. (1/108).

The above direction given by sage Yajyavalkya are mainly intended for proper distribution of wealth. Another view is that a householder does not earn wealth or cereal etc for himself only. The maintenance of the entire society rests on his shoulders.. It is expected that he will not become poor by providing meals to the needy and the guests who visit his place. Such a theory of social distribution of wealth is a unique thing and is present even to-day in the Indian society.

The Fundamental principle of Indian economy is that nothing is earned for self. In the earning of every body even of the share of his family members as well as guests is there. The most valuable feature is that majority of the Indian society believe in this principle with full heart, the burdensome honour to the guests has no meaning.

Further, Sage Yajyavalkya gives emphasis over the observance of Dharma, Artha and the Kām at the proper time. It means that he is of the opinion that these three elements are the constituents of ancient Indian economy and one has to follow the rules pertaining to them for success in the life.

Sacrifice and The Economic Progress

The wealth of a king i.e. state is primarily meant for sacrifices. Further, the philosophy behind a sacrifice is that when a king would perform the same he will give donations and gifts to the priests and poors. In this way state-wealth would be distributed among the people. The tendency of accumulation of wealth would also be under control. Most of the ancient sages did not accept the donations of wrong doer kings. For them sacrifice was the good sacred means for giving donations to great souls. The principles of such a philosophy have well been depicted in the Mahābhārat Anushāsanparva as a dialogue between Bhishma and Yudhisthir.

Mahābhārat Anushāsanparva

King Yudhisthir wanted to know which one of the donation and sacrifice was eternally beneficial after the death from Prince Bhishma. To bring his curiocity at rest he put the question to him as follows:–

O Bhārat (Bhishma)! Which one out of donation and sacrifice provides spiritual benefit after the death? Whose result is said to be great? Which Brāhmaṇa is to be given in donation and when? And how and when a sacrifice should be performed? I want to know these things in reality. Ȯ learned! Tell this curious person the law pertaining to the donation in detail. (61/1-2).

O grand father! Which one donation is the cause of well-being; whether the donation given at the sacrifice place or out of that place being inspired by hearty kindness? (61/3).

Replying to king Yudhisthir's questions Prince Bhishma said—

O Son! A Kshatriya has to take up cruel work. Therefore, sacrifice and donation are the means to make him pious. (61/4)

Great persons do not accept the donations (ordinary) of a sinner king. He should, therefore, perform sacrifices by giving sufficient gifts. (61/5)

If great men accept his donation, then the king should give him donation everyday with full devotion. Because donation given with devotion is the good means of purity of the self. (61/6)

You give donations to satisfy Brāhmaṇas, who are having good conduct, truthful, austere, have good knowledge of Vedas, friendly to all, and of saintly nature. (61/7)

If they will not accept your donation then it would not be sacred to you, so you perform sacrifice with tasty food and sufficient gifts for such great men. (61/8)

By giving donation to the person who perform sacrifices you find yourself shares of sacred results of sacrifice and donation. You always honour the Brāhmaṇas who are engaged in sacrifices. By doing this you will get a part of sacred results of the sacrifice. (61/9)

Such donations of the Kshatriyas provide more good result than Rajasuya and horse-sacrifices. (61/15-II part)

From the above discourses it is clear that the donation and sacrifice are at par in the matters of sacred result, but when a donation is accepted by a great soul i.e. Brāhmaṇa of high conduct. As a king has to do right and wrong both in the public administration sacrifices have been recommeded for them to perform as the regular ceremonies with sufficient donations and gifts according to their capacity or by righteous collection of taxes from rich persons, according to Prince Bhishma.

The persons, who are rich and are capable to pay tax comfortably only their money or the money collected by liberal means should be utilized in the sacrifice and not by utilizing the tax collected by putting the subject in trouble. (61/23)

Thus by all means a king should assure himself that the money to be utilized in the performance of a sacrifice has been obtained by righteous means. The object of a sacrifice being spiritual benefit after death, so that the next life be comfortable and pleasureful, the sacrificer should be cautious about the source of money. The other thing to be kept in mind that no pious Brāhmaṇa or saintly person be dissatisfied by his share in the donations and gifts. His dissatisfaction may cause harm to the sacrificer spiritually. But such a faith has a worldly meaning also and that is the economic well-being of the persons engaged in the search of knowledge and the propagation of righteous path to the mankind. They, being non-earning member of the society, should be financially hononoured like that. Such a rule of law attached to a religious rite is based on social justice. There can be no social harmony in a state if its economic policy is framed only to benefit the rulers and not the ruled. For the achievement of all the goodness in the life time as well as economic prosperity of the concerning state sacrificial ceremonies should be performed at the regular intervals. So that the learned class of the society may get chances to be honoured properly. The sacrifices were the proper ceremonies during the performance of which the learned person found time to express their knowledge publically. The wealth used for the performance of sacrifices and donated as shares of gods attain the divine character.

Salvation Through Sacrifice

A sacrifice being the good, the wealth utilized for the performance of that attains divine character as said earlier. But how the sacrificer achieves salvation by performing sacrifices is a wonderful concept of the Hindu Shāstras. It may be a faith only but a story regarding that is available in the Bhāgwatpurāṇa.

Bhāgwatpurāṇa

There is a description is the Bhāgwatpurāṇa how Nābhāg a son of Nabhag the Son of Vaivasw at Manu acquired wealth as gift given by the Āngirās in lieu of his (Nābhāg's) services in completing a sacrifice which was being performed by them. The story runs as follows:–

O Parikshit! says Sukadeva, Nābhāg was the son of Nabhag who was son of Manu. When he returned back after observing Brahmacharya for a long period, then his elder brothers gave him, though younger yet learned, their father in his share. (9/4/1)

He (Nābhāg) asked his brothers — Brothers! What have you people given to me in share? Then they replied, We are giving the father to you in your share. He told his father, 'my elder brothers have given you father in my share'. The father told, 'Son! do not agree with them: (9/4/2)

Look! The great Āngirā Brāhmaṇas are performing a very good sacrifice at this time. But my learned son! They commit errors on every sixth day (9/4/3).

You go to those great souls and let them know two Suktas concerning to Vaishvedeva. When they would be going to the heaven they would then give the remaining wealth of the sacrifices to you. (9/4/4)

Therefore, you go to them. He did it as told by his father. In return the Āngirā Brāhmaṇas too gave him the entire remaining wealth and proceeded to the heaven. (9/4/5)

The above story throws light on the question whether or not a sacrificer makes himself able to proceed to heaven by performing a sacrifice even though of a special kind. As the result of the sacrifice performed by the Āngirās was in affirmative, it may be said that it is a means to attain salvation. But one thing must be remembered, as said in the foregoing pages, that the wealth which is to be utilized in performing the sacrifice must have been acquired by righteous means and only that wealth has a divine character.

It would be worthwhile to mention here that the above story of Āngirās going to heaven by performing a special kind of sacrifice finds place in the two Suktas of Rigveda, Book ten, Sukta sixty one and sixty two (10/61 and 62). The sage of these Suktas being Nābhānedistha Mānavā and the name Āngirās appearing in meters (Richas) it is presumed that the learned scholars of Vedas would have taken a view that the same pertain to the aforesaid story.

So it can be said that the Vedic sages were also of the opinion that the sacrifices of special nature were helpful in achieving the eternal goal. As huge quantity of wealth was required to accomplish such sacrifices the same was given the divine character even by them. The logic behind the notion of Artha i.e. wealth was that it should be earned righteously mainly for the purposes of sacrifice and things which remain unused as oblation etc. should be consumed by the earner–sacrifice. It was that logic which prevailed upon the learned persons to forcefully depict that only remainders of a sacrifice be used as food material.

The object of economic prosperity in India in the olden days was not only to uplift the way of life but also to equip oneself for the performances of various kinds of sacrifices to appease the gods and through those ceremonies to attain salvation. When the cereals and other products of vegetations as well as products of cows were used as oblations to the fire assuming the same as carrier of shares to the various aimed gods. Those things turned to take the character of divine ones, unless any kind of divinity prevailed in the things which were being used as oblation to the fire gods could never accept it.

Apparently offering of oblation to the sacrificial fire was nothing but to cause burning of the things which were earned with hard labour and trouble. The person who earned the things must have developed some kinds of attachment with them. But inspired by eternal benefits emotionally the hard earned wealth was used as oblation and to part with it in the form of donation, gifts and food to the Brāhmaṇas, guests and poors invited to witness the ceremonies. Some kinds of religious and social duties were attached to the wealthy persons and kings to remain active for the sake of sacrificial ceremonies, so that there might not develop attachment to their riches.

With such intentions in mind the saints and sages always inspired to the kings, landlords and businessmen to perform sacrifices at regular intervals. So that economic harmony be maintained in the society of their locality, and through that eternal benefits be obtained after death. The philosophy that the country of Bharat, that is, India as a land of deeds evolved in the society of sages and seers as well as in the learned class. The poverty as a curse was, infact, treated not only with a view to resolve economic problems but also with a view not to remain away from such religious rites, which were helpful in getting spiritual benefits after death. The notion of Indian economy was that every individual should be capable to perform at least simple sacrifices to achieve the eternal goal.

Even a poor person should try to earn money for the sake of sacrifice even by begging. Most of the Brāhmaṇas to the past resorted to begging for the purpose of simple sacrifices and they took their meal after providing (Bhog) to their aimed god. Through that they expected salvation and getting of the bondage of poverty.

Economy According to the Ages

There are four ages or Yugas according to the Hindu Shāstras. It has been assumed that the long spell of a given period cannot remain static either in the matters of thoughts or in the matters of economic growth. The line of thinking of ancient Indian scholars being different, they assumed that in the beginning the people were pious minded in thought, intention and deeds. They were truthful by mind, words and deeds. So the beginning of time cycle was fully good. The first quarter of a given period is called Krit as Satya age (full of truth), the second quarter was also good but one step less, which means that the society became twenty-five present corrupt, that period is called Tretā age (Triage), the third quarter which is called Dwāpar age was two steps less than Truth age. It reflects that fifty per cent of the society became corrupt, the fourth or the remaining quarter begins with one leg, that is to say that three legs of this quarter already vanished. It means that the society has become seventy five per cent corrupt. These are the wordly meaning of the terms. Even though such meanings of the respective names of the four yugas reflect the socio-economic condition of the society to a great extent, yet the texts describe the said conditions separately of each ages in detail.

Matsyapurāṇa

In the Matsyapurāṇa the four ages, which are under study

here have been described at two places. In the chapter one hundred sixty five of the said Purāṇa a brief sketch of each yuga has been given. Whereas, in the chapters-142, 144 and 145 detail description of each yugas has been given. Even the periods of change-over have been described to make the readers fully aware of the conditions, socially and economically, as well as how the changes occur in the society effecting the mind and heart of the people in respect of the economic growth too.

A general description of the four ages in the chapter -165 of the Matsyapurāṇa is thus–

O son of sun (king Satyavrat)! the period of Krit age (Satyayuga) is said to be of four thousand divine years and its evening is said to be of two times i.e. counted in century (eight hundred years). (165/1)

In that age religion, that is, duties or righteousness remain standing on the four legs and that unrighteousness is of one fourth. All the men born in that age are engaged in the performance of their duties and also the saints born in that age follow their path. (165/2)

Brāhmaṇas follow religious path and the Kshatriyas (kings) follow political duties or laws. Vaishyas are engaged in agricultural work, whereas, Shudras are engaged in the state and individual services. (165/3)

At that time truth, purity and righteousness increase in all the fields. All the persons follow the path shown by good persons and praise that. (165/4)

O king! The conducts of Krityuga are found in every living being (human) whether they belong to Brāhmaṇas or to the lower Varṇas. (165/5)

After describing the social conditions of Krityuga, the conditions of Tretā age is described thus.

Thereafter, comes the Tretā-age, the length of the period which is of three thousand divine years and that the evening of this age is said twice the period in century (i.e. six hundred years). (165/6)

In this age the righteousness has three legs and the unrighteousness has two legs. The religion of Treta is said to be based on truth and of good qualities. (165/7)

There is no doubt that there comes deformity in the conduct and duties in the Tretā yuga pertaining to the Varṇas. Due to the entrance of the badness in the duties of four Varnas their counterpart Āshramas are also effected by the same and get weak. (165/8)

It is the wonderful feature of the God-created Tretā age. (165/9 I part)

From here God began to describe the salient feature of the Dwapar-age which is as follows:-

O king, son of sun! The Dwāpar-age is of two thousand divine years. As said, there are four hundred year in its evening. (165/10)

O son of sun! In that age all the (human) beings become economic minded being effected by Rājas quality. All the persons born in that age are inactive and mean minded. (165/11)

The religion (duties) has only two legs in that age and that unrighteousness get three legs. Thus by gradual change the (righteous) duties completely vanish in the Kali age. (165/12)

During the course of change in the Dwāpar age people's faith in Brāhmaṇa also vanishes and they keep away from fast and other religious rites. (165/13)

At that time there enters cruel Kali age in which as said there are one thousand divine years with two hundred years as evening. (165/14)

The effectiveness of nonrighteousness increases during that age and it reaches the extent of four feet. The religious life remains upto the extent of only one quarter. The persons born during that age have lust of desire with no austerity. (165/15)

None of the persons born during the Kali age is truthful or good natured or truth speaking. They are all non-believer in God, but expresses himself as devotee of God. (165/16)

People become proudly having no affection to each other. All the Brāhmaṇas begin to observe the conduct of Shudras (by adopting services for livelihood). O son of sun! There occurs changes in the Kali age and by the end of that age their varnas become doubtful (because of no proper identity). (165/17-18).

A similar description of four ages are available in the other chapters of this Purāṇa. It is no use to repeat the same in this context. But the process of change-over which affects the very nature of mankind is given here.

As the Krit-age and the Tretā age are similar in nature and deeds, their salient features are not to be described distinctly. (142/37)

The information which is apparent from the above description is that there is no change over in the basic character of mankind when the age of Truth is changed into that of the age of Tretā. They continued to observe the same religious rites even for the economic growth and prosperity to which they were performing in the age of Truth, even after its end. But when Dwāpar-age begins after the end of Tretā even then no sign of change is visible. The description of the Matsyapurāṇa regarding this is thus–

In the beginning of Dwāpar age the nature of people remains the same as that of Tretā-age. But when the effect of Dwāpar prevails completely then the nature of Tretā age is switched over. (144/2)

At that time attachment, impatience, business, war, indefinity of principles, merger of Varṇas, exchange of deeds (of various varnas), begging, devastation, difference in self and others, penal administration, proudness, jealousy, rudeness, use of force as well as Rājas and Tāmas qualities–increase. (144/3 to 5 - I part).

More clearly badness becomes effective on the nature and the reasons of man with the passage of time during the age of Dwāpar. It gradually increases with the passage of time. At the time of end of this age bad qualities reach at a considerable height as said in the following sloka:-

At that time people lack the righteousness. In the likewise condition (of society) its evening comes. (144/28)

At the time of end of Dwāpar-age there remains only indication of goodness and only then enters the Kali age. (144/29 II part)

During the Kali age Vedas though present, loses their entity and that sacrifices, which are the only cause of religious rite, vanishes. (144/47)

It is clear from the above Purāṇic depictions as to how the norms of various ages get changed gradually in accordance with the cycle of time. But one thing unique has been revealed, from the above description which is the decreasing value of goodness by effecting the nature and behaviour of mankind. As such this is the process of growth of corrupt practices in the earning of wealth. The Hindu Shāstras are of the view that the root cause of growing malpractices during the age in which we are living is the effect of time. The entire mankind is completely in the grip of Kali age.

Mahābhārat - Anushāsanparva

But the turning of mind from goodness to badness can be controlled well by performing yogas and by concentration of mind. Our Shāstras are not passive spectators of the time cycle. Apart from the above solutions to remain away from the affects of time, muttering of names of God has also been said as good solution. The same has been described in the Mahā bhārat Anushāsanparva as follows in a dialogue between Shiva and Pārvati–

O Goddess! Setting the mind strongly is the sign of accomplishment of Yoga. Therefore, mind should always be kept stable effortfully. Skin, nose, tongue, ear and eye should be detached from their subjects. Consolidating all the five sense organs (at one place), the learned person should place them in mind. (Page 6017 (b) of Gita Press Ed.)

One whose mind is engaged in the concentration thus, the heart of such a yogi becomes glad soon. (P. 6018-b)

A person who is engaged in performing yogas gets rid of the effect of badness of Kali age. It is no good to submit to the time cycle. A Karma yogi moulds the time toward goodness by resorting to the concentration.

2

Divine Character of Wealth

It is not only the movable and immovable beings which have been created by the supreme divine power but also the cereals and other kinds of wealth. The material world can not run without wealth. It is a necessity for all the living beings whether it be in the form of food or otherwise. But it has been the general thinking of the ancient Indian scholars that the wealth being a worldly material creates obstruction in the way of spiritual benefits. Such a thinking is partially true and that too in respect of the sages who perform yogas and observe concentration and lead their lives in the state of nature. Even if they live in total barrenness, they take food to remain alive. So it can be said that there is some natural relation between the plants and the man.

Prashnopanishad

This aspect has well been explained in the Prashnopanishad in the form of a dialogue between sage Bhāradvāj's son Sukesh and great soul Pippalād on the issue of as to who is the god having knowledge of sixteen arts of creation. The exchange of thoughts went on between them are as follows–

Sukesha son of Bhāradvāj asked from the said renowned sage (Pippalād) – O God! A prince named Hiranyanābh, resident of Kaushal, (state) come to me (one day) and asked this question– O Bharadvāj (son of Bharadvāj)! Who is the man of sixteen arts? Then I told that prince that I did not know him. If I had known him then why not I told you: That man definitely perishes who tells a lie. Therefore, I am not able to tell a lie. That prince mounting on chariot (then) went away. I am asking the same question to you. Where is that man? (6/1)

That (sage) told him, O affectionate! He is in this body, from which these sixteen arts evolve. (6/2)

(Then) he thought by whose getting out I would be gone out and by whose entrance I would have come into being? (6/3)

He (first of all) created soul, thereafter, devotion, then sky, wind, heat, water and earth respectively, then mind, thereafter (evolved) sense organs, then cereal, semen, austerity, meters (mantras), deeds, world and (in the last) names (of the things so created). (6/4)

The aforesaid is the order of creation as described by the great sage Pippalād. In this order of creation cereal was created after the sense organs and before semen, the fluid which causes rebrith by cohabitation. An austere or even a householder should know this order of creation for acquiring on-ward knowledge of creative power of god Nārāyaṇa, who is known in the society of saints as a powerful personage of sixteen arts. He was so named because of the sixteen creations to accomplish the Sristi in the early days.

But latter on that creative divine power was named as Lord Brahmā by personifying the same. Not only this after creation there arose the problems of sustenance of the living word. Even non-living beings required some energy in them to remain in existence for indefinite period that is to say till the end of Kalpa and the divine power which so imagined was called Vishṇu. Thus with the march of human society ahead there evolved the concept of sustenance of the world. The matter did not end here. The human intelligence carried on thinking on the events which were virtually happening in the world in the form of death of living beings as well as destruction of the non-living beings for instance food material and other consumable things. It was thought that such happenings were the result of the activities of the destructive divine forces, when it was personified it was given the name Rudra (Shiva or Shankar). It was called Rudra because it resulted in weaping. All the three divine powers are jointly called trinity of gods. In the Māndukopanishad those three forces of the nature are defined as the limbs of Om.

Mādukopanishad

It has been explained in the Māndukopanishad in this way–

All that are seen or in existence are Brahma, which is the great soul. Whether it is Braḥma or soul, it has four feet. (meter-2)

That which is said four footed soul being described in the form of letter Om which has three parts, i.e. Aa, Ou, and Ma. Accordingly Brahma has three feet only. (meter-8).

The said three parts of single letter Om (ॐ) have been explained in the Nāradpurāṇa which represent Brahmā, Vishnu and Shiva or Rudra respectively, (i.e. Aa, Ou and Ma).

Nāradpurāṇa-1

In has been said in this Purāṇa that a person must have knowledge of the three forces of the nature, viz. creative, sustenative and destructive so that he may earn, preserve and consume the things needed consciously. It has been explained like this–

O sages! Now I am telling you another kind of concentration, listen, which is in the world like shower of nector to the persons who are burnt (by worldly problems). (33/153)

The great pleasure Nārāyaṇa should be remembered as a unique voice like half vowel placed over Om (ॐ) i.e. Praṇava. (33/154)

The 'Akār' i.e. letter Aa (of Om) is the form of Brahma, the 'Ukar' i.e. letter 'Ou' represents Vishnu and that 'Makar' i.e. letter 'Ma' represents Rudra (Shiva) as well as half vowel i.e. point with moon (ँ) is the form of Nārāyaṇa called great Brahma. (33/155)

All these three letters are called representatives of Brahmā, Vishnu and Shiva and that O Brāhmaṇa! The joint form (the Om) denotes great Brahma. (33/156)

Great Brahma is the meaning and Praṇava (Om) is the word. O Brāhmaṇa! Their relationship interse as meaning and word is only to make it understandable. (33/157)

In fact there is indivisible relation between the two. One who worships the Praṇava by way of muttering gets rid of sins and by being engaged in the concentration one achieves salvation. (33/158)

Thus it is clear from the above explanation that Brahmā, Vishnu and Shiva, are the three divine powers of Almighty God Nārāyaṇa which remain active from the beginning of the Kalpa or Sristi i.e.– from the day of creation till the day of dissolution or destruction thereof. It is not merely the matter of belief or faith but is scientically true that there must be such natural forces which may help in the creation of thing, maintenance of the so created thing; and that destroy it when the same becomes obsolete. Virtually all these three forces are present more or less in every person. That is the reason why he or she makes any thing of his or her choice, preserve it and neglect it when not needed. Likewise wealth or riches are earned, preserved and consumed by a person. Had these forces not present in the body of a person nobody would have been in a position to earn his or her livelihood and that life of a man would have been similar to that of an animal. The art of reproduction, the creativity, and preservation for future use would have never come to light even in the mankind. So it can well be said that the divine powers, which are represented by Brahmā, Vishnu and Shiva are severally as well as jointly present in the body of human being to make the life pleasurefully comfortable and the world meaningful.

Moreover, the story teller Sanak, a great sage of repute has explained the basis of the creation of the above three powers in the form of trinity in the chapter three of Nāradpurāṇa.

Nāradpurāṇa-2

In the beginning of creation Vishṇu (Nārāyaṇa), who is in the form of world, selflighted, divided the three qualities and that on the basis of those qualities created trinity (of gods). (3/3)

That ancient God first of all created Prajāpati (Brahmā) from the right part of his body for accomplishing the work of creation. O sages! (He) then created Vishṇu from the left part of his body for sustenance there after (He) created Shiva from the middle part of his body for the destruction. Someones say that god (Vishnu) as Shiva and someones say to Him as Vishṇu and others always say Him Brahmā the truth. (3/4-5)

That great or supreme power is vested in Vishnu (i.e. Nārāyaṇa in true sense), which is called in the form of present or non-present, knowledge or non-knowledge. (3/6).

When the world is felt different from Vishṇu (Nārāyaṇa) then non-knowledge is to be understood as effective which is the cause of various troubles. (3/7)

It is to be understood here that in the efforts of the economic prosperty or well-being whatever action is done it is the act of creative force present in the body of man. His action is like that of Brahmā, whatever he thinks to find out ways and means to achieve his goal in the form of earning or reproduction or production is like that of austerity of Brahmā which He performed before taking up of creation. The intelligence of a man when transformed into action brings out the desired results.

When it is said that Vishnu, that is Nārāyaṇa created Lord Brahmā from the right organ of His body, it means that creative power is present in the said part. The right part should always be used righteously for building anything or for earning of wealth. As Brahmā never uses foul means while making creation so is to be done by a man. He should never adopt any foul means in the efforts of earning. These are the directives of our Shāstras.

Likewise the earnings and production or reproduction of a thing should be preserved by righteous means; it is the work of left organ of our body. As Lord Vishnu was created by God Nārāyaṇa by using his left organ, who possesses the power of sustenance, so a man should preserve the things for future use. Otherwise he would be put in troubles. The other meaning of the right and the left organs is the parallel activities regarding accretion of wealth and its preservation from loss etc. to be done.

The middle part of the body of Nārāyaṇa which is said to be the place of origin of Lord Shiva is meant, in the context of economic growth, that it bears the risk of destruction or physical loss all the time so it should be used or consumed properly before it vanishes. Keeping this aspect of risk in view ascetics or austeres never liked collection of food stuffs or other things for many days to come.

Vrihadāranyakopanishad

Where the Prashnopnishad deals with the science or order of creation based on scientific principles and that the cereal is one of the basic elements so created by God, the Vrihadāranyakopnishad depicts that it is a creation of the basic elements by applying science and art. Both the theories of Upanishads are complementary to each other. Their object being different, it appears that whatever Vrihadāranyakopnishad describes it is onward description of creation of cereals by God. The creator being the same the divine character of cereal is apparent.

So far as developing nature of 'Om' is concerned, no cereal can be developed as seed of plant with the development of 'Om'. The philosophy is that it was Om which developed in three forms, viz, god, soul and nature. When nature came into the existence and the creation of earth became a reality, then the developing tendency of earth became active the plants of various kinds grew up from within that. The plants of cereal were among them.

Therefore, it can be said that apart from the desire of God regarding creation of plants and trees there are some natural forces which help Him by their inner activities for onward creation, development and reproduction to cause the created elements or things for remaining in the existence for indefinite period or till the end of Sristi. In the context of evolution of cereals the depiction of Vrihadāranyakopnishad is worth to be cited here which is as follows–

Father (Prajapati Brahmā) created seven (kinds of) cereals by his deeds and (applying) science, from amongst them one (kinds of) cereal is general; two (kinds of) cereal He distributed to the gods; three He possessed for himself; one (kind of) cereal He gave to animals. Within that (cereal) there includes, those who breath and those who donot breath. Why the cereals donot perish even by taken as food material? He, who knows the imperishable characteristic of this (i.e. cereal), take it by mouth. That is received by gods and enjoys nectar. In this regard these are the slokas (i.e. Mantras).(1)

It is known that father (Brahmā) produced cereals by (applying) His knowledge and deeds. There is one general of those cereals. In other words, this is what taken as food stuff is its general cereal. One, who is attached to this is not away from sin, because this cereal is mixed. Two cereals which He gave to gods are (one as) an oblation of fire and (the other as) an offering of food to all created beings. Therefore, a household man offers an oblation to the fire and a portion of daily food to the gods. Some others so say that two cereals of gods are (one as) appearance of new moon and the (other as) full moon, therefore, these (two) should not be performed with any desire. A cereal, given to animals, is milk. Men and animals first of all take milk to remain alive, therefore a newly born baby is made one lick of ghee or breast sucking is caused, and a newly born calf is called now eating grass. Those, who breath or do not do, they all, exist by these two (methods). Therefore, it is said so, that a man who offers an oblation of milk to the fire win over the unnatural death, which should be understood so; because on the day he offers oblation to the fire, only that day he wins over the unnatural death. A man who knows this offers cereal etc. to the gods; but eating away all the time why the cereals donot perish? The reason of this is that the soul (of a man) being imperishable, he produces the cereals again and again. He who knows its imperishable characteristics only he produces this cereal by his knowledge and deeds. If he would not have produced it, then it would have extinguished. The mouth is its symbol, therefore (he) eats cereal by mouth. That goes to gods (with the result that he) enjoys the nector this (result) is admired. (2)

He took three cereals in his share. My mind was somewhere else, therefore, I did not see; my mind was somewhere else, therefore, I did not hear, (as such) one sees with mind and hears with mind. Desire, determination, suspicion, reverence, non-reverence, firmness, infirmness shame, intelligence, fear, these are (the elements of) mind. That is why a man touched at the back feels it by mind. Whatever is word–it is voice only; because it is engaged in the expression by words. Therefore, it is not to be lighted, but it brings to light. Inhale, exhale, winds coming down, going up, winds in stable condition and moving winds (in body), all these are breath. This soul (i.e. body) is entirely mental and living breathing. (3)

The sage by the above three meters not only describes the creation of cereals by Lord Brahmā. He is called father because of his creative activities not only with regard to the living beings, but also with regard to cereals and that too of seven kinds. It has been explained in these meters that Brahmā did not create cereals as the food stuffs of mankind only; the animals also have their share in the same. Even the religious rites and sacrifices are performed by offering oblation etc. in which cereals of various kinds are basically used. The oblation offered to the fire mainly consists of cereals. The most valuable principle which has been described in the meter number three is that even mind, voice and breath have been defined as cereal because of their life giving property. Air and cereals having the life giving property are divine wealth.

Aitareyopnishad

In the Aitareyopnishad it has been depicted that god desired to create cereals for the gods and the world, as divine wealth. The Hymns are thus:–

God thought that the creation of the world and the controlling gods had been complete and that He should then create cereals for them. (1/3/1)

(Then) that god caused heat to water, there came into being an image (idol) from that warmed water, that image which come into being is certainly cereal. (1/3/2)

The cereal, so created, began to run away from that place in opposite direction then (that person) wanted to take it by speech but he could not do that. If he could take the cereal by the speech then he would have been satisfied by describing the cereal. (1/3/3)

(Then that person) wanted to take that cereal by means of inhale, (but) he could not take it by inhale. If he could inhale that cereal then certainly one could be satisfied by its smell. (1/3/4)

(Then that person) wanted to take that cereal by eyes, (but) he could not take it by eyes. If he could catchhold of that cereal by eyes (then) surely he could be satisfied by seeing it. (1/3/5)

(Then that person) wanted to take that cereal by the ears, (but) he could not catchhold of that cereal by ears. If he could catchhold of that cereal by ear, (then) surely (one) could be satisfied by hearing its name. (1/3/6)

(Then that person) wanted to take that cereal by the skin (but) he could not catchhold of that cereal by the skin. If he could catchhold of that cereal by the skin (then) surely one could be satisfied by touching the cereal. (1/3/7)

(Then that person) wanted to take that cereal by the mind (but) he could not catchhold of that cereal by the mind. If he could catchhold of that cereal by the mind (then) one could be satisfied by thinking that cereal by mind. (1/3/8)

(Then that person) wanted to take that cereal by the urinery organ, (but) he could not catchhold of that cereal by the penis. If he could catchhold of that cereal by the penis then (one) could be satisfied by discharging the cereal by the urinery organ. (1/3/9)

(In the end that person) wanted to take that cereal by means of the anus (or the life wind) called apān, (at this time) he took that cereal. It is that apān (the life wind) which is the taker of the cereal. That winds, being known as life, is the life wind (breath=Apan Vayu). (1/3/10)

The aforesaid hymns of Rigvedic Aitareyopnishad while depicting the creation of cereals by God, the supreme power, also describes the trial and error method which was adopted by the men of primary creation or creation by will of God. It is natural that firstly the knowledge of any thing as acquired by mankind by way of trial and error method. After getting the right path it is settled.

Taittīriyopnishad

When the men of earlier age came to know the importance of the cereal as the life or life saving element, they began to worship the same in the form of a divine power. It comes to light by hymns of the Taittīriyopnishad (1/5/3). It is thus:–

(The utterance of words) Bhuh is the life or inhale (Prāna); 'Bhuvah' is the exhale (wind), Swah is the vital air (vyan) in the body that which is diffused through the body, 'Mah' is cereal (Anna). By the cereal all the life airs (Prānas) become great. That four utterances (of the said words) are of four kinds, (therefore) that four are of four kinds (each) which comes sixteen (utterances).

That, who knows them, in reality, is the knower of Brahma. All the gods offer oblation, that is to say gifts to this (person) having knowledge of Brahma (God in the minute form). (1/5/3)

As such the Taittīriyopnishad keeps the cereals at par with the minute God 'Brahma'. Accordingly a person must have vertual knowledge of cereals and the method of their reproduction as well.

That was the reason why when sage Bhrigu was 'seeking knowledge from his father Varuna about Brahma, then by applying his logical intelligence, he reached at a stage that cereal is 'Brahma'. The Hymn of Taittīriyopnishad (3/2) is as follows:–

Cereal is Brahma, he (sage Bhrigu) knew it this, because really all the living beings i.e., men take birth from the cereal, after being born they live on the cereal, and while going (to heaven), they enter into the cereal.

Therefore, it is clear that ancient sage did practise austerity in the field of economic knowledge too to know its reality and the relations between the cereal and Brahma as well as the cereal and the human body.

Mahābhārat Vanaparva

A story regarding the evolution of cereal has also been told in the Mahābhārat, Vanparva, chapter three as a dialogue between sage Vaishampāyan and king Janamejaya. The teller of the story is priest Dhaumya, who accompanied to the exiled king Yudhisthir of Indraprastha. It is described thus:–

King Yudhisthir asked to his Priest Dhaumya in the following words (3/1)–

O great Vipra! These Brahmanas, well versed in the Vedas are travelling with me (in the jungle). But I am not in a position (incapable) to feed them, thinking this, I feel trouble. (3/2)

O lord! I cannot leave them; but I have no capacity to provide them cereals. In this state of affairs what should I do? Please tell me. (3/3)

Vaishampayan says: – "Janamejaya! Among the spiritual souls, a great sage, Dhaumya on listening the question of Yudhisthir came in a thinking mood for two moments and after finding out the means in the righteous way told him thus. (3/4)

O king! In the primary period of creation when all the (human) living beings were in trouble feeling hunger. Then god sun, mercifully, like father, of all of them going northward sucked up the juice (water) of earth by means of his rays and by returning to southward covered the earth by that juice. (3/5-6)

Thus, when the field is made out or prepared, in the entire world, then moon, the lord of herbs, produced cereals and herbal plants from the rain which was showered by the sun from the space taking the form of clouds. (3/7)

When sun, being coronated by the rays of moon, (in this ways), comes in the state of nature, then pious herbal plants grow up filled up with six kinds of juices. That is the cereal for mankind in the earth. (3/8)

Thus cereal, as the protector of life of the living beings, is in the form of sun. Therefore, god sun is like a father of all the living beings, hence, you go in his shelter. (3/9)

The above story conveying the thoughts of sage Dhaumya suggests that the life of the vegetations fully depends upon natural help of sum and moon. These two planets are the cause of life as well as cause of plants to grow up in the earth.

As such the vegetation has been a primary source of economy that is to say agriculture for a very ancient time in India.

Mahābhārt Anushāshanparva

Another source of livelihood has been milk of cow. The renowned Rajkumar Bhishma is of the opinion that Surbhi cow was created by God Himself at His will as a source of food material (milk) to the people of early age. Replying to a question asked for by Yudhisthir relating to the donation of red cow to the Brāhmaṇas Prince Bhishma says thus:–

Son! I am telling you a story relating to the birth of red cow as I heard it from the elderly people, which is a description of olden days. (77/10)

In the beginning of the creation Lord Brahmā gave an order to Dakshaprajapati 'to cause birth of children (offsprings)', but (instead of producing off springs) he raised a questions (relating to their livelihood) and for the provision thereof (livelihood). (77/11)

O great! As gods lead their life taking the recourse of nector, in the same way all the people lead their life with the support of livelihood. (77/12)

Movable beings are greater than the immovable beings. From amongst them men (are great) and amongst men Brāhmaṇas are great, because in them sacrifices are established (77/13)

Soma is obtained from sacrifice and that sacrifice lies in the cows, from which gods get pleasure. Therefore, (the place of) livelihood is first, thereafter the children. (77/14)

Coming into existence all the living beings began to make noise (began to demand) for the livelihood. As the thirsty and hungry boys go to their mother and father, likewise all the (living) beings went to Dakshaprajapati for livelihood. (77/15)

On this state of affairs of the people god Prajapati began to think in the mind and took nectar for the livelihood of the people. (77/16)

When he become fully satisfied, by taking nector, then a good smell began to come out of his mouth (called Surabhi). With that good smell (Surabhi) a cow named 'Surabhi' appeared to which Prajāpati looked at as his daughter being appeared from his mouth. (77/17)

That Surabhi (cow) gave birth to so many cows named 'Saurabheyee', they were like mothers for the entire world. Their colour was brighting like (colour of) gold. Those cows were to give milk to the people in the form of livelihood. (77/18)

It may be recalled here that at the time of churning of sea of milk, to be described latter on a cow named 'Kamdhenu', that is to say, 'a cow fulfiller of desire', appeared from the same sea. As such the Shastras depicts the appearance of two kinds of divine cows. The appearance of both of them is said to fulfil the needs of livelihood to the mankind. This is the reason why the entire ancient

Indian economy revolves on the two axises of the tending of cattle and the agriculture. In these two kings of livelihoods some thing divine is seen and spiritual benefit is expected from the same.

Mahābhārt-Shāntiparva-1

In a dialogue between king Yudhishthir and Prince Bhishma of Hastinapur state a discussion on the religious character of wealth went on between them. King Yudhishthir who, himself, was aware of the Shāstric philosophy of wealth wanted to get his knowledge regarding wealth corroborated by the discourse of Prince Bhishma lying on the bed of arrows in the battle field of Kurukshetra. It is the philosophy of the Vedas that wealth was created by God for performing sacrifices. The said discourse is reproduced below:–

Yudhishthir asked (to Bhishma), O father! I want to listen your definite opinion regarding righteousness (dharma), wealth (artha) and desire (kām), depending upon which journey of life is accomplished? (123/1)

What is the origin of righteousness, wealth and desire? What is the reason of these three (elements)? Why these three are sometimes joined and some where several? (123/2)

Bhishma answered– O king! when the mind of the people are pure in the world and they are engaged in the earning of the riches righteously, at that time proper moment, cause and deed those three (elements) are seen mixed because of the same. (123/3)

Those (three) righteousness or religious rites are always the causes of wealth and enjoyment as the fruit or the result of wealth. But the determination is the root cause of these three and that the determinator is in the form of worldly pleasure. (123/4)

All the worldly pleasures are entirely for the enjoyment by the sense organs. This is the origin of religious rite, wealth and the desire. To get rid of all these is called salvation. (123/5)

The righteousness or the religious rites protect the body (of a man), for performing the religious rites wealth is said to be needed and the fruit of enjoyment is the sexuality. All these are material substances (rajas). (123/6)

The way these may become causes of welfare that way be followed. These should not be given up even by mind. Only by austerity rites, wealth and desire should be left over. (123/7)

By giving up attachment and desire of result from mind, the efforts are done for the sake of those three, it is great. Often, even rightful effort does not produce wealth and often it produces the same. (123/8)

Other than this even various other means become the source of acquisition of wealth and sometimes actual means of acquisition of wealth go against. Often people get engaged in wasteful activities even after getting riches and in performing religious rites other things become helpful. The person who does not believe in the principle that the wealth causes religious rites is a stupid person and being less intelligent gets nothing. (123/9)

Desire of fruit is the refuge of religious rites, storage is the refuge of wealth and enjoyment is (also) the refuge of wealth. The demerits of these (three) are prohibited. (123/10)

O king! He, who only has desire after leaving away religious rites and (means of acquisition of) wealth his intelligence perishes owning to giving away the other two (elements). (123/15)

It is nothing but the religious character of the wealth which prevails in producing good fruits of a person's deeds. Even sacrificial performances require wealth and the utilization of one's money in such a work is always fruitful. It develops an ideal economy in a nation.

Mahābhārat-Shāntiparva-2

Yudhishthir as a king appears to be more anxious about the proper use of triad i.e. righteousness or performance of sacrifices etc; acquisition of properties by righteous means and reasonable utilization thereof. He, being a religious minded person, was more conscious about his kingly duties regarding the application of religion based economic policies in his state, so that he might set an example of righteous rule in the Indian subcontinent for others to follow. It was the result of this consciousness that he placed the matter of triad before his advisor and uncle Vidur as well as his brothers to invite their comments on the said subject. The entire chapter-167 of the Mahābhārat Shāntiparva deals with their comments and the views of Yudhishthir on triad. Their comments and opinion are as follows:–

Yudhisthir questions– Generally people have an interest in the religious rites, acquisition of properties (wealth) and desire or enjoyment which of these three is great, medium and little? (167/2)

At which one the mind should be concentrated especially to win over all the three (triad)? You people should think over gladly and enthusiastically on this question and answer whatever result come (in the mind) and tell the thing in which you have full faith. (167/3)

Vidur on Economics –

Then Vidur well versed in the economical matters with the knowledge of the realities of the same after studying the question in mind began to answer first of all. (163/4)

O king! The property of the soul are study of Shastras, austerity, giving up, faith, sacrifice, forebearance, purity of emotion, mercy, truth and self-control. (167/5)

O Yudhishthir! You try to achieve all of them. Your mind should not be diverted from them. These are the roots of religion and wealth. In my opinion these are the supreme things. (167/6)

By adopting righteousness sages crossed the ocean of world. It is the righteousness or religion at which entire world is founded. The gods have progressed on religion (religious ceremonies) and the wealth has its existence in the religion only. (167/7)

O king! Religion is the great virtue, wealth is medium one, and the desire or enjoyment is minor than other two, such is the verdict of thinkers. (167/8)

So, having control over mind religion should be primarily aimed at and all the living beings should be behaved in the same way as we want to be behaved. (167/9)

The opinion of learned Vidur is clear. He gives superiority of the religion over wealth and desire etc. In his view a spiritual person achieves other two things by the performance of the sacrifices.

Arjun on Economics –

O Janmejaya! When Vidur completed his discourse, then the great economist Arjun began to put up his opinion. (167/10)

O King! It is the land of deeds. Here the means of livelihood is admired in which agriculture, business, cow tending and various art and crafts are included. (167/11)

It is only the riches which are helpful in carrying out the deeds of various kinds. Without wealth neither performance of the religious rites can be done nor the desire can be accomplished, this is the saying of Vedas. (167/12)

A rich person can perform good religious rites by utilizing his wealth and can even accomplish his desire which are difficult to be attained. (167/13)

It is the verdict of the Vedas that religion and the enjoyment are the two organs or parts of the wealth, with the accomplishment of wealth the other two are also accomplished. (167/14)

As all the persons worship to Lord Brahmā so the persons of all the caste praise the wealthy man. (167/15)

Even a man practicing perpetual abstinence and chastity wearing matted hair (on head) and also muddy bodied bald headed men live with the desire of wealth. (167/16)

Learned men having no belongings, hesitant, peaceful and wearing saffron grabs, having the beard and moustache grown (long) are seen having desire of wealth. (167/17)

The other kinds of persons having ambition of heaven and observing rules of Kulāchār (family traditions or law) and also rules of their varṇas and āshramas have also desire of wealth. (167/18)

There are some others having faith in God or not and restraints, are desirous of wealth. Knowledge of importance of wealth is a light and unawareness (non-knowledge) of importance of wealth is darkness of knowledge. (167/19)

(In my opinion) he is rich, who is capable of giving facilities to his employees and keeps under control enemies by penalizing (them). O great king! In my view such opinion is good. Now, you listen other two (brothers) who are in a hurry to tell. (167/20)

Nakul and Sahdeva on Economics

O king! Therefore, the sons of Madri, Nakul and Sahadeva, having good knowledge of economics placed their views, jointly. (167/21)

O king! A man, even if he is awakened, asleep, sitting or walking or standing, should think for the means to increase earning whether it be big or small. (167/22)

The wealth is lovely and unattained thing. When it is accomplished, he can fulfi all his desires in this world. All the persons have practical experience of these things. (167/23)

The wealth, which is earned righteously and the religious rite has good finance are definitely like nector to you, this is the opinion of we both. (167/24)

A poor person can fulfill no desire and a person performing no religious rite how can he get wealth? A person who is deprived of wealth, all the persons are depressed in mind with him. (167/25)

Therefore, a man having control over mind should perform religious rites first of all, then earn wealth; because all the people have faith in righteous person and when the people began to believe a man his entire work are accomplished automatically. (167/26)

So, first of all religious rites should be performed then righteous wealth be earned, thereafter keeping both favourable desires should be fulfilled. When triad is earned by this way one becomes a man of successful ambitions. (167/27)

O Janamejaya! Nakul and Sahadeva after telling so much they kept mum. Then Bhimsen began to say thus, says Vaishampāyan. (167/28)

Bhimsen on Economics –

O king of religion (Dharmaraj)! A person, who has no desire, he only likes to earn nothing, nor, is interested in the performance of any religious rite. Having no ambition, a person does not like enjoyment also; therefore, in the triad the place of desire is greater. (167/29)

Even having desire the sages perform austerity and live by chewing leaves and fruits as well as roots of plants. By inhaling air (they) keep the sense organs under control. (167/30)

For fulfilling the desire the people study Vedas and sub-Vedas and become expert in them. Their interest develop in the oblation to manes, sacrificial performances, donations and accumulation (of wealth) by way of the desire. (167/31).

Businessmen, agriculturists, milkmen, Artisans, and craftsmen even doers of work pertaining to gods are engaged in their work with desires. (167/32)

The divers in the sea entered the same having desire (to fulfill the same). There are several forms of desire and all the work are joined with desire. (167/33)

Every person or being has desire or ambition. There is nowhere unambitious being, nor there was any ever, nor there will be in future. So it is the desire which is the essence of triad. O King! Religious deeds and wealth are also present in the same. (167/34)

As the essence of curd is butter likewise essence of wealth in desire (Kām). As oil is greater than oil cake, as ghee is better than butter-milk or butter and flowers and fruits are better than wood of a tree likewise desire is better than religion and wealth. (167/35)

As juice is better than flower likewise desire or enjoyment is called better than religion and wealth. Desire is the cause of religious rites and wealth, so it is in the image of the religion and the wealth. (167/36)

Without any ambition Brāhmaṇas do not take food even of good cereals and none gives donation of wealth without any ambition (desire). No activity of any living being takes place in the world without any desire. So in the triad (trivarga) the place of desire is seen first and important. (167/37)

Therefore king! By taking the support of desire you enjoy with the beautiful ladies wearing attractive clothes and ornaments. We should give importance to the desire in the world. (167/38)

O son of eternal judge (Dharmaraj)! I have decided so by diving deep. You should not think otherwise in my such saying. My this word is nice, soft, great, free from meanness and essence (of all). So great men may also agree with this. (167/39)

In my opinion all the three i.e. religious rites, wealth and desire should be brought into practice at a time. Who has faith in only one (of them) is mean, who has skill in the two is medium and he, who has equal faith in the triad (trivarga) is good enough. (167/40)

The intelligent, friend and having been under discussion as sandal paste besmearer and wearer of wonderful garland Bhimsen told to his brave brothers in brief which was comprehensive also. Thereupon, he became silent. (167/41)

When all his younger brothers expressed their views king Yudhisthir then began to say his conclusion.

Yudhisthir on Economics –

Dharmaraj Yudhishthir, who by now patiently listened to the discourses of his brothers after considerable thinking for some moment, smilingly said the following–(167/42)

Brothers! There is no doubt in it that you people after giving due consideration on the principle of Dharmashastras have reached at a decision. You people have knowledge of the proofs also. I wanted to know the views of all of you, that is why you people have told me your definite views, which I have heard with full concentration. Now you listen, what I am going to place. Necessarily listen my views with concentration. (167/43)

A person, who is neither engaged in sin nor righteousness, nor earning of wealth, nor religious rites, nor desire, he gets rid of trouble and pleasure giving accomplishments for ever. At that time he maintains similar views regarding a lump of clay and a piece of gold. (167/44)

Those, who remember the happenings of the previous life and are infirm due to old age, they being in trouble due to various worldly sufferings admire the salvation. But we know nothing about that salvations. (167/45)

Self created God Brahmā says that those who has attachment in mind, they never get salvation. The learned persons having no attachment get salvation. So persons desirous of salvation should do no good or bad to anyone. (167/46)

To think thus is the means of getting salvation and no conduct done according to one's will. I do the same work which has been allotted to me by creator. The creator inspires all the beings for different works. So you people should know that the creator is strong enough. (167/47)

A man cannot get the wealth by deeds which is unable to be achieved. Which one is to be happened; only that happens. You people get acquainted with this. A man even being deprived of the triad gets the necessary things. So the secrete measure to get the salvation is to do good in the world really. (167/48)

Vaishampayan says — Janamejaya! Whatever king Yudhishthir said was appealing, good and reasonable. Understanding it fully all the brothers became glad and joyful and saluted the chief of Kuru family brave Yudhishthir with joint hands.

In the family debate of king Yudhishthir on the subject of economic policy in general what result came out from their discussion is that nothing is in the hands of man but depends upon the will of God or supreme divine power. Even then the conclusion of Bhim is more appealing and more practical. In modern time it is only the desire of mankind which compelled to work hard for the scientific progress and industrial as well as other developments to become economically well off.

Mārkandeyapurāṇa

There is a description of dialogue between Madālasā, the

mother and her son Alarka on the subject of triad (trivarga) in the Mā rkandeyapurāṇa. This dialogue also throws light on the divine character of wealth. So it is reproduced below:—

Alarka asks (his mother) Madālasā – O head of the family! I like to hear from your mouth which of the good conducts is the means of pleasure in this world as well in the next world (heaven) for a man. (31/5)

Replying the above question Madālasā says —A householder always observe good conduct, a man who lacks the conduct there is no possibility of pleasure for him in any world. (31/6)

The man enters in the worldly life violating (the rules of) conduct, his sacrifice, donation and austerity become the cause of non-good. (31/7)

A man of bad conduct never lives long; therefore, one should effort- fully observe good conduct. Bad signs are removed by observance of good conduct. (31/8)

O son! I narrate the shape that good conduct. You listen to it by concentrating your mind and do your work accordingly. (31/9)

The householder should do efforts for the acquisition of triad (of Dharma, artha and Kām). When triad is accomplished the (concerned) householder gains benefit of this world as well as of the next world. (31/10)

It is the duty of a householder to store the fourth part of earned wealth by the contentment of self, for the sake of the rites (religious) pertaining to the next world. The half of the so earned wealth should be spent in the maintenance of self (and the family) and the routine religious rites. (31/11)

The rest (one fourth) should be utilized to increase the wealth. O son! Doing such a conduct the success in the acquisition of wealth is achieved. (31/12)

The same amount of good conduct which is observed in respect to the subject of wealth, so much good conduct should be observed for spiritual gains also to remove the sin. Religious rites are of two kinds – with desire and without desire. A religious rite which is performed without desire provides benefits in the next world and the one which is performed with desire provides benefits in this world. (31/13)

Due to obstruction and expenditure both the religious rites with desire and without desire should be performed with no objection. With no objection of the triad (Trivarga) the desire or enjoyment is of two kinds. (31/4)

As the religious rites (Dharma), wealth (artha) and desire or enjoyment (kām), these triad, are joint in interest likewise these are several as well. I narrate the jointness of these three, listen. (31/15)

The religion (worship) and the thing pertaining to the religious rite do not obstruct the self. So, there are the two kinds of religion. Likewise the desire (or enjoyment) is also of two kinds — one is for worldly benefits and the other is for eternal benefits and both are included in the righteousness. As wealth is used for the above two religious performances, it is also divided in the two parts likewise. Kinds of these three should be known thus. (31/16)

A householder rising (from the bed) before the sun rise, should think over the religious rites, means of earning of wealth (and about the proper enjoyment) and also (to minimize) the bodily trouble as well as elements of Vedas. (31/17)

Whatever preachings Madālasa has given to her son Alarka it is of general nature. This Purāṇic depiction provides a guideline to the householders to whom our study is mainly concerned in respect of the application of principles of triad (Trivarga) in the day to day life. However, if a king applies these principles in his day to day life as guidelines his state and the citizens residing therein will naturally be benefited. In the present age of democracy such principles of triad are the guidelines to the council of ministers and the members of the administrative machinery. Such principles which control the lust of wealth are everlasting. They also inspire a person to remain away from corrupt practices.

Bhāgwatpurāṇa

The merits of the triad have well been explained in the Bhāgwatpurāṇ, Book one as follows—

The riches cannot be the end of righteousness (Dharma) through which the worldly bondage is removed. So wealth is the means of earning the religious merits. Sensuous enjoyment has not been recognized as its consummation. (1/2/9)

Again, gratification of the senses is not the end of sensuous enjoyment. Keeping the body and soul together, is the only use of sensuous enjoyment. An enquiry into the truth is the object for keeping the body and soul together and not the attainment of heaven etc. through the performance of pious deeds. (1/2/10)

As in the performance of pious deeds or religious rites or sacrifices wealth is needed, its utility in such matters could not be ignored even by sages. The divine character of the wealth, has thus been given recognition in the Bhāgwatpurāṇa also. In this contest one aspect of the wealth is, also, to be kept in mind that when earned righteously it has the divine merit and provides spiritual benefits when utilized in sacrifices.

Moreover, it is believed by the learned class of people, particularly by the thinkers and yogis, that the wealth, though is a worldly thing, yet, is a divine gift to the mankind. It has a divine origin totally dependant upon the will of God, the creator of the world, the worldly beings, whether living and non-living ones. No precious stone could or can be created by man. Had God, as a creator of the wealth, not created such stones in the form of riches, the man could not have been, even, aware of those things.

The mind of man rotating around this control point reached at a stage that there is a power in the nature which controls the creation and extinction of the wealth also. It being of divine character has been given the name firstly 'Shri' thereafter 'Lakshmi', as goddess of wealth.

■

3

Acquisition of Wealth and The Divine Control

The concept of wealth as depicted by the Shāstras is mainly related to the goddess Lakshmi as the controller of wealth. It is generally believed that She came out of the milk-sea (Kshir-sagar) as the goddess of prosperity during the course of its churning by the joint efforts of gods and the demons in the remote past and liked Vishṇu as her spouse. Goddess Lakshmi's relation as pair of Lord Vishṇu goes to establish that He also needed such a spouse who may help him by means of riches for the sustenance of the world as His primary duty entrusted by God Nārāyaṇa.

As there are two other stories regarding her birth available in the Purāṇas, they should also be discussed here in this concept. In a story as described in the Kūrmapurāṇa it is clearly depicted that goddess Lakshmi came into being in the beginning of creation i.e. Sristi. After coming into being as such she preferred to be the spouse of Vishṇu.

According to the third story which is related to her birth, she was the daughter of sage Bhrigu (father of sage Shukrāchārya) from his wife Khyāti and that she was married to Lord Vishṇu.

It appears that the author of the said three stories intended to throw light on her worldly connection pertaing to the wealth. As Lord Vishnu holds the reign of sustenance of the world and the beings living on the earth. He required to be equipped by such a divine power to perform His duties well. Lord Nārāyaṇa too, would have felt such need and under His planning His Maya, the virtual power, joined hands with the other power meant for the purpose of sustenance of the living world. The story tellers narrated this jointness of the two complimentary powers in their own ways as Vishṇu and Lakshmi.

All these three stories are given below in the order of birth of goddess Lakshmi:-

Kurmapurāṇa – 1

In reply to a question asked by the sages Shri Kurma said —

I, Nārāyaṇa, was present in the earlier period there was nothing other than me. I was asleep on the bed of a serpent, named Shesha. When I awoke up after the end of night, I began to think on the subject of creation of the Sristi. At that time all of a sudden I became happy. Thereafter, Lord Brahmā, the grandfather of the world, came into being. In the meantime due to some reason there came into being Anger. O' great sages! (at that time) as the son of Anger Lord Rudra came into existence lighted like three eyed sun for the destruction of the three worlds, with a Trishul (a three fork weapon) in his hand. (2/3 to 6)

Thereafter, alike lotus great eyed with a beautiful body and mind and smiling face as well as attracting all the people Goddess Lakshmi took birth. With pious smile, very much happy, good doer, established with her greatness, divinely lighted wearing a divine garland etc. imperishable Mahāmāyā (Lakshmi) having original nature She Nārāyani lighting (the world) by her own (divine) power came nearer to me and took her seat. After seeing her Lord Brahmā father of the world; said to me–O Mādhava! Appoint this beautifully bodied (goddess) for the attraction of entire (human) beings, so that my creation go on increasing considerably. (2/7 to 10)

When Brahmā said like this, I smilingly told Goddess Lakshmi–O Goddess! By order of Mine you by attracting gods, Asuras and men of the whole world engage (by apply your Māyā). (But) those who are engaged in jyānyoga (acquiring knowledge), winner of sense organs, have faith in God (Brahmanishtha) and have knowledge thereof, lacking anger, and are truthful, you give leave to such people (from your Māyā, the divine power). (2/11-12)

You should also give leave from a distance to those who are engaged in the concentration of mind (dhyān), having no lust, are peaceful, and spiritutious, well versed in the Vedas, performing prayer, and hermit Vipra (Brāhmaṇa). You give leave from a distance to those, who have especially a definite knowledge of the Vedas and Vedānta and those, who are engaged in the performance of great sacrifices. Those, who perform Japa i.e. to say mutter prayers, offer oblation (homa), perform sacrifice (day today) and also perform sacrifice, being aimed at God-head Maheshwara (Shiva), you give leave to them effortfully from a distance. (2/13 to 15)

Those who are performing yogas of devotion (Bhakti-yoga) and have surrendered their mind to god and are engaged in performing yogas, to those who are of pure mind, you give leave (to them) from a distance. Those, who have concentrated their minds being strongly attached to in the worship of Praṇava (OM) and those, who are performer of Rudra (mantras) and worshippers of Atharvashiras (An Upanishad dealing with Brahmavidya i.e. knowledge of Brahma), you give leave to such righteous persons. And what to tell more, (O goddess!) you do not attract the minds of such people who are observer of rites and worship God regularly everyday. (2/16 to 18)

Thus inspired by me Mahāmāyā, the beloved of Hari (Haripriyā) did what I gave order to her (to do); therefore, goddess Lakshmi should be worshipped. God's wife (goddess Lakshmi) on being worshipped shower glory or great wealth (Aishwarya), power (Shakti), intelligence, prominence (Yasha) and strength (Bala). Therefore, the worship of Goddess Lakshmi should be fully performed. (2/19-20)

The above story indirectly says that the people or the person who want to become economically well off should faithfully and devotedly worship to goddess Lakshmi. So that her illusionary power (Māyā) may have no effect in diverting the minds of good doers in any way. Lord Brahmā's instructions to goddess of wealth, as described above, throw light on this subjects also, which are self-explanatory.

Kurmapurāṇa-2

In another story, which is a description of sea churning, there is a tale of goddess Lakshmi's coming out of milk-sea during the course of that. It is a story which was told by Romaharshaṇa suta to a group of sages who assembled at Naimishārṇya (presently located in the District Sitapur, Uttar Pradesh). The churning of sea of Milk was a joint efforts of gods and demons to obtain nectar for becoming immortal. It was like that of churning of curd to take out butter from the same. The story is as follows:-

In the ancient time the gods churned the sea of milk together with the sons of Diti (called) Daityas and Dānavas making the Mount Mandar as churner to obtain the spiritutious liquor (nectar). At the time of churning the sea of Milk, for the well-being of gods, God Vishṇu taking the form of Kūrma (Tortoise) held that Mount Mandar (Mandrāchal) (on his back). (1/27-28)

Looking upon the universal visitor imperishable God Vishṇu, Gods, Nārad and other sages worshipped Him, (that God). At the same time Nārāyani, the goddess (named) Lakshmi the beloved of God Vishṇu, came into being. Supreme God Vishṇu took her. Being fallen into love by the light of Lakshmi (sage) Nārad together with Indra and other sages told to unexpressed in these words– O God! O Godhead! O Nārāyana! O Lord having world in you! You tell us, the asking people, correctly, who this big eyed goddess is? (1/29 to 32)

Listening the words of those gods and sages Lord Vishṇu the conqueror of Dānavas, looking towards goddess Lakshmi told to Nārad and other pious sages–She is my true form, supreme goddess, the supreme power. She is Māyā (goddess of wealth) endless and my beloved, who has fascinated the entire world. O great Brāhmaṇas! Through her I fascinate the world full of gods, Asuras and men, destruct and recreate it. (1/31 to 35).

(Learned persons) after knowing the origin and destruction of the whole world) and rightly understanding the birth and salvation of the living beings and looking at the self they get rid of the bondage of this Mahāmāyā (Lakshmi). O Brāhmaṇa! She is my all kinds of power by taking the shelter of (even) the parts of her power Brahmā and Shiva as well as other gods have (divinely) became powerful (1/36-37).

She is the (combination of) three qualities (Sattva, Rajas and Tāmas) of the three constituents of the nature and She gives birth to the entire world. In the Shri Kalpa of the ancient period She came out from me in the form of a lotus seated (goddess). She has four hands holding conch, wheal and lotus. She is full of blessings, her facial light is like crores of sun, enchants all living beings. There is no living body on the earth, who has capacity to cross this Māyā, whether he be god, mane, man or Vasugaṇa (a group of gods, who are eight in number). (1/38 to 40)

The above theory of the appearance or the coming into existence of goddess Lakshmi brings to light that She is nonetheless, but the nurshing and creating power of the worldly beings of Lord Vishnu, who is believed to be the divine controller of the world. Her divinity is part and partial of Vishnu being the Lord of nourishment of all beings.

Vishṇupurāṇa -1

In Vishṇupurāṇa there is a description that goddess Lakshmi took birth as the daughter of Sage Bhrigu from his wife Khyāti, who latter on become the wife of Vishṇu. The sloka pertaining to this is as follows–

Khyāti, through (her husband) Bhrigu gave birth to two gods named Dhātā and Vidhātā as well as Lakshmi, who became wife of Nārāyana (Vishnu): (1/8/15)

Thereafter, sage Maitreya to whom sage Parāsher was giving his discourse asked him–

O Lord! It is heard that Shri (Lakshmi) came in to being at the time of churning sea of milk for the sake of nectar, then how you say that She took birth from Khyāti by Bhrigu? (1/8/16)

Sage Prāshar said, "O Maitreya! What you asked at this time to me, I heard Shri (Lakshmi) relations from sage Marīchi, and that (story) I tell you (please) listen. (1/9/1)

At one time Durvāsā, an incarnation of lord Shankar, was travelling on foot on the earth. During his journey on foot he saw a divine garland of the flowers of Santānak (one of the five trees of Indra's paradise) in the hands of a Vidyādhari. O Brāhmaṇa its (good) smell which was spreading through out the jungle made it a charming place for the residents thereof. Then the said great Brāhmaṇa of a frantic nature after looking the handsome garland demanded it from the beautiful Vidyādhari. On his demand the big eyed single-bodied Vidyādhari after respectfully saluting him gave that garland (to him). (1/9/2 to 5)

O Maitreya! The said frantic great Brāhmaṇa after taking that garland put on it in his neck and started to walk on foot on the earth. At the same time he saw Indra, the ruler of three worlds and the husband of goddess Shachi, riding on the furious, Erāvat (elephant) coming (towards him) with gods. Looking upon him sage Durvāsā putting off the said garland from his head which was clunged with black bees thrown it on the god king Indra. (After) taking it Devarāj put it on the head of Erāvat (elephant) its look then was such as (holy) river Ganga seated on the mount Kailāsh. That intoxicated elephant smelled it with his trunk on being attracted from its (good) smell he threw it away on the ground. On seeing this great saint god Durvāsā became very angry and told to Indra (1/9/6 to 11)–

O poluted minded Indra! Being mad by the glory (of your position) you did not honour the most beautiful garland which I gave to you. Oh! you neither after saluting (me) told, "you were so kind", not put it on your head happily. You stupid ! You have not valued that garland given by me, therefore, your glory of the three worlds will vanish. Indra! Certainly you placed me at par with other Brāhmaṇas, that is why very proudly you have insulted me. Well, you have thrown away the garland which I gave to you, on the ground, therefore, this three world will go gloriless very soon. O Devaraj! Whose anger makes the movable and immovable world afraid, you have insulted that one proudly, as such. (1/9/12 to 17)

Sage Parāshar told- "Then and there Indra came down from Erāvata elephant and pleased sinless sage Durvāsā (by entreaty). Then being pleased on his entreaty and salute sage Durvāsā told– (1/9/18-19)

Indra! I am not kind hearted, there is no place in my heart for foregiveness. Those sages are differents ones; you understand, I am Durvāsā? Gautam and other sages (of the repute) uselessly have given you too much liberty, but you remember, it is my all not to foregive (you). You have become so proudy because of the good many admire of merciful Vasistha and others that you have dared to insult me to-day. Oh! To-day which one other is in the three worlds, who would not be afraid to see my frowning face and matted hair. You Shatkrato! Why you are making many entreaties hyprocratically? I cannot foregive you. (1/9/20 to 24)

Carrying on his discourse Sri Parāshar told-O Brāhmaṇa! Saying so the great Brāhmaṇa (Durvāsā) moved therefrom and Indra too went to Amaravāti (his capital) riding on Erāvat (elephant). From then trees and creepers etc. became feebly virtueless and began to decay. The performance of sacrifices stopped. The saints left to practice austerities (tapasya) and the people had no place in their heart for donation etc. O great Brāhmaṇa Total world became incapable and remained wisful even for small things. Where lies virtues there stays Lakshmi (Shri). Virtue is the associate of Lakshmi. No virtue lies in indignified (person)? Without virtues no quality stays: (1/9/25 to 29)

Without qualities a person has no strength and bravery etc. and a weak as well as incapable person is insulted by all. Being insulted intelligence of (even) a dignified is spoilt. (1/9/31)

Thus, after becoming virtueless and gloriless demons (Daityas and Dānavas) began to fight with gods, who became already virtueless and gloriless by all means. The end was that the gods were defeated by demons. (1/9/32)

Bhāgwatpurāṇa

From here the connecting story on this subject from Srimad Bhāgwatpurāṇa is given below:-

When pressed hard on the field of battle with sharp edged weapons the gods fell dead in large numbers, they did not rise again. As a result of the imprecation pronounces by the sage Durvāsā, O ruler of men, (all) the three worlds along with Indra were divested of their splendour. Sacrificial and other performances disappeared (from the society of gods). (8/5/15-16)

Observing this, the great Indra, Varuṇa and other hosts of gods, though deliberating through consultations did not arrive at any definite conclusion by themselves, thereupon they all went to the

Sabhā of Brahmā on the summit of Mount Meru and made every thing knowns to that supreme ruler submissively. On looking at Indra, Vāyu and other destitute of strength and shorn of splendour the world devoid of auspiciousness as it were and the demons getting strength and splendour unlike the gods, vested with all powers, Brahmā began contemplating on the supreme person with a fully concentrated mind. With a cheerful countenance that supreme Lord said to the gods (as follows). (8/5/17 to 20)

Lord Shiva, myself, you (gods) as well as the demons and other beings, men and animals, the vegetable kingdom and the sweat born creatures have been evolved by the manifestation or by a friction of the latter or by my own rays. Let us all seek refuge in that immortal Being. There is none deserving of death or protection of His hands and no side worthy of neglect or respect in his eyes; yet, for the purposes of creation, continuance and the dissolution of the universe, He severally assumes at the proper time the qualities of Sattva, Rājas and Tāmas. And the present is the time for maintaining the equilibrium of the universe. On the part of the Lord, who is embracing the quality of Sattva for the welfare of embodied souls. We, therefore, seek shelter in the perceptor of the universe. The beloved of the gods, He will ensure the welbeings of us, His own people. (8/5/21 to 23)

Shri Shuka went on; having thus addressed the gods, O chastiser of foes, the creator along with the gods went to the realm of Lord Ajita Himself, that lies beyond the darkness of Māyā. There, indeed, with a collected mind, O lord, he uttered hymn, of course, in the divine language, intended to propitiate the Lord, whose essential nature had not been perceived but about whom he had already heard. (8/5/24-25)

Thus extolled by Brahmā and others and having fully known their heart just as it was, the lord spoke a voice deep as the rumbling of clouds, to the good, who stood with joined palms and had fully controlled their senses. Though capable of accomplishing the purposes of the gods all alone. Lord Vishṇu addressed them, eager as he was, to divert himself with the churning of the sea and other efforts. (8/6/16-17)

The Lord said: O Brahmā! Oh lord Shiva! O gods and heavenly beings! Listen you all attentively to my words, so that good may come to you. Go forth and let peace be concluded with the Danāvā s and Daityas, who are favoured by time, till prosperity returns to you of its own accord. In the event of the object to be accomplished being of great moment, enemies too much be won over (through alliance). Once you have achieved your purpose, O gods, you may certainly behave with your enemies even as a serpent does with a rat. Efforts should be putforth without delay for producing nectar by drinking which even one who is in the jaws of death would become immortal. (8/6/18 to 21)

Casting into the sea of milk all plants, grasses, creepers and herbs and making Mount Mandar a churning dasher and (serpent) Vāsuki as a cord for whirling it round, churn the said ocean unweariedly, with myself as your helper. The Daityas will reap, toil while you shall, enjoy its fruits, Approve you heartily of that which the Asuras want, O gods. All ones objects are not accomplished well by anger as through kind words. You should not be afraid of the poison, called Kalkūta, that will come out of the sea. Nor, should ever evince covetousness or greed with respect to the objects nor give vent to anger. (8/6/22 to 25)

Having thus duly instructed the gods, the Almighty Lord, whose movements are guided by His own free will, disappeared out of their sight. Bowing to the Lord, Brahmā as well as Lord Shiva then each returned to His own realm, while the gods called on Bali. King Bali, who was praiseworthy and knew when to wage war and when to make treaty with the enemy, even though the latter were not prepared for action. The gods approached Bali, who sat guarded by leaders of Asura troops and having conquered all, was vested with the highest splendour. Having conciliated with his polished language the highly talented Indra told him all that he had received instruction from Lord Vishṇu. The proposal found favour with the Daitya king as well as with whosoever were present there viz. Shambara, Arishtnemi and other demon chiefs and denizens of Tripur. (8/6/26 to 31)

Arriving at an understanding, the gods and the Asuras, who

cultivated friendship, thereupon but forth their best energies for (obtaining) nectar. O chastiser of foes! Then, uprooting Mount Mandar by their might and roar, the arrogant gods and demons, who had full energy and whose arms were strong as budgeous, proceeded to take it to the seashore. Being exhausted by carrying their load to a long distance and unable to carry the same further, Indra, Bali and others helplessly dropped it on the way. While falling down, that mountain, which resembled Mount Sumeru, crushed under its huge weight numerous gods and demons on the spot. (8/6/ 32-35)

Finding them disheartened and their arms, thighs and necks broken, the Lord appeared thereon on the back of Garuda. Perceiving the gods and demons badly squeezed by the falling down of the mountain, he revived the gods by His look as though they were unhurt. He placed the mountain on (the back of) Garuda with one hand as if he was playing a game and mounting the bird. He flew to the seashore, surrounded by the gods and demons. He took down the mountain from his shoulder and placed it on the seaside. The celebrated Garuda, the foremost of winged creatures, withdrew, when discharged by Hari. (8/6/36 to 39)

(Thereafter) Vāsuki, the king of serpents, was summoned and assured of his (due) share in the rewards and he was twined round the mountain as a cord, the gods and the demons then being full of joy commenced the churning of sea for the sake of nectar. O scion of Kuru! fully prepared Shri Hari, first of all, grasped the serpent in the five part and the gods then ranged on that side. (Bhāgwatapurāṇa 8/7/1-2).

The Daitya generals did not like this act of the Supreme Person. 'We, enriched with the study of Vedas and other scriptures and renowned for birth and deeds are not going to hold the tail, the inauspicious limbs of a serpent': Perceiving the Daityas standing quite after uttering these wards, the Supreme Person and gods left the fare part, with a smile, and caught hold of the tail. With their positions as such the sons of Kashyapa (gods and Demons) began to churn the sea for the sake of nectar to their utmost exert. (8/7/3 to 5)

During the course of churning the mountains having no support began to sink in the sea due to its weight, even through it was held by the mighty gods and Asuras. O Scion of Pāndu! (Ibid 8/7/6)

Perceiving the hand of Vighnesh Lord assumed the wonderful and gigantic form of a tortoise and then plunged into the water (of the sea) and bore up the mountain. (8/7/8)

Vishṇupurāṇa - 2

Such a description finds place in the Vishṇupurāṇa (1/9/88) also. The other description is as follows:-

Thus the sea of milk being churned by the joint effort of gods and demons first of all a heavenly cow (Kāmdhenu) appeared (from the sea), which is worshipped by gods, in the form of sacrificial offering. O sage! gods and demons became very happy at that time and being attracted towards that their eyes remained open without dropping the eyelid. Thereafter, before the anxious Siddhas, saying, what is that? What is that? in the heaven, there appeared goddess Varuni with revolving eyes by intoxication. By again churning spreading good smell in the three world and making (the heart of) gods and goddesses cheerful there appeared Kalpatree (a tree of heaven.) O Maitreya! Thereafter, Apsarās came into appearance from the sea of milk, who were most beautiful and have liberal qualities in them. Then appeared moon which was held by Lord Maheshwar. Thus, there appeared poison from the milk-sea, which was taken away by the Nāga serpents. (1/9/92 to 97).

Bhāgwatpurāṇa - 2

It would be worthwhile to mention here that it is described in the Bhāgwatpurāṇa that Lord Shiva swallowed that poison (8/7/41) and while He was drinking it, scorpions, snakes and poisonous herbs as well as what other biting creatures were there, took in what little leaked from His palm. (8/7/46).

Vishṇupurāṇa - 3

Then arose a white clad personage named Dhanvantari holding a jar full of nectar in his hand, O Maitreya! At that time all the sages together with Daityas and Danāvās with healthy mind became very cheerful. (1/9/98-99)

Next arose goddess Shri (Lakshmi) holding in one of her hands a rath of lotuses with a most charming face seated on a fully developed lotus. (1/9/100)

This is the story of appearance of goddess Lakshmi from the sea of milk. As she chose Hari that is Lord Vishnu as Her husband, the most worthy of all from the point of view of His everlasting vertues, the people worship Her as Goddess of wealth. It also brings to light that two states or societies even if both are inimical to each other should take up joint venture for the common cause in respect of economic developments.

Saubhagya Lakshmiupnisad

According to the Padmapurāṇa (Chapter - 5) Goddess Lakshmi was worshipped by the sages with the chanting of 'Shri Sukta' allegedly finding place in the Rigveda. But the same finds place in the Saubhagya Lakshmiupanished having fifteen Richas, as follows-

O omniscient god fire! (You) in a golden colour, often greenish, wearing garland of gold and silver, you offer oblation to goldy and moonlit Goddess Lakshmi for me. (1)

O fire! offer oblation to that indestructible Goddess Lakshmi, whose arrival will provide me gold, cow, horse and sons. (2)

That goddess, whose forepart is of horses and chariots are her rearpart and who becomes cheerful by hearing the roaring sound of elephants; I offer oblations to her, I may get from her (wealth). (3)

Who is visibly in the image of Brahmā feebly smiling, covered with golden cover, merciful, spiritually bright, satisfied, kind to her devotees, seated on the seat of lotus and is lotus bodied, I offer here to that Goddess Lakshmi. (4)

I take the patronage of such Goddess Lakshmi, who is like a good moon light, beautifully lighted, bright with glories, worshipped by the gods in the heaven, liberal and having lotus like hands. My poverty may go away. I pray you as my patron.(5)

O (goddess) in the form of bright light of Sun. By your asceticism or austerity the great tree of marvelous (wood apple) among the trees has evolved. Its fruits may keep away my internal and external poverty. (6)

O goddess! I get the approach of gods' friend Kuber, His friend Maṇibhadra and Kirti, the daughter of Dakshaprajāpati. I have taken birth in this nation I may have reputation and wealth. (7)

I want the disappearance of poverty which is the elder sister of Lakshmi (wealth), which is the cause of hunger and thirst, which remains filthy. O Goddess! Get away all kinds of poverty and non-goodness (evils) from my house. (8)

I offer oblation to such Goddess Lakshmi who is the mother of all beings and cowpat smelling earth, and is evil turmeric as well ever strong. (9)

I may get all desires and my vow be fulfilled as well as truth. My expression be achieved. Animals like cows etc. and various cereals and conferring glory Goddess Shri (Lakshmi) may arrive at mine. (10)

We are scion of sage Kardam son of Shri (Lakshmi). O sage Kardam! you take your birth in my family and wearing garland of lotus mother Goddess Lakshmi (Shri) to whom you establish in my family. (11)

You create tender watery things (vegetations). O Chiklīta son of Lakshmi! you also reside in my house and get (your) mother Goddess Lakshmi to reside in my house. (12)

O fire (god)! You offer oblation to Goddess Lakshmi at my place, who is tender by nature, having lotuslike hands, in the form of strength, pale bodied, and wearing garland of lotus.(13)

O (god) fire! Goddess Lakshmi is tender hearted, showers goodness, is like a shelter, beautiful bodied, wearing golden garland, sun like and golden, you offer oblation (to her) for me. (14)

O (god) fire! You offer oblation to indestructable Goddess Lakshmi for me, whose arrival causes too many wealth, cows, maid servants and sons etc. (15)

One who is desirous of Goddess Lakshmi (wealth) should offer oblations of ghee (in the sacrificial fire) every day remaining pious and keeping sense organs under control and regularly reads the above Shri Sukta having fifteen Richas. (16)

Kurmapurāṇa - 3

There is another story in the Kurmapurāṇa which brings to light the appearance of Goddess Lakshmi before a Brāhmaṇa named Indradyumn being pleased with his austerity (tapasya). The story is described thus:-

One day (while performing austerity (tapasya) Indradyumna (the Brāhmaṇa) came to know that Avināshwar (immortal God Vishnu) in whom Knowledge (Vidya) and ignorance (Avidya i.e. no knowledge of Brahma) both are vested and to whom learned people (The Rishis) know Parbrahma by name, but coming to know my name as Vasudeva Indradyumna worshipped me as the only shelter of all the living beings by means of vow (Vrat), fast (upvās), rule, offering (homa) and the satisfaction of Brāhmaṇas. (1/50-51)

He used to salute him with good wishes, had loyalty in him and to none others. He began to worship in the dependency of yogis, who had Mahādeva in their heart. During the course of his austerity the Vaishṇavi power (divine power of Lord Vishṇu) evolved from Lord Vishnu one day and showed to him her divine image, Having a look of beloved goddess of Lord Vishṇu Devi Vishnupriya he (Indradyumna) bowed down benevolentally saluting her and prayed Her by various prayers with joint hands. (1/52-54)

Indradyumna asked from her, resembling Vaishaṇava, good doer and big eyed goddess you are who? At this time you tell me your real image. (1/55)

Listening the words (request) of Indradyumna with a happy mood that good wisher goddess remembering Lord Vishṇu told to lovely Brāhmaṇa with smile. (1/56).

I am Parāmāyā (divine power relating to nature) of Lord Vishnu as his nature: Even sages, Indra and other gods cannot see me, the Nārāyani, who is with no second of Nārāyaṇa. I am as His nature. That Vishṇu is Parbrahma (Higher than the Highest Brahma) who is not visible even to Lord Indra and also to sages. By way of deep thinking no difference between me and Shri Vishṇu is seen. I am His resemblance (Pratirupa). That Vishṇu is Higher than the Highest Brahma (Parbrahma) God head (Parameshwar). He being shelter of all the living beings, those, who worship Him by yoga of knowledge (Jyanyoga) or yoga of deeds (Karmayoga), I have no control over such devotees (Bhaktas). Therefore, taking the path of yoga of deed (Karmayoga) you perform the worship of Vishṇu by way of yoga of knowledge (Jyanyoga). He has no origin or end. You will get salvation (by way of that).(1/57 to 60).

After being so (answered) said that very intelligent great sage (Brāhmaṇa) benevolently saluted the goddess by joint hands and told (asked) her again- "O Parameshwari goddess! Everlasting, indivisible and untaken father of all, how that God can be known? You tell this. (1/61-62)

When the Brāhmaṇa (Indradyumna) said so, the goddess residing in the flower of lotus said to the sage,- "Nārāyaṇa will teach you directly (that subject matter)". Therefore, She touched the sage by her both the hands and disappeared at the same place remembering the great Vishṇu. (1/63-64).

Though the Goddess told Indradyumna the means of worship to Vishṇu to achieve solvation, yet before disappearance she blessed him. By touching his body all the worldly benefits which a person in the world needs for a happy life. As the salvation is a matter which is under Vishṇu, She directed him to take His shelter.

Agnipuāṇa

In the Agnipurāṇa the method of worship of goddess Lakshmi has been described in the chapter-308 for the purpose of economic prosperity of an individual or a state. The meters given in the said Purāṇa are as follows. But before them derivation of the term 'Shrin', meaning wealth in general sense is given. In particular sense it is the name of goddess of wealth. The purpose of the prayer to goddess Lakshmi has also been given in a sloka before the praise in this way:-

God Fire says–O Vasistha! By addition of (letters) S,R,I and anuswar (•) (to make one word) there becomes a term 'Shrin' which is a (small) meter (mantra) of goddess 'Shri' (Lakshmi) and provides all the prosperities or accomplishments. (308/1).

The Hymns are of two kinds, which run thus:-

First Kind

O! the great Goddess of wealth, the great illuminating light, I offer oblation, bowing to you heartly.

O Goddess of wealth, O Victor, I offer oblation to you and also oblation with mind.

O the white coloured goddess, having great strength, fastened —fastened, offer an oblation, and also I offer an oblation to you O goddess of wealth, with top hair of head.

Take (my) offering of oblation, as moon like safeguard.

O great bodied, having lotus like hands: I loudly praise, protect me, protect me soon.

Second Kind

O goddess of wealth! I offer oblation, bowing with heart, you goddess of wealth (come) soon. I offer (you) oblation with head.

I am bowing O goddess of wealth, I am offering oblation to you by mind. O goddess wealth, I bow to you, be pleased, protect me-protect me. You come soon and give me protection by weapon.– (308/2)

Thus anyone of the above (two) kinds may be adopted (for the purposes of praise to goddess of wealth). It be muttered to a tune of one or three lacs times with a garland of Padmāksha i.e. beeds of lotus. It provides glory (to the mutterer). The sacrificer (of such a muttering) in a temple of Lakshmi or Vishṇu may gain wealth by worshipping goddess of wealth. (308/3).

With such a muttering prayer the goddess of wealth is effortfully tried to be pleased to shower blessings and wealth for the pleasureful worldly life, so that household life may not be dry.

Rigveda - 1

It is not only the goddess of wealth who is, conceptually; the lone divine power controlling the economic world as depicted by Purāṇas, but also there gods, who have been recognized as the wealth giver to the human beings. The Rigvedic concept of wealth does not rotate around any single divinity. There are five gods who have been supposed to have control over the wealth. Out of five gods four are individual gods, namely, Fire (1/1), Indra (2/12 and 2/23), Prajanya (5/83), Vaishvānara (7/5) having qualities of fire in one form or the other. Whereas Vishvedevā (7/35), as the group of gods, has also been praised as gods of the wealth. Such a description finds place in the Agnipurāṇa. (Chapter-259).

All the five Suktas of the Rigveda, as said above, are reproduced below serially:-

Rigveda - 2

In this Sukta (1/1) god fire has been worshipped as a carrier god which is thus–

I pray to such fire (god), who is lighted foremost, sacrificer, the emissary of gods and effortful. (1)

O Fire! You are the medium through which gods were offered oblations in the sacrifice by the sages in the past and are so offered in the present too. (2)

O Fire! You are the giver of wealth, you are feeder and give bravery. (3)

O Fire! You are all over present in a sacrifices no obstruction is possible over there. That sacrifice satisfies the gods of heaven. (4)

O Fire! You are the carrier of offerings, inspirer of Knowledge and deeds. You be present in the sacrifice with immortal and glorious gods. (5)

O Fire! You do welbeings to the offerer of oblations. Essentially that deed (offerings of oblation) reaches you. (6)

O Fire! Certainly we reach nearer to you by saluting (praying) you throughout the day and night by the heart and mind. (7)

O Fire! You are the expresser of the sacrifice (physically by burning), protector of truth, Self lighted, and normally comes to the intelligence. (8)

O Fire! As (a) father reaches to the son at his own accord, so you are within our reach simply. Therefore, you become well doer to us. (9)

In the above Sukta (hymn) where one to eight Richas (meters) are the prayers to the god Fire the ninth one–is the object of the prayers.

Rigveda - 3

The next Hymn (Sukta) of Rigveda (2/12) is aimed at to god Indra. It is the Hymn of fifteen Richas which are as under:–

O Indra! Expressing yourself by your own (divine) power, you have become (number) one in the men (mankind). You have vested the gods with the heroic deeds. The heaven and the earth become afraid of your strength. (1)

O Indra! You are Indra by giving firmness to the trembling earth, making exploding mountains calm and giving base to the sky by making space. (2)

You are that Indra, who by killing (Asura) Vritra, you have let the seven rivers flow (on the earth) which were confined by the Rākshasas (demons), (you) generates fire in the clouds, (and) kills the enemies in the battle. (3)

You are that Indra, who has created world, habitated the wrong persons in the lower caves, (and) wins the wealth (properties) of enemies. (4)

You are that Indra, in respect of whom people are eager to know and discuss, who takes away the properties of the enemies like that of ruler (of a state). (5)

Indra is that, who gives wealth too much, giver of wealth (to those) who ask (for that) and who prays (for the same) and maintains to the good sacrificers. (6)

He is Indra, from whom (sacrificer) expects horses, cows,

chariots and who is the controller of sun and Dawn (Usha) as well as inspires (clouds) to rain (water). (7)

Who is invoked in the war, who is invoked by uppers and lowers, enemies and friends, is Indra. (8)

By the neglect of whom there happens no victory or gain, who is invoked for protection, who is capable of vanishing the firm mountains, that is Indra. (9)

Who has vanished the sinners and bad or wrong doers, who provides accomplishes to self respected and kills the bad (persons), that is Indra. (10)

Who has killed to a Daitya named Shanber hidden in the earth (under ground) and great powerful 'Ahi' while he was asleep. (11)

Who is like a lightening and imposing (personalty) like electric current, full of rays, shower desired (things) and causing flow of seven rivers, holds 'Vajra' (a weapon) and who obstructed Rohini desirous of heaven, is Indra. (12)

In front of whom mountains trembles, to whom sky (heaven) and earth salute, who is drunkered of Soma, firm bodied and have strong hands, is Indra. (13)

Whose prayers are like cereals for us and whose prayers are accomplisher of two dash (an offering) as well as protector of those who squeeze soma, is Indra. (14)

O Indra! You provide cereal to sacrificer and those, who squeeze soma, you are like Turth. We having sons chant your prayers. (15)

Rigveda - 4

Another hymn (Sukta) of Rigveda (2/22) is also aimed at to god Indra which is chanted for the fulfillment of all kinds of desires in a sacrifice. It has only four meters (Richas), which are as under:–

Very powerful Indra has made for soma (सोम) Vishnu (called Trikadra) in the sacrifice. The Soma pleased Indra for accomplishment of (a) great work. The white soma which is like truth may cause Indra, who has bright appearance, to please. (1)

Brighted Indra has won 'Krivi' (a country of Pānchāl State)

by His own strength. He fulfilled the heaven and the earth by his own brightness. He became strong by the strength of Soma. Indra has taken one part of the (juice of) Soma in his abdomen and rest parts he gave to gods. (2)

O Indra! You came to appearance from a weak sacrifice. By increasing your physical strength you have won the nonviolent bad persons. (You) provide the desired glory to accomplish the deeds of the prayers. (3)

O Indra! You let the world to dance i.e. to come into activity. What good work you did in the past is admirable in the solar circle. By killing Vritra by own strength you let the water flow. You are hundred doers and have knowledge of cereal and strength. (4)

In this Sukta God Indra is worshipped as a god of strength and cereal who is expected to accomplish the desires of sacrificer in these regards.

Rigveda - 5

A Rigvedic Sukta eighty three of Book (Mandal) five (5/83) is addressed to god Parjanya. Who is believed to be the god of rain. Lord Indra is also said to be the god of rain. As such both the gods have inter- relations in matters of rains. The Sukta (5/83) is as follows:–

O praisers! You praise (or pray) to powerful (god) Parjanya (god of rain) to be present before Him. You praise or pray Him with good praise. You serve Him with the offerings of cereals. He, as a liberal god of rain with thunder, cause the vegetations to conceive (for reproduction). (1)

God Parjanya, you let the trees grow in the earth, kill the Asuras (bad persons) and being large you cause fear to the world as well as perish sinners (i.e. wrong doers). Therefore, who are not wrong doers they also become affraid (of you), they do not come before the raining Parjanya and flee. (2)

As a charioteer (you) encourages the horses by applying a hunter which in turn inspires the braves, likewise Parjanya inspires the clouds (which are to rain) for raining. While Parjanya collects the dark clouds in the space, by then their thunder is heard from long distance like roars of a lion. (3)

So long god Parjanya nourishes the earth by rain, by then the wind, which contributes in the rains, blow. The lightning shincs everywhere, the sky rains, vegetations grow and the earth becomes to do welfare of all. (4)

O Parjanya! You give me pleasure. By your actions the earth bows down. It is your work that the vegetations grow in various forms. (5)

O hosts of god air! You inspire rains in the sky for us, cause clouds to rain from all over (the sky). O Parjanya! you come before me being showerer and full of thunder because you are nourisher of us with the rain. (6)

O Parjanya! You become thunder. You roam in the space by your chariot of rain. You inspire the clouds, having water, to rain. You make, the uneven landmass even. (7)

O Parjanya! You instigate the clouds being in the form of treasure of water. (So that) currentful rivers may flow. You drench the earth and sky by water. There should be no lack of good water for drinking to the cows. O Parjanya! You disturb the clouds by loud thunder, then the whole world and the living beings of the earth get strength. (8)

O Parjanya! By causing rain you make the desert furtile and it is filled up with water. You are worshipped by the prayerer for causing the vegetations to grow (appear) for the well-being of men. (9)

It is seen from the above Sukta that Parjanya is worshipped the Vedic sages as a Lord of clouds rather dark clouds which are likely to rain. Agricultural economy basically dependent on rain, the learned persons inspired the common men to perform sacrifices addressing to such a god who is believed to have control over the same.

Rigveda - 6

The god of Sukta (Hymn) five of Book seven of Rigveda is Vaishvānar, a form of fire (Agni). It has been personified as god and is worshipped in a sacrifice for the sake of wealth in the form of cereals, property and physical strength. The Richas of this Sukta are thus:–

O Prayerer! You pray or praise that kind of fire which is divine and physical and is active with the awakened gods in the sacrifices:(1)

That Vaishvānar fire which leads the rivers, is the cause of rains, and by worship appears on the earth and in the space. It grows by offering of the oblation and gets beautiful. (2)

O fire! When you destructed the city of the enemy of (king) Puru and became lighted by your brightness then evil doers being affraid of you ran away. (3)

O fire! Sky, earth and the space work for your well-being. You prosper the sky and the earth becoming lighted by your brightness. (4)

O fire! you are Lord of men and flag of the day. The horses desirous of you, serve you. The friendly and sinless words praise you. (5)

O fire! you respect friends. Vasugaṇa (eight gods) have made you strong (powerful). For the protection of active persons you have caused to demons (Rākshasas) to run away from their place (of residence).(6)

O fire! Expressing yourself in the form of sun, you drink (juice of) soma, first, like wind god (Vāyu). Evolving water, you give expectations to those who are desirous of cereals and before thunders like lightnings. (7)

O fire! You are the choice of all (for the worship). You give me that great cereal by which you strengthen the wealth and donot let (or give any chance) to become feeble the glory of offerer of oblations. (8)

O fire! You be auspicious together with Rudras and Vasugaṇa to us and provide cereals, wealth and admirable strength to the sacrificer of oblations. (9)

Rigveda - 7

In the Sukta thirty five (35) of the Book seven (7) of Rigveda Lords Vishvedeva in a group of gods have been worshipped or prayed for the economic prosperity. It is the hymn of fifteen Richas which are as under:–

O Indrāgne! You become showerer of peace for the sake of my security. O Indrāvaruṇa! The sacrificer has offered oblation, you become auspicious (for him). Indra and Soma be auspicious. Indra and Pūshā provide pleasure to me. (1)

God Bhaga give pleasure. We get pleasure by speaking truth. Aryamā do good (auspicious to me). (2)

Gods Dhata (holder), Varuṇa, Earth, mountain and Svadha may become giver of pleasure to me. (3)

Volcanic activity (of the earth) be cool to me. Mitrāvaruṇa, Ashvinī Kumar brothers (two in number), wind and good doers be giver of peace. (4)

Sky, earth and space, herbs, trees, and Lord of the worlds Indra give me peace. (6)

Rudradeva with Vasus, god Twastā with goddess may become giver of peace to me. (7)

Soma, stone on which soma is grinded, sacrifice, praise (prayer), pot of sacrificial fire (yup) herbal plants, place of sacrifice etc. give us peace. (8)

"The sun, which brights too much, directions, rivers and water be peaceful for me.

Aditi (mother gods), Marudgaṇa, Vishṇu, Pūshā, space and wind be peaceful. (9)

Savita (rising sun), Usha (before sun rise), Prajanya, and Lord of regions be peaceful. (10)

Vishvedeva, Sarswati, performance of sacrifice, donations, earth, sky, space, gods, Ashvinī brothers, cows and Ribhugaṇa may become peace giver to me. My manes may also shower peace to me. (11 and 12)

One who is not subject to birth, god Ahirbudhna (lightning like serpent in the cloud), ocean, Apannapat (not fallen) and Prishni may give me peace. (13)

Adityas, Marudgaṇa may listen to this, I have written this new prayer (praise); the gods sky, earth, and all the sacrificial gods may pay attention to my offerings. (14)

O gods! Manu, Prajapati, imperishable and expressed gods may give me son and protect me with good auspicious (things). (15)

Thus most of the prime gods of the society of gods have been addressed in the above Sukta for the prosperty and well-being.

Moveover, almost all of them are the species of fire, which is a prime elements of nature. It was natural for the author of Agnipurana to give emphasis on such powers of nature in which element fire played an important role for causing the vegetation to grow in the earth. The fire is an element which caused the earth, as a planet, to come into existence in the universe with all sorts of treasure for the economic well-beings. Had the fire (as god) not come out with freehand to create natural wealth either on the ground or under the ground nothing could be done as regards to the economic progress. Apart from the physical form of fire, in every sort of energy right from solar to electrical, the element of fire is present. It is the element of fire which causes the over ground water to come in the form of clouds and to rain on the earth in the help of the vegetation to grow.

If the Vedic sages wrote several hymns as praises of natural powers like that of divine ones it reflects their intelligence and knowledge. It also reflects their intention to pay due attention for the maintenance of equilibrium in the nature and the economic well-being till the end of Sristi. They had their eyes on the issue of survival of mankind with all the natural treasure for the full span of Sristi. With such an object in the mind, they wrote hymns of praises to those powers of nature which were supposed to have upper hands in the economic growth and the reproduction thereof. The form and method of sacrifice as well as offerings of oblation to the burning fire with the praises of aimed gods also brings to light that the economic prosperity had been kept in the mind by the sages to the last limit of their intelligence.

■

4
State Economy

It is believed that Lord Indra was the first king to be coronated on the throne of a state in the Himalayan region called Trivishtap (heaven). That was the state of divine race of the people (gods and Marutgaṅas). In the present time that region perhaps, is called the Tibet. As a King of gods, He had to explore the sources of economy through the development of which His territory could be enriched in the ancient time. For which He thought to praise Goddess Lakshmi i.e., Shri. The hymn of praise, which He used to pray Goddess Lakshmi in this regard, is available in the Agnipurāṇa in the discourses of sage Pushkar to sage Parashurām.

Agnipurāṇa

According to the above Purāṇa, chapter 237, the praise referred to in the said discourse is as under –

Pushkar says — O Parashurām! In the ancient time as Indra praised to Shri (Lakshmi) for the stability of His State. (prosperity i.e. Rajyalakshmi, or His own power, likewise a king (of men) should also worship for his victory in the same form. (1)

Indra praised like this– who is the mother of worlds, who appeared from the occean of milk, who is lotus eyed and who is seated in the chest of Lord Vishnu, I salute that Goddess Lakshmi. (2)

O goddess of making the world pious! You are the oblation of food (swadhā i.e. food offered to the manes of deceased ancestors), offering of an oblation made to all gods through god fire (i.e. swāhā), honey (nectar or sudha, which is used in the offerings), the Sandhyā i.e. Gāyatri meter (uttered in the morning and the evening i.e. when the day and night joins), night (darkness), shineness (brightness), the intelligence, in the existence or being, veneration or reverence and Sarswati (goddess of learning or knowledge, or voice). (3)

O shining goddess! You are sacrificial knowledge, great knowledge, secret knowledge and giver of the knowledge of the self which provides salvation.(4)

You are the logic (ānvikshikī), triad (three Vedas), profession of agriculture, cattle tending and business, and penal policy also. Goddess! you yourself are of benign nature. Therefore, this world is looked benign because of your presence throughout. (5)

O goddess! Who is the other woman to make her residence to sacrificially disturbed body of godhead Lord Vishnu who bears club in His hand, and the sages (yogis) think for. (6)

O goddess! By your desertion, the three worlds reached at a point of devastation. But with your again support these three worlds are looked prosperous. (7)

O goddess! By your mercy men always get woman, son, house, friend and wealth. (8)

O goddess! To whom you look with merciful eyes, for them bodily fitness, glory, harm to enemy side and all kinds of pleasure are not difficult to achieve. (9)

You mother! You are the mother of all and Vishnu is the father of all. You and Vishnu have persuaded the entire moveables and immoveables world.(10)

O goddess making pious to all! You are my (all kinds of) respect and honour, treasure residence, domestic goods like cereals, you give up nothing. (11)

Living in the chest of god Vishnu O goddess! You do not give up my sons, friends, cattles and ornaments.(12)

O spotless goddess! When you desert the men, so deserted, are also deserted then and there by the qualities like truth, equality, purity and virtues etc. (13)

On putting your merciful eyes, men of no quality become virtuous and full of qualities as well as get everlasting glory for generations. (14)

O goddess! To whom you once looked with your merciful eyes, become praise worthy, men of merit, of thanks, of good family, intelligence brave and heroic deeds. (15)

O beloved of Vishnu! You are mother of world. From whom you turn your face, their vertues and other qualities are immediately, turned to disqualities. (16)

You lotus eyed goddess! The tongue of Brahmā too cannot be capable to describe your qualities. Be pleased on me and donot desert me. (17)

Pushkar says—After Indra's praise like this, Goddess Lakshmi (Shri) gave boons to him for the stability of His state and victory in the battle as desired. She gave other boons of enjoyment of pleasure and salvation to those men too, who utter or hear her praise. (18 and 19)

As such Devaraj Indra showed the path of worship, to the gods and men, and to pray Goddess Lakshmi for their economic prosperity and also its stability. In the above hymns of Her praise it is also clear that Goddess Lakshmi has her association with Lord Vishnu. The hymns also bring to light that Indra prayed Goddess Lakshmi in the capacity of a king of His state with the aim of its prosperity and economic stability to which Kings of men should follow suit. The Hindu society even today worships Shri for the prosperity.

Shivapurāṇa – 1

So far value of wealth to a state is concerned, Lord Shiva also realized it and shifted from Mount Mandar to Mount Kailāsh, an adjoining territory of the state of Yaksharaj Kuber. A story in this connection as described in the Shivapurāṇa, (Shristikhanda ch.19-20) is reproduced below—

Brahmā said —O Narad! In the Padmakalpa Vishravā took birth from my son Pulastya who was born by my will and from that Vishrava, a son named Vaishravaṇa was born. (1)

Who enjoyed (city of) Alakāpuri, built by Vishwakarmā and satisfied Lord Shiva by the performance his great austerity. (2)

After the end of Padmakalpa when Meghvāhankalp a began then son of one Yajyadatta, named Gunanidhi, who became Kuber latter on performed a great austerity. (3)

Knowing the effect of devotion to Shiva by lone burning of clay lamp i.e. lighting of a (mustered oil) lamp, he went to Kashi (Varanasi), a city of Lord Sada Shiva which enlightens the mind (mental power). (4)

He started concentration (of mind) in the eleventh team of Lord Shiva after enlighting the lamp capable of giving wealth (Ratnadeep) in the form of mental power. (5)

Regarding that lamp of Shivāshiva lack of difference wealth giving was great sin. That lamp was burning all along by the fire of austerity. It also prohibited the attack of great obstruction of desire and anger. (6)

By the control over breathing he (Gunanidhi) was free from the action of wind (in the body), his knowledge was spotless. He was shining by the light of the same. He worshipped the Shivalinga with the flower of good thoughts. (7)

Thereafter, he (Gunanidhi) performed austerity, for ten thousand years. With the heat of that his body remained in the form a skeleton covered with skin only. (8)

Being pleased (with his austerity) Lord Vishveshwar (Shiva) himself with Vishālākshi (his wife) expressed (appeared) before him. (9)

He placed himself in the Shivalinga with the concerning hymn and told Alkāpati (Gunanidhi) to ask boon from him. (The object of His appearances before him was the same). (10)

When that devout opened his eyes, then he saw a shinning divinity alike thousands of suns' rays. (11)

He (Shiva) so looked bright that his (Gunanidhi's) eyes could not remain open. (12)

He (Gunanidhi) told god head (Shiva) in his mind– O Nath (God) make me capable to look upon your lotus like feet. (13)

O Shashishekhar ! I have no expectation of other boons, I offer my salute to you. (14)

Listening the words of Alakāpati (Gunanidhi) god head Umāpati (Shiva) touched him with his feet and made him capeable to have a look on Him. (15)

Thus Gunanidhi son of Yajyadutta being capable of having a look he looked firstly to goddess Uma after opening his eyes. (16)

Looking at Her he (Gunanidhi) began to think who is this

beautiful goddess having the closeness of Shiva. What austerity she has performed, an austerity more than myself? (17)

Oh! Her body, Her lovely good luck. Her astonishing and not earlier seen beauty is great or lucky enough. Being astonished many a time, after looking at Her as son he began to say like that. (18)

Saying so being jealous, when he began to see one after the other with cruel eyes, his left eye became lightless then and there. (19)

Then Devi (goddess) told God Shankar – who is that devout? Who tells me one after the other to make his austerity more bright. (20)

He looks at me all the time and has jealousy with my beauty, love and prosperous luck. (21)

Listening the words of Goddess, God Shiva smilingly began to say, O Uma! He is your son, he does not see you with cruel eyes. (22)

But he is looking at your prosperity which you have obtained by performing austerity, the description of which is difficult for him. Saying this to Goddess, Shiva began to say to the devout. (23)

O my son! Being pleased by your austerity I offer my blessing that you would be the lord of wealth and guardian of demigods, Yakshas (Guhyakas). (24)

Not only this you will be the King of Yakshas, Kinnaras (deformed men) and King of Kings. You will be guardian of pious doers and also giver of wealth to all. (25)

I will always reside near to you by making friendship. And O Friend! for the sake of your love I will always reside adjoining to this Alakāpuri. (26)

O son of Yajyadatta! come here, She is your mother. O great devotee! you salute in Her feet". (27)

(The teller of this story) Brahmā said— Thus blessing with boons, Shiva told to Pārvati (Shivā), O Goddess you make your this son happy. (28)

Listening the words of Lord Shiva Pārvati, the mother of the world with happy mood told to the son of Yajyadatta. (29)

Goddess said, "O son! Your devotion in Sadā-Shiva be spotless. Owing to your left eye becoming lightless you will be known as Yaksheshwar having the name 'Ekapinga' (one eyed). (30)

"Whatever blessings have been showered by Shiva will remain right in the same way. What jealousy you have shown to see my beauty, (with that reason) your name will be KUBER, O my son! (31)

By showering blessings like this godhead (Shiva) went to Kāshi (Varanasi), with Goddess (Uma), the place of His residence. (32)

Thus a friendship developed between Lord Shiva and wealth giver (Kuber). And Kailash, became the place of residence of Shankar adjoining to Alkāpuri. (33)

Shivapurāṇa - 2

After making Kailash as His place of abode, Lord Shiva thought it proper to get a residence erected for Him as well as for His gaṇas, He liked to take the help of gods' engineer Shri Vishwakarmā in this regard. A description on this subject in the Shivapurana, Sristikhanda-I, chapter 20, is like this:—

Shiva summoned Vishwakarmā and asked him to build houses (for himself), for gods, gaṇas and other his devotees as suitable to them. (35)

O sage (Narad)! Getting the orders from Lord Shambu (Shiva) Vishwakarmā built (required number of) houses as their residence very soon (at Mount Kailash). (36)

At that time Shiva became pleased by the praise of Hari Vishṇu). (37)

Thus by the kind favour of Kuber Lord Shiva came to reside at Mount Kailash and entered this palace at the auspicious moment. (38)

In this way Shiva extended His blessings to His devotees and associates. Thereafter , Vishṇu with other gods, sages and siddhas happily coronated Shiva. (39)

All of them offered gifts to Him of various kinds and worshipped as well as waved lights before Him with other ceremonies. (40)

Such ceremonial functions arranged in the honour of Lord Shiva's coming to Mount Kailash to make it as His permanent abode go to establish that He was received by the gods of that place with full heart and mind. They liked Shiva's presence over there as their guardian. So far Kuber was concerned, He being a devotee of Lord Shankar could have no objection against His (Shivas) settlement over there. Moreover, Kuber was elevated to that position by the grace of Lord Shiva, Being a wealthy region it was most suited place to Lord Shiva as a donor god.

After establishing His state in the Himalayan region at Mount Kailash Lord Shiva thought it proper that any other kingdom be established there.

Shivapurāṇa - 3

Going a step further the Shivapurāṇa depicts that Lord Shiva arranged to appease Lord Vishṇu by way of His coronation as a King. The story as described in the Shivapurāṇa, Rudra-Samhita, Sristikhand-2 chapter 25, is in the form of a dialogue between Ram, the exiled prince of Ayodhya, and Goddess Sati, the wife of Lord Shiva who went to him, while he was in the search of his kidnapped wife Sita in the Dandkāraṇya, to take his examination about the reality of his divinity as the supreme Lord. The concerning story is the reply of Ram to Goddess Sati about the true status (divine) of Lord Shiva and also of himself, as incarnation of Lord Vishṇu. The story in question. (chapter 25) is as under:—

Ram Said, O goddess! At one time Lord Shambhu (Shiva). Who is the Lord creator of entire Sristi invited Vishwakarmā in His territory, which is beyond all the landmass (of the world).(1)

He got erected a palatial residence with a throne from Him (Vishwakarmā) having a beautiful look and good for comfortable living in His (Shiva's) cowshed.(2)

Over that throne a divine and wonderful umbrella was also got made by Vishwakarmā. (3)

He also invited all gods including Indra, Siddhas, Gandharvas, Nāgas, Āgams (Learned ones), and sons of Brahmā as well as sages and Apsarasas. They attended (the court of) Lord Shiva with the gift articles of various kinds. (4-5)

Girls sixteen in number from each of the countries like Divine, sage, siddha, and Nāga also attended with gifts, in their hand, of auspicious articles. (6)

At that time musical instruments like Vinā (lute) and Mridanga (drum-like) and other important (instruments) of various kinds began to play. With that musical instruments a ceremonial function was performed.(7)

Shankar then arranged the required material for the coronation (ceremony) like money (valuable metals), herbs, waters from auspicious places in five golden pots (kalas) and other divine material from other places through His associates (gaṇas). His orders were loudly cheered like the speech of Brahmā. (8-9).

Then, O goddess! Lord Shankar by inviting Lord Vishṇu from Vaikunth (place of Vishṇu's residence) expressed his happiness. Looking at the devotion of Vishṇu (in him) he became very happy. (10)

Lord Shankar decorated Vishṇu with various kinds of ornaments (divine) after getting Him seated on the great throne (so prepared as described above) at the auspicious moment. (11)

(Lord Shiva) Himself put on crown on the head of Vishṇu and blessed His curiosity (and thereafter) coronated Him (Vishṇu)— in that Brahmānd Mandap (open or divine ceremonial hall). (12)

And His entire glory, which never goes to others, dedicated to Vishṇu. Then He began to praise Godhead Vishṇu, who is independent with all potentiality. (13)

And after praising Shankar, being kind to devotees, expressing his dependence to them said to me (Brahmā). (14)

Mahesh said – O Lokesh (God of world)! You people listen – It is my order that this Vishṇu is, ours and others, praiseworthy. (15)

O Father Brahmā! you salute Him (Vishṇu) with (other)

gods. The Vedas also praise His glory as they praise me according to my orders. (16)

Ram said – Saying so to Brahmā, Lord Shiva Himself saluted Vishṇu. Thus being pleased from the devotion of Vishṇu, Shiva blessed Him to be worthy of His salute. (17)

From that day, Brahmā and other gods competent to appear in any image, sages, and Siddhas began to praise Vishṇu. (18)

Lord God (Shankar) praised to Vishnu in the presence of gods and being pleased with Him. He blessed Him with several boons. (19)

It is worthwhile to mention here that by coronation of Lord Vishnu in the presence of gods and His praise, thereafter, while He was enthroned was to invite the attention of Goddess Lakshmi to have Her kind hand on Him (Shiva). He being divinely sound a God. He was fully competent or capable to march ahead of any kind of economic prosperity, yet He intended to adopt the worldly means and liked to praise Vishṇu and through Him to Goddess Shri or Lakshmi. So that Her merciful hands may always remain on His state. With this intention in mind, Lord Shiva, perhaps, arranged Lord Vishṇu's coronation in His cowshed, which was located within the limits of His territory.

In this connection Ram's view is worth to be noted as desenbed in the onward story of Shivapurāṇa. Ram said to Goddess Sati in this way:–

Vishnu obtained unbroken glory from Lord Shiva (as described above) and thereafter He (Lord Shiva) began to enjoy Kailash with His gaṇas. (30)

From that time husband of Lakshmi (Vishnu) took the image of Gopa and to become the guardian of Gopas, Gopis and cows. He made His residence in the 'Goloka' (cow-country). (31)

He (Vishnu) began to bring up this world from that time and by taking incarnation He protects the earth according to the orders of Shiva. (32)

As such both Lord Shiva and Lord Vishnu hold the reign of

economic progress of the world as kings in their field of work divinely as well as worldly. The concerning stories of Shivapurana referred to above bring to light that Shiva a great austere in the trinity of Gods (Brahmā, Vishṇu and Mahesh), Himself realized the necessity of a Government in the particular region of Himalayas, where there was treasure of valuable metals. As said earlier in this chapter a Brahmaṇa youth Guṇanidhi, who went astray in the early age, by resorting to austerity and through that pleasing to Lord Shiva became the first king of the aforesaid hilly region. Lord Shiva finding something good and pure in the heart and mind of Guṇanidhi one of His devotees, selected him to shower His blessings in the form of a worldly position of a king and that too which was full of treasure naturally. He was so much impressed with the purity of Guṇanidhi's heart and mind that He moulded the views of His wife Sati by accepting him (Guṇanidhi) as their son, though with the effect of Her curse his (Guṇanidhi's) left eye became lightless. Guṇanidhi became king of the precious region of Himalayas with the blessing of Goddess Sati also, but with the changed name 'Kuber', as named by Her meaning deformed body.

After appointing Guṇanidhi, with the name of Kuber, as king of riches and treasure, Lord Shiva Himself liked to hold the reign of power and to carry out His intention. He shifted to Kailash from the Mount Mandar, where He was performing austerity. He Himself arranged His coronation ceremony in the presence of Lords Vishṇu and Brahmā through His gaṇas.

In this series Lord Shiva, thereafter, thought it proper and reasonable to arrange coronotion ceremony of Lord Vishṇu also. With this view in the mind He managed to coronate Him (Vishṇu) as king to bring up the living beings of the earth. Lord Vishṇu's coronation was arranged in Shiva's cowshed on a throne in a beautiful palace erected by Shri Vishwakarmā under the direction of Lord Shiva Himself. Later on Lord Vishnu made the said area as His permanent territory with the name Goloka, meaning a country of cows.

As such these three god kings, namely, Kuber, Shiva and

Vishṇu command the reign of riches and treasures as well as cows, believed to be the life saver of mankind. The concerning stories of Purāṇas place guidelines before the human kings that they should follow the path shown by kings of Deva race of people.

Brahmapurāṇa–1

In the context of improvement of fate of Kuber as Yakshraj and god of wealth a story somewhat different to the above one is described in the Brahmapurāṇa, chapter-97. He is described therein as a elder step brother of Rāvaṇa, the king of Lanka on whom Ram, the son of king Dhasharath of Ayodhyā attacked. This story is as follows-

Brahmā said, the eldest son of Vishrava named Kuber, the king of North was before that king of Lankā. He was a sage and prosperous with full glory. (2)

He had three step brothers, named Ravaṇa, Kumbhakaraṇa and Vibhishaṇa. They were very brave and strong. Being born from a Rakshasi wife of Vishrava, they were Rakshasa sons. (3)

Kuber come and go every day by a plane given by me with his brothers with the cooperation of each. (4)

Looking at this devotion (to their brother Kuber) everyday, the mother of Ravaṇa became angry and told to her sons. (5)

Sons, looking at (your) work which is against the nature, neither I die, nor I get pleasure of life. Devas and Dānavas were (also) step brothers. (6)

With the intention of victory and glory they wanted to kill each other. Lives of those are in vain, who live as the followers of step brothers. Therefore, you people are, neither male, nor powerful, nor desirous of victory. (7)

Brahmā told— O sage! Listening the words of mother, the three brothers, went to jungle for the performance of austerity and they did perform austerity too much, (8)

The Rākshasas received boons from me (Brahmā) also. Thereafter, being inspired by words of maternal uncle Marichi, maternal grandfather and mother, they demanded power of Lankā from their (elder) step brother (Kuber). So, there, became enemity between them because of the disqualities of their mother as well as being Rakshasas. (9-10)

With the result that the brothers of both the branches fought against each like Devas and Dānavas. Ravana took into possession Pushpak plane, city of Lankā and other properties defeating his peace loving elder brother donor of wealth (Kuber) and made a declaration in the entire world, that whoever will give shelter to his step brother would be killed. Thus he (Kuber) could not get shelter and Vaishravana (Ravana) exiled his brother (step). (11-13)

Being compelled (by the circumstances) he went to his grandfather Pulastya and told him after salute:-

Kuber told— I have been exiled by my own evil brother (Ravana). What should I do now, you tell me, whether I should depend on fate or to take the shelter of pilgrimage? (14)

Brahmā said—After hearing the words of his grandson, Pulastya said– (15)

Son! Go to the bank of river Gautami and praise Maheshwar there. He (Ravana) will get no entry in the water of river Gangā at that place.(16)

You will essentially get success there for your welfare. Therefore, you come with me and begin the said work. (17)

Brahmā said— Kuber saying that I will do according to your advice, he went to the bank of (river) Gautami Gangā with his father, mother, wife and old Pulastya and made himself pious by taking bath in it. After taking consecration (*diksha*) of vow he started the praise (prayer) of godhead Shiva, the donor of enjoyment and salvation with concentrated mind. (18-19).

He started to praise by the following hymns—

You are the Lord of this moveable and immoveable world. Shambho (Shiva)! None is great than you. If in this world any body neglecting you becomes proud by affection then he is mean and pitiable. (20)

You hold the entire world by your eight images. The universe is conducted by your orders. Only learned persons know you the primeval being, ignorants can never know your greatness. (21)

Mother (goddess) told a boy born out of her bodily impurity (dirt) by jock as your brave son, but (You) God! He became obstruction king Vināyaka by your merciful vision. Oh! This is the result of your kindness. (22)

The body of Girija (Parvati) being covered by tears of Rati, who had separation with her husband Madan, knowing this fact you very kindly gave Madan his desired place and Rati got her pleasure of good luck. (23)

Brahmā said— Being engaged in the praise three eyed Shankar himself appeared before Kuber and showered blessings on him, but donor of wealth Kuber being over happy did speak nothing. (24)

Kuber and Pulastya, who kept mum like this, Shankar becoming very please told many a time "toast for boon" (25)

In the mean time a voice from heaven told Shankar that he wants the place of Lord of Wealth. (26)

The voice from heaven expressed the wishes of Pulastya and Vaishravana (father of Kuber) which was in their mind. (27)

The voice from heaven came for the things which were to be given in the past and may be given in the future, which was full of prosperity, obtainable as well as like obtained, given and to be given. (28)

Kuber having number of enemies, troubled by so many pains obtained the place of a direction with god, good quality of wealth, power of unlimited donations and also wife and son by worship of Someshwaralinga. (29)

On hearing the voice from heaven as said above, Kuber said to holder of Trident,(trishul) god of gods 'be like this'. (30)

God head Shankar also supported the voice from heaven and said 'be so'. Thus honouring to Pulastya, Vishrva and Kuber, with pious and good blessings, godhead Shankar disappeared. (31)

The above story relating to Kuber's going out of power of

Lankā and his austerity with his father and grandfather for the achievement of a new state by appeasing Lord Shiva is a different one. But the ultimate result is similar to that of the earlier story. Moreover, this description comes to an end with the blessing of Shiva's boon that Kuber will become a king of wealth in the coming days. It goes even a step further to narrate the effects of the said boon in its continuity. But his wishes for accomplishment of a state of riches is clear.

For any information regarding the improvement of fate of Kuber, one has to refer the earlier story of Shivāpuraṇa cited in the foregoing pages. The concerning story of Shivāpuraṇa has its relevancy in bringing to light that he was a man of pious soul and a historic personality. He had not only a desire of wealth but his wishes were to become a king of a wealthy state or territory, which he achieved in his life time. He was effortful for the governance of wealth as the King of riches. This is the reason why Kuber is known as a giver of wealth (Dhanada).

Shivapurāṇa - 4

The following is a tale of ruling style of a king, who was follower of Shavism, through which he gained the throne of Kuber as an eternal benefit.

There was a king Dama son of king Arindama of Kalinga state, who was devotee of Lord Shiva from the childhood and always discussed it with his friends. (Shivapurāṇa, Rudra Samhita, Sristikhanda-I, 18/52-53). The life story of king Dama, as described in the Shivapurāṇa, Rudra Samhita, Sristikhand-I, chapter 18 with respect to his devotion to Lord Shiva, is as follows—

He (Dama) became king (of Kalinga), after the death of his father (king Arindama), in the young age. He made a state-wide campaign of Shiva worship with a great zeal. (54)

He being suppresser of wickedness did know no path of worship other than Shaivism.(55)

He commanded to the village chiefs of those villages where no (earthen) lamp was being lit in the Shiva temple, to get it lighted by the same. (56)

He made a state declaration thus— I say it truth, those who will not do this, I will punish them. It is said in the Vedas that by lighting a lamp Lord Shiva becomes very much satisfied. (57)

Whenever there are Shiva temples around a village, lamps must be lighted in them with no thinking. (58)

Who will violate my order, I will cut his head. As much with the fear of that king (Dama) all the Shiva temples were being lighted by lamps. (59)

In this way king Dama 'remained' prosperous and accomplished so long he was alive. Thereafter, he died (living full span of life). (60)

(After death) He became king of Alkapuri in the name of Kuber (when took rebirth) due to campaigning of lamp lightings in the several Shiva temples. (61)

As such any religious rite done in the name of Shiva becomes much fruitful at the proper time. So anybody desirous of pleasure (in life), must worship Lord Shiva. (62)

This story also puts emphasis on Shiva worship for economic well beings.

Brahmapurāṇa - 2

A sage named Mudagala had a son named Maudagalya according to the chapter-136 of Brahmapurāṇa. That Maudagalya taking a vow took bath in Ganga regularly in the morning (according to sloka 3). The rest of the story is thus--

O Munīshreshtha (elder sage)! It was his daily routine. Every day he offered oblations of Vishṇu in his lotus like heart on the bank of Gangā with Kusha (a sacred grass), soil, flower of shami etc. in accordance with the rules as told by his father. (4)

On his invocation the Lord of world Vishnu who is the husband of Lakshmi also come everyday holding conch, wheel and mace, very soon riding on Garuda. (5-6)

Sage Maudagalya with full devotion very well worshipped Him. Being pleased with worship Lord of world told various stories to him. (7)

Thereafter, in the afternoon Vishṇu tells Maudagalya, son! You are tired now, you go to your house. (8)

Thus on the spell of Vishṇu that Brahmaṇa went to house. Then god Himself went to His temple with gods.(9)

Having full devotion in the feet of Vishṇu that learned Maudagalya is graced by the appearance of Lord everyday. Thereafter, what he earned (by begging in the way) he gave that to his wife, while returning home. (10)

His wife, was a very pious lady. Whatever her husband brings, she keeps it in the feet of great Vishṇu. (11)

She welcomed the guests with the vegetables and fruits brought by her husband after cleaning them. She took her meal when her husband, children and the guests took it. Thereafter, in the night Maudagalya told the stories heard from Vishṇu (in the day) with happy mood. Thus a long period elapsed. One day his wife very wonderfully said to him at a lone place. (12 to 13)

Jābāla, the wife of Maudagalya, asked him, When Lord of the world Vishṇu himself comes to you, then why we suffer from so much trouble? (15)

When He comes this time then O learned sage! Ask Him when by remembering to whom (Vishṇu) people get salvation from the birth, death and old age, why not our trouble, even by gracing His appearances for long? Wife of Maudagalya said so to her husband. (16)

According to Brahmā, (I) will do so, telling this, Maudagalya did perform the worship of Vishṇu like everyday and benevolently asked by joint hands. (17)

O Jagannath ! By your simple rememberance, sorrows, poverty and sinful deeds come to an end, then why my troubles remain as it were, even by seeing you? (18)

In reply to the above question of Maudagalya Lord Vishṇu said, Always all (the people) suffer (the results of) their deeds. Nobody in this world does favour or disfavour to any person. (19)

As the seeds are sown the fruits are obtained likewise. No plant of mango grows from a seed of margosa (neem). (20)

Those, who never served Gautami (a river), did not worshipped Vishnu (Hari) and Shiva and did not donate food to the Brāhmaṇas, how they can get the right of wealth. (21)

You have given nothing either to me or the Brahmanas so far. Whatever, is given to others that is gained in this world and other world. (22)

What pious deed you do always with soil, Kusha (a kind of grass), and hymns (mantras), so you are (a man of) pious soul even by suffering trouble bodily. (23)

Without donation man gets no pleasure (of goodness). By doing good a man becomes pure. Thereafter, he becomes detached. (24)

After that, he acquires unobstructed knowledge and then gets salvation from life. By devotion in me and 'Purta' work (i.e. digging pond and well etc) salvation in this world is available to all (men). (25)

By giving donation and solving the problems of other beings one gets essentially enjoyments (of life) or salvation, but only by devotion enjoyment is not obtained.(26)

When Lord Vishṇu completed his reply Maudagalya put supplementary questions to him—

How there can be obtained salvation by enjoyment? Salvation by enjoyment is very very difficult. If man can get salvation by the way of enjoyment then nothing is required? O Lord of the world! If the salvation can be achieved by way of enjoyment and is recognized then I want that. (27-28)

Replying to the above supplimentary questions of Maudagalya Lord Vishṇu said —

There are several ways of giving donations. O Brahmaṇa! There are differences in those ways. The donations given to Brahmaṇas taking my name is imperishable and that which is donated without taking my name produces only that much results, that donation is a donation by name only. That does not become the cause of enjoyment and pleasure in the life. Therefore, O great intelligent! Either you give something to me or give to the great Brahmaṇa at the bank of Gaumati. (29 to 31)

According to Lord Brahmā, when Maudagalya heard so then he said to Lord Vishṇu, that he had nothing to offer Him at that time. There is nothing except the body. That too is already dedicated to you, thereafter, Lord of the world Vishṇu gave orders to (his carrier) Garuḍa, "You bring some grain of corn so that by donating the same this my devotee reasonable enjoyments according to his desire can achieve. Listening the orders of His Master bird king soon obeyed it. Then observer of vow Maudagalya put the grains of corn on the hands of Vishṇu. In the mean time Vishṇu told to Vishwākarmā, (32 to 35) (thus) -

O great intelligent! So long there are seven male members in his family-tree may remain, there must be available desired things like cows, gold, corn, clothes and ornaments and other things in his house. (36)

According to Lord Brahmā, whatever things there could be whether ornaments or other material all those became available to Maudagalya by the effect (of mercy) of Vishṇu and Ganga. Then Vishṇu gave order to Maudagalya to go home and he went home, the sage said (to his wife and children) Oh! Whether it is the effect of donation or it is the effect of worship of Vishṇu or the effect of Ganga. Who can know this great effect? (37 to 39)

Whatever sage Maudagalya thought in his mind and what conclusion he drew, at that juncture, is something else. In the context of economic development of a state through a ruler this story brings to light that worship of Lord Vishṇu is one of the means to make the same prosperous It else throws eight that God Vishṇu is not opposed to the material object of a worship, rather He places a guideline before a worshipper, that what one should donate and to whom its accomplishment. A King may also adopt this guideline shown by Vishṇu for the economic prosperity of his subjects as well as of state for regular donation to a deity or Brahmaṇa.

Mahābhārat Shantiparva - 1

From the very beginning of the statehood wealth played an important role on the public administration and proper management of the territory. Even its security needed public finance either from natural resources or with the help of the people in general. With the lapse of time the statehood reached at a stage that on some occasions the people required financial help from the King, i.e., state.

In this regard Prince Arjun is very clear on this point. His opinion as finds place in the chapter-8 of Mahābhārat Shāntiparva is given below-

As the rivers flow from mountains, in the same way good deeds are performed from the increased accumulated wealth. (16)

O king (Yudhisthir)! Religious rites, desire and heaven are accomplished from wealth. Even the life of the people does not run without riches. (17)

As the small rivers dry up in the summer likewise wealthless and people with short of intelligence leave all the activities. (18)

(A person) who has wealth has too much friends who has riches, has the brethren. In the world, who has wealth, he is called man and who has riches he is known as learned. (19)

O king of men! It is wealth from which observance of religious rites, desires and heaven are accomplished, happiness increased, anger become successful, study and hearing of Shāstras as well as suppression of enemies are accomplished. (21)

"O King! Those who are short of riches, cows and servants as well as visitors are in lesser number, in fact, he is the weak. Those who are bodily weak are not called weak. (24)

(If) you think of judicially and look upon the conduct of Suras and Asuras, O king! Then you will find that except killing of their brethren, what more they want! (25)

If the taking away of others property is improper for a king then how he can perform the religious rites? The learned persons have given their decisions in the Vedas and Shāstras that a king should study the Vedas everyday, be learned, collect all kinds of riches and effortfully perform Yajyas. (26-27)

The gods have taken possession of all the places of heaven by going against their brethren. From whom gods desire to obtain riches or state (territory) is nothing but malice against them. (28)

This is the decision of gods and also ancient principles of Vedas. Brāhmaṇa read and teach Vedas and the Shāstras with the money, by money they perform Yajyas and get it performed. The kings bring the riches by winning others in the battle with that they do all the good deeds. We do not see any kind of property, which has not been brought by doing misdeeds to others. (29-30)

Likewise all the kings win the territory and after winning they began to say – "It is mine". Right in the same way as a son tells the properties of his father as his own. (31)

All the king sages of the ancient period, who are no more, those, who reside in the heaven, in their opinion the state law has been defined like this. As the water of ocean rising up in the form of clouds (by evaporation) rains in all the directions, in the same way the riches coming out from kings spread throughout the territory (of their states). (32-33 first part)

This earth (territory of Bharat) has been in the possession of one by one king Dilīp, Nriga, Nahush, Ambarīsh and Māndhātā earlier, the same has come now under you, therefore, an occasion has come to you for performing moneyed Yajya by giving offerings (to the Brahmāṇas) in totality. (33-II part-34)

Whether the above principles are the opinion of Prince Arjuna or are the thoughts of Vedavyās, the writer of Mahābhārat, it matters little. Its relevancy in the present time is that a state must manage to be enriched in all the branches of wealth for its economic stability and to strengthen the security of the country as well as citizens. But it should be kept in the mind that righteous path be adopted even in taking away the property of others. The war was considered to be the righteous path if fought for reasonable and proper cause. The acquisition of properties by means of that was considered rightful in the ancient period. But in the present time this view has become obsolete.

One thing more should always be remembered that collection of moneys or properties by a state must be spent for the welfare of the people or the citizens. The object of various Yajyas was the distribution of wealth in the society by way of gifts or offerings to the priests and poors, the first part of stanza –33 referred to above which says, "the wealth (vittam) coming out of ruling family (king) spreads throughout the earth (territory)" is relevant even today. People residing in a wealthy country receive benefits from the state finance in several ways.

Mahābhārat Shāntiparva - 2

A renouned sage Devasthān supporting the views of Arjun said to king Yudhisthir as follows as described in the chapter-20 of Mahābhārat Shāntiparva-

O king! The views of Arjuna that nothing is great than wealth', in this connection I too would like to say something. You please listen with concentration. (2)

O king! Having no enemy! You have won the earth (the territories of enemy) according to law. It is no good to you to give away it, which is won so. (3)

O, Son of Kunti! You perform great Yajyas (sacrifices) in which too much offerings (fees) are given (to priests and poors). Sacrifices in the form of acquiring knowledge and study are performed by sages (not by kings). (3)

O king! You should be aware of that there are two branches in (the society of) sages, one is of deed believers and other is of austerity believers. O, Son of Kunti! The words of Vaikhānas sages are heard in this way. (6)

They should not effort too much for the gain of wealth, who do so especially for that, because they began to worship the wealth, which generates evils. (7)

Brahmā has created wealth with the object of sacrifices, and for its preservation mankind was created. Therefore, entire wealth should be utilized in the performance of sacrificer. It accomplishes all the desires of the sacrificer very soon. (10)

After describing the material and eternal utility of riches in the performance of sacrifices Sage Devasthān cites examples of Indra and godhead Shiva who are shinning in the heaven and the world by means of the same. He says thus:-

The shinning Indra by performing sacrifices of various kinds utilizing His treasure is elevated too much than the entire gods. He is lighted in the heaven getting the seat of Indra (i.e. King of gods). So entire treasure (of the state) should be utilized in the performance of sacrifices. (11)

The great soul godhead Shankar by dedicating Himself with all His belongings in the form of a sacrifice, became God of gods. He by His own great deeds is shinning in the world (universe) from the brightness of the same (i.e. by giving up all for the cause of Devas and mankind and living in the state of nature). (12)

It is no secret in the society of mankind now that godking Indra is known for his performance of various kinds of sacrifice in multiple numbers, that is to say more than hundred. He is called 'Shatkratu' due to this sacrificial performances numbering one hundred. In the society of Hindus sacrifices are highly regarded for the accomplishments of worldly and heavenly gains. In the modern age the shape of sacrifices may be remodelled in the form of various projects of the public interest for which our Shāstras do permit. To bring the sources of water on the ground and the projects of plantations on the barren land have been depicted as means of eternal benefit. Such religious or Purānic principles have their roots on the earth and in the earthly prosperity. Such projects, as described in Shāstras, are not in the form of hypothesis of a religious philosophy.

The life style of godhead Shiva is an example before the worldly kings or the governments that the treasure of a state is not for personal use, but to a certain limit. It is for the cause of the people to whom they represent. He has no belongings and is living in a state of nature even though his position in the society of gods and men as well as in the demigods is that of an emperor. He is regarded as the chief controller of riches and donor with open hand. Likewise a government must not be a miser in helping the needy persons.

However, in practice, no Indian king even in remote ancient time adopted the living style of Emperor Shiva. Initially, the aim and object of the economic development of a country would have been to make the people so much prosperous that they could sustain any loss of crop due to a natural calamity. The king was expected to help the needy persons at the time of any natural calamity according to his capacity. It was also expected from a king that he would be in a sound position to come forward for giving help in the matter of food etc. Accordingly, there developed a principle in the mind of the people in ancient India that the position of a king is like that of a father to maintain his subjects as his children . Later on this principle was widely accepted and was given prominent place in the Shāstras as well.

■

super divine power had to intervene. The Daityas lost their territories in His hands because of their misrule and misdeeds. It is a warnings to every ruler to run the government according to the norms of the time in the interest of the people it governs and also guide them to prosper in every walk of life righteously.

Vālmīki – Rāmāyaṇa – Uttarkānd – 2

The above citation of Valmīki – Rāmāyaṇa has a link with a latter description in the canto seventy six (76) of the Uttarkānda of the Vālmīki – Rāmāyaṇa in which it has been depicted that Indra was appointed as king of gods. This story, though in brief, runs as under —

O Rām! There was time during the age of Satya, the entire (society of) mankind (the prajā) had no king. Later on Indra was installed as a king of gods. (37)

Then the people went to God Brahmā in order to have a king (and prayed to Him); O Lord! you have appointed Indra as king of gods. Similarily, for us also,(you) make a worthy man as our king, so that by worshipping him we could move about in the world becoming sin-free. (38-39)

We shall not live without a king, this is our firm decision. Then Brahmā, the god head, after calling the lords of the regions along with Indra (Shatkratu), said – All of you give me a portion of your authority. Then all the lords gave away a portion of their powers. (40/41)

Then Brahmā sneezed, whence from was born king Kshupa. He was vested with the entire power (might) of the lords (of the region given away by them). (42)

Thereafter, He made Kshupa, the ruling king of the people. Kshupa after being installed as a king ruled the earth (territory under his control) by virtue of the portion of might given by Indra. (43)

The king (Kshupa) nourished the people by the portion of power given to him by Varuṇa, by the portion of the mighty Kuber. He then lent to the people the glory of Kuber, the lord of riches. By the portion of Yama, he used to punish the wrongdoers (i.e. when the people committed sins). (44-45-I part).

The above depictions of Vālmīki – Rāmāyaṇa is clear on the subject of welfare statism. Lord Brahmā who asked the various gods of prominence to part with a portion of their authority to equip Himself for vesting a consolidated power or authority of such gods in king Kshupa who was to be coronated as a king of mankind. The root of the principle that a king of men is the consolidated ruling authority of the portions of prime gods lies in the above depiction. The said depiction provide, a guideline to a human king that he should also look by his rule that he is vested with such authorities divinely.

Shukranīti

As regards a king being the collective form of the portions of divinitis which they parted with the object of vesting their powers in him has been fully explained by Āchārya Shukra in the Shukranīti (Chapter- 1). He goes to explain naming such gods whose portion of power vests in a human king. The same is cited below —

A king becomes lord of movable and immovable worlds by taking a portion of the individual divine power of various lord of directions (Lokā-pāls), namely Indra, Vāyu (wind or air), Yam (eternal judge), sun, fire, Varuṇa (lord of water), moon and Kuber (lord of wealth), in him, which remains in them (respective gods) for indefinite period and also with the effect of his austerity. He is skilled like Indra in the matters of protecting his territory and thus takes his portion (as tax). (1/72).

After describing the power of Lord Indra as above, Āchārya Shukra explains the divine power of the other individual gods the portion of which vests in a human king and the effects there of, as follows —

As the wind inspires the good and bad smell likewise a king is the inspirer of good and bad deeds. As the sun is the remover of darkness and the propagator of rightousness (dharma), so is the king. He is the remover of unrighteousness and propagator of the righteousness. (1/73)

A king, by giving the punishment of wrong deeds, is like Yama (eternal judge) because he (Yama) also punishes wrong deeds. A king by becoming himself pure like fire and taking his portion, for the public cause (Loka-protection), from the people, becomes user (of the same). (1/74)

A king brings up the people by (using) his riches as Varuṇa makes all (the beings) healthy by means of his waterlike juices. As moon by its (cool) rays makes the world happy, likewise a king also makes the world (territory) happy by his good deeds. (1/75)

As Kuber has a skill to protect His riches, likewise a king also has the (same) skill to protect his wealth or treasure. If a king has no qualities of a moon by taking its portion (so given), then by (taking) the portions of various lords of directions, he will not shine (in his territory). (In other words he should be the cause of happiness like moonlight). (1/76)

In the modern time, where there is no kingships in almost all the countries of the world barring a few, above described qualities of a king, to make a state welfare one, have no relevancy. But the existence of a government in a nation is still there. If the aforesaid qualities are transformed into the government, that is to say, in the cabinet as the policy maker of the state economy and also as the executors thereof, a nation may easily come under the category of a welfare state. These principles are everlasting and cannot become obsolete by the lapse of time.

Placing his views in the field of the political management and administration Āchārya Shukra, who was the supreme priest of Asura kings in the very ancient time, goes on saying that a king must have some other qualities to build the territory under his rule as a welfare state. His views are thus —

A king should have qualities of a father, a mother, a teacher, an elder brother, a younger brother, Kuber, and Yama, in him and by developing the qualities (in respect of the said relations and gods) in him he becomes able to be called a king. Otherwise, if he lacks the said qualities, he is unable to be called a king. (1/77)

As a father is skilled to build his son able likewise a king should also be of the same skill. And that as a mother is forgiver to her children for their wrongs, and makes them healthy , in the same way a king should be so. (1/78)

As a teacher preaches his pupil whatever lesson is in his interest and also teaching of goodness rightly in the same way a king should be for his subjects. As elder brother takes his share in properties of the father according to the (law of) Shāstras, so also a king should collect his share (as tax) from his subjects (1/79)

As a (younger) brother protects the body, wife, riches and other secrets of his brother (elder) like a friend, so should a king protects (such relations and things of) his subjects. When need be a king should be a donor like Kuber (to his subjects) and should be imposer of reasonable penalty to the wrongdoers like Yama (eternal judge). (1/80)

In the good intelligent kings all the said qualities lie. So it is proper for the kings never to leave the above seven qualities. (1/81)

In spite of the above qualities, a king is expected to be willing of forgivingness. What Āchārya Shukra opines in this regard is as follows —

One who is willing of forgivingness is called forbearer and who suppresses the evil doers is called powerful. But if king, having all the qualities, lacks forgiveness does not shine. (1/82)

Whether it is a divine principle or a worldly political principle that a king is a person of having joint powers of various gods. This principle of political philosophy of Shāstras goes to throw light on the divinity of political system of our country. At the same time Āchārya Shukra is also of the opinion that a king, who is not forebearer by nature, is not a good one. It is, therefore, clear that cruelty in the rule has no place in a welfare state. Even hardness in the criminal justice has to be avoided in every kind of political system. In the present period of democratic rule the principle of divinity is applicable to the judiciary. The penal laws should be framed in accordance with the nature and gravity of the offence. The government should remain faithful and helpful to the people it represents.

Even being the priest of Asuras Āchārya Shukra is firm in his opinion that a king must be careful in the matters of welfare of his subjects. On this issue he says thus :—

A king after giving away his disqualities (badness of nature and habit) should become bearer of his criticism and also honour his subjects by donations and welcome so as to feel them pleasure. (1/83)

Though Āchārya Shukra has been a priest of bad natured Asuras, he was clear in his mind that a welfare state was the only solution in those days too to establish peace in the societies of the both, Suras and Asuras, who were interse at dagers drawn. With this state of mind he expresses his views in this way —

If no remedial deed is done fruits of (wrong) work done have to be suffered and if such a deed is done then it neutralizes the effect of misdeeds (giving relief to the doer). (1/88)

Āchārya Shukra has given his verdict as cited above in the context of the behaviour of a king towards his subjects, who is interested to establish a welfare state by his rule. His above opinion is relevant even today in the democratic set up in the sense that a bad government can be voted out of power.

Vālmīki – Rāmāyaṇa - Bālakānd

The ancient Indian sages did not only reduced into writing what they imagined or opined during their propitiation to God, but also tried to give it a practical shape on the earth. They never believed in any philosophy which was true only in principle and could not be adopted in practice. The concept of a welfare state is one of them. A dialogue between Devarshi (god sage) Nārad and ascetic Vālmīki will throw light on this subject, which is described in the beginning of Vālmīki – Rāmāyaṇa. The celestial sage Nārad narrates to sage Vālmīki the story of King Ram of Ayodhya regarding his virtues, knowledge and style of his rule. His narration, though in brief, yet, it covers the framework of a welfare state which is to be dealt with here. The same is as follow—(chaper3)

The ascetic Vālmīki puts up the following questions to Nārad, the foremost of those skilled in expression, who remains engaged in austerity and self-study (of Vedas):-(1)

Who can possibly be full of virtues in this world at present? Nay, who possesses bravery and knows what is right? Who is conscious of services done, truthful of speech and firm to resolve? (2)

Who is of right conduct and is friendly to all living beings? Who is a man of knowledge, powerful and is of singly lovable appearance? (3)

Who has subdued his self? Who has conquered anger? Who possesses splendour and is above faultfinding and from whom even gods dread when his wrath is provoked in the battle? (4)

I like to hear this; because of curiosity in my mind about the same, while you are capable of knowing such a man, O eminent sage! (5)

Listening the appeal of Vālmīki, the sage Nārad who had knowledge of the three worlds and greatly delighted, said–Listen? And began to address in the following words:– (6)

I shall consider and tell you. Be pleased to listen about the man endowed with the manifold and rare virtues which have been asked by you. (7)

There is one descendent in the line of Ikshwaku known by name as Rām, in the (society of) mankind. He has, fully, controlled his mind, is very powerful, radiant, resolute and brought his senses under control. (8)

He is intelligent, sagacious, eloquent, glorious and an exterminator of foes. He is distinguished with broad shoulders powerful arms, a neck shaped as a conch and a stout chin. (9)

He knows the secret of virtue, is true to his promise and intent on the good (welfare) of the people. He is illustrious, full of wisdom, pure in his dealings, a man of self control and concentrated mind. (12)

He is supporter of creation like Brahmā, affluent, the slayer of his enemies, a protector of living beings, and a staunch defender of faith. (13)

He is vindicator of his own virtue and the protector of his own people. He is in know of the truth of the Vedas and the science auxiliary to them and is a past master in the archery. (14)

He has the knowledge of the real meaning of all the scriptures, possesses a sharp memory and quit wit. He is popular in all the worlds, pious, high-minded and shrewd. (15)

He is always sought by the righteous (even) as the ocean is by rivers. He is noble, alike to all and always appears pleasing. (16)

He is endowed with all excellences and enhances the delight of (his mother) Kaushalyā. He vies with the ocean in profundity and compares with the Himālayas in the firmness. (17)

He is a replica of Lord Vishṇu in powers and pleases like moon. In the (show of) anger he resembles the destruction fire and is a counterpart of earth in the forbearance. (18)

He equals Kuber in liberality, is Dharma as truthful it were and with all such qualities Ram is full of truth. (19)

The qualities of Ramā as narrated by the great sage Nārad to sage Vālmīki is not in his praise as a future king of Ayodhya and incarnation of Lord Vishṇu, but it is his (Narad's) expression what ability he at that time saw in him for shapping the state of Ayodhya as a welfare one. The questions of Vālmīki were in general, which actually arise in the minds of a person, who is in search of knowledge, about a clean, pious and truthful personage. Sage Nārad's reply was also in general character. He foresaw–in Ram the qualities pertaining to promoting the welfare of the entire country. The great sage placed a pictorial description of a king, who could be accepted by the society of sages and learned men in general as a popular ruler. If such a rule is developed in a state it will come in the category of a welfare state.

Vālmīki – Rāmāyaṇa —Yuddhakānda

Moreover, after his coronation as a king of Ayodhyā Rām effort- fully tried to rule his territory as a upright ruler. A picture of his rule is also described in the Vālmīki Rāmāyaṇa, Yuddhakānda, chapter-123, which is as follows:–

Having attained a sovereignty which was unsurpassed by any other Rāghava (Rām), whose mind was set on virtue, further propitiated the Lord through many kinds of sacrificial performances with his friends, relations and kinsfolk. (97)

While Rām ruled over the kingdom there were no widows to lament, nor, there was any danger from beasts of pray or snakes, nor, again was there any fear of diseases. (98)

The world (territory) had no robbers or thieves, nor did anyone suffer harm. Nor, did again old people perform obsequies relating to youngers. (99)

Every creature felt pleased, (nay) everyone was devoted to righteousness. Turning their eyes towards Rām alone, creatures did not kill one another. (100)

So long as Rām ruled the country, people lived to an age of thousands of years, were blessed with thousands of sons and remained free from diseases and grief (of any kind). (101)

So long as Rām ruled the country, the talks of the people centred around Ram, Ram and Ram (as such) the country appeared as transformed into Ram. (102)

Trees (in Ayodhya) ever remained firmly rooted, bore fruits and flowers perpetually, clouds rained when desired and the wind was delightful to the touch. (103)

Remaining entirely free from avarice and satisfied with their own avocations, the Brahmanas, the Kshatriyas, the Vaishyas and the Shudras remained engaged in their own duties or deeds. (104)

So long as Rām ruled, the people remained devoted to pious observances and never told lies. All were endowed with auspicious bodily marks and all were given to righteousness. (105)

With his brothers the glorious Ram ruled for ten and one thousand years. (106)

Vālmīki Rāmāyaṇa— Uttarkānd-3

In respect of the quality of rule of Ram, the description of Bharat (his younger brother) is worth to be mentioned here.

Addressing Ram he narrated the condition of Ayodhya in the following words—(Chapter-41)

Beings, which do not claim their descent in the humanly line, speak again and again like men under your reign. O valiant one ! Having a divine soul! Only more than a mouth has elapsed since you took the reign in your hand. (17-Part and 18).

O Rāghava ! Mortals have become straingers to diseases, death does not over take, even men worn out with age, women undergo no labour pains during parturition and human beings are well built indeed. (19)

An abundance of joy has fallen to the lot of every citizen dwell in the town. O king! Pouring down nectarean clouds rain at the proper time.(20)

Even the winds which blow here are capable of giving a delightful touch, are pleasing and healthy people living in the city and in the country (i.e. in rural area), arriving in the capital, declare, 'May such a sovereign be our ruler for long', O king! (21)

Whatever condition of rule of Ram in the state of Ayodhya has been described by Valmiki in the Rāmāyaṇa either by himself or through the words of Bharat brings to light a clear picture of an welfare state. The views of sages or the ancient poets were somewhat different regarding the welfare of the people. The welfare of the people or human society was not viewed with the angle of economy or economic stability only. But the spiritual benefits, righteousness, general behaviour with the fellowmen as well as their deeds were also kept in view to categorize a country or state as a welfare one. They never believed in one-sided evaluation or study of a country's prosperity.

Yajurveda

In the Yajurveda an ideal picture of a welfare state has been depicted in this way:—

O Brahmana! In our nation brightly intelligent and learned persons may take birth, who may have possessed of knowledge of divine power is knowledge of the great soul (Brahma). So take birth such persons who can protect the nation from the attack of enemies having been brave and well versed in the science of archery. The cows of the sacrificer be milch ones. The oxes be able to carry load. The horses be quick runner. The women should be beautiful and skilled (in household affairs). The chariot mounter hero be victorious. The youths so born be brave and well versed in Shāstras to be able to get seat in the assembly or court (of the king). Whenever the people of the country desire, the clouds (Parjanya) rain. The vegetations and herbal plants be flowery with ripe fruits so that the people be well off. (22/22)

The above hymn of the Yajurveda defines a welfare state keeping in mind the general prosperity of the territory under the management and administration of a political power. How the goal of such a nation can be achieved? The above hymn leaves it on the ruling power. The policies to achieve the said goal are to be framed by the political power governing the country on the guideline shown in the hymn.

Vālmīki – Rāmāyaṇa – Uttarkānd –4

In a discourse of Ram's council, the duties of a king regarding the welfare of the people and the state have been surmised (in the Uttarkand of Rāmāyaṇa, chapter-2, said to be interpolated one) in the following way:—

The king is the creator of all living beings and the king is the leader (of men). The king remains awake, when others (i.e. Subjects) are asleep. The king protects the subjects. (4)

The king, being the protector (of all) protects Dharma (Righteousness) by pursuing right policy. When the king does not protect, the subjects perish soon. (5)

The king is the creator, protector and father of the entire world. The king is the time, (i.e., sets the trend of the times) and the 'yoga' (a particular age of the world). The king is the whole world. (6)

The people call it religion (Dharma) for it sustains (the world). The created beings are sustained by 'Dharma'. Since it supports the three world together with all the movable and immovables.(7)

He sustains his enemies, puts them on the right path and

delights his subjects by the religion (Dharma). Therefore, he is known as religion (Dharma). (8)

This act of religion (Dharma) or sustaining is religion (Dharma) the conclusion is this. O king Ram! This is the highest 'Dharma', It yields reward after death. My view is that nothing is unattainable by the religion (Dharma). (9)

Charity, compassion, honouring nobles, straightforwardness in behaviour, O Ram! Are the religion (Dharma) in this life (even in social set up) and the life here after that accrues from protecting the subjects. (10)

O Ram! You are the strict observer of vows. You are the authority par excellance. You are coversant with the righteous duties (Dharma) which is practised by the good people (and the kings). (11)

You are the supreme abode of the duties (Dharma) and the ocean of virtues as it were. I spoke out of my ignorance. (12)

Bowing my head I pray. You should not get angry on this account. (13)

At the conclusion of the speech, the person, who was addressing it, apologizes to Ram in view of his knowledge and capability etc. But the subject of his address was befitting to a welfare state. If a ruler practises the 'dharma'or his duties in the said way he will be known as an architect of an ideal state. Even if the canto under reference allegedly an interpolation, yet its content being relevant to the subject under study the concerning stanzas (slokas) have been cited above.

Vālmīki – Rāmāyaṇa – Uttarkānd – 5

A question generally arises in the mind of a scholar as to why Ram is known as an ideal king? The answer to this question is that there were certain qualities in him which made his rule superior (in the form of a welfare state) to other rulers of his time. One of his qualities was to give before hand word to any visitor of his court for the purposes of any help. A story pertaining to Ram's such a character is also described in the chapter-60 of Uttarkānd of Vālmīki Rāmāyana. It is as follows:—

Thus (as the day passed by) with Ram and Lakshamana conversing themselves the vernal night appeared which was neither cold nor causing heat. (1)

After dawn in the morning; after performing the modern duties, Ram, the scion of Kakutstha, approached (the place) who could see his subjects. He was desirous to know the activities of his citizens. (2)

Then Sumantra (his charioteer) having come near Rāghava (Ram) and spoke thus — O king some ascetics stand at the door for entry. (3)

O tiger among men! Great Rishis, who dwell at the banks of the (river) Yamunā and rejoice among themselves, placing Chyavana, the Bhārgava as their leader, implore us in the haste for your hearing. (4,5-Ist part)

Having heard to him Ram, the righteous one, spoke, 'Please let the Brāhmaṇas, headed by Bhārgava, enter. (5-II part)

He then went near the door obeying the orders of the king and caused the ascetics to enter. (6)

More than a hundred holy ascetics, glowing with their own luster entered the palace. (7)

Those Brāhmaṇas accompanied with pitchers full and sanctified with all the Tirthas (pilgrimages). (8)

They offered to Ram fruits and roots, Ram accepted them in pleasing mood. (9)

Accepting the gifts (of ascetics) in the form of water of Tirathas and fruits, He (Ram) of long arms, then addressed all the great ascetics thus:—(10)

These are the special seats, please be seated as it suits you. Hearing the requests of Ram all the great Rishis seated themselves on the lovely golden chushions. (11,12 Ist part).

Seeing them thus seated, the conqueror of the strong- holds of enemies, Rāghav surely (calmly) with joint hands uttered these words:— (12)

For what purpose you people have come here? What should

I perform for you? I am at your commands. I shall perform, happily, all that is desired by you people. (13)

This kingdom, my entire life and even what dwells in my heart, all are for the (enjoyment) of Brāhmaṇas. I tell you the truth. (14)

Hearing these words of Ram and his assurance (to fulfil their objects), the Rishis performing austerity and dwelling at the banks of Yamunā arose. (15)

With great joy the noble ones said — O best amongst men! It befits you alone in this world and none others.(16)

Many powerful kings have gone by looking at the greatness (gravity) of the task did take no interest to promise (to fulfil them). (17)

You, respecting the Brahmanas, made your promise, without giving a second thought about the task. No doubt, you will, therefore, dispel all the fears that haunts the sages (Rishis). (18)

As is seen Ram made a first hand impression in the mind of sages in his favour by blind assurance to fulfil their task. It was best known to the sages (Rishis) seeking Ram's help that he was capable to solve their problems easily. A question, as to whether Ram was capable to solve their problem, is something different but promise to solve the same reflects the idealism of the concerning ruler. A government which is all the time ready to help its countrymen can establish its state as a welfare one. As the visiting sages were not the inhabitants of Ayodhyā, their satisfaction with the style of Ram's work is meaningful.

Mahābhārat– Ādiparva

An information of the rule of king Dushyanta of Hastinapur state and the condition thereof, which is described in the chapter – 68 of the Mahābhārat, Adiparva, also throws light on the framework of a welfare- state as well as on the duties of a king in that regard. The concerning story is as follows :—

O great lord the scion of Bharat (king Janmejaya)! There had been a king named Dushyanta extending the scion of Puru. He was a great hero and the ruler of entire earth surrounded by the four oceans. (3)

King Dushyanta fully ruled the four parts of the earth and all the countries covered by the oceans. He won many wars. He alone ruled and protected the four classes of people spread over upto (the coast of) the ocean and also adjoining landmass extended upto the boundary of the Malechchha country. (4-5)

Though the above citation simply defines the territorial limits of the then Hastinapur state ruled by king Dushyanta, yet its mention here is relevant for the sake of the study of the subjects of this chapter. The author has made such a reference here in the context of the onward citation, which is as follows —

During the period of rule of the said king (Dushyanta) nobody produced children of cross-breed. The earth produced cereals without ploughing and sowing. Therefore, none was active to think for cultivation and finding out the treasure (of the earth). Even there was none to commit wrong or sin in his state. (6)

O king! All the people had faith in the righteousness and did observe it. Therefore, they got both righteous things and wealth with no labour. O son! When king Dushyanta was the ruler of this country, then there was no fear of thieves. The fear of hunger was also not there even nominally. During the rule of Dushyanta over this country, there had been no fear of disease at all. (7-8).

The people belonging to various Varnas (classes) remained engaged in the observation of the religious rites of their Varnas. They performed the worship of gods and other deeds with no desire. Taking the shelter of king Dushyanta all of his subjects became fearless. (9)

The clouds rained at the time of need and the corns were full of juice. The earth was full of riches and animals from all sides. (10)

The Brāhmaṇas took keen interest in performing the rites of their Varna (class) and Ashrama (hermitage). They lacked lie and deceit etc. King Dushyanta was himself an youth. His body was firm like 'Vajra' (a divine weapon). He was full of wonderful and the great heroic deeds. (11)

Mahābhārat – Sabhāparva – 1

What the Yajurveda depicts as a guideline, as referred to above, and expects from a king to build his state as a welfare one, Dushyanta effortfully tried to give a shape accordingly to his territory during his rule. In the ancient India nothing remained unpractised. The learned kings with the help of their priests, the council of ministers as well as courteers transformed the directives of Vedas and Shāstras into action on those grounds. Sage Vaishampāyan simply describes the economical framework of the Hastinapur state of his time in the form of a story told to king Janamejaya, a great grand child of king Yudhisthir descending through the branch of prince Arjuna, his third brother.

Great sage Nārad was in favour of the establishment of welfare states in India. As a roaming sage he should have no interest in the economic policies of the kings or the government. But he took interest in economic affairs of the country whichever he visited. His interest in the state economy can well be imagined from the descriptions of chapter – 5 of Mahābhārat, Sabhāparva. He parried many questions to king Yudhisthir when he visited his court after his coronation as king of Indraprastha, His questions are given below. Narad asked (Chapter – 5) :—

O king! Whether your wealth is sufficient to meet your expenses? Whether your mind is pleasurely concentrated towards righteousness? Whether you feel pleasure of enjoyment according to your desire? Whether your mind is not caused hurt? (17)

O king! Whether you behave in the same way as your ancestors behaved with the subjects in the matters of profession and performance of righteousness and economy? (18)

Whether or not to be tempted by wealth or engaged in the performance of religious rites or by attachment with desire you cause harm to the righteousness and the riches? (19)

You great king amongst victorious heroes and blesser of boon! Whether you have the knowledge of the proper time of enjoying triad (trivarga)? Therefore, by division and allotment of time properly, whether you enjoy (the usufruct of) triad (trivarga)? (20)

By means of the above question sage Nārad wanted to know from king Yudhishthir, whether he had knowledge regarding the time for resolving the problems pertaining to righteousness (dharma), economy (arth) and desire (Kām). In this context it may be said here that he had full knowledge of the routine duties of a king of his age.

Now again we come to the parries of questions of Sage Nārad to the king Yudhisthir relating to the state economy.

Mahābhārat – Sabhāparva – 2

Whether after taking a decision you adopt such a means in which there needs less capital and the production is comparatively high, with the object of economic progress and that you act upon the same recourse soon? Whether you do not come in the way of such work or in the way of persons doing such work ? (5/31)

Whether you are not ignorant about the labourers, like agricultural ones or so of your state? Have you an eye on their work and the activities? Are they persons of your disbelieve? Or, whether their duty of work is broken of and on? Because in the rise (of a state) their affectionate contribution is the (real) cause. (5/32)

Whether you have engaged in the agricultural work or so such experienced elderly persons who are reliable and not greedy and coming down from the time of your ancestors? O king! Whether accomplishment of any of your work or approaching accomplishment, the people (like foe) know it? (5/33)

O son of Kunti! Those who come to you with fear of the loss of their property or (even) after (actual) loss or defeated by you in a battle, do you take care of such persons as your offsprings or not? (5/56).

Sage Narad's enquiry about the agricultural conditions of king Yudhishthir's state is as follows—

Whether tanks full of water have been dug in all the parts of your state? Whether the agriculture in your state does not totally depend upon rain water? (5/78)

Whether the cereals and the seeds of the agriculturists of

your state do not perish (due to bad maintenance)? Whether you advance loans to your agriculturists on the interest of rupee one per hundred (per month) gratuitously? (5/79).

O son! Whether the Vārtā (agriculture, cow tending and business) kind of profession, is done in your state by good or skilled persons ? Because only the persons dependant upon Vārtā kind of profession do progress pleasurely. (5/80)

Whether, O king!, in the every village of your state (Janapada) there is committee of five persons having knowledge of peoples welfare and are brave, intelligent and skilled to deal with the problems of said nature and they (members of the said committee) actually take interest to solve them (problems)? (5/81).

O Lord of the subjects! Whether you awake in last part of the night after getting asleep in the first two parts of the night and that you think about the righteousness as well as economic problems and the solution thereof? (5/86)

Sage Nārad feeling that only a king having practical knowledge of Vedas, Shāstras and household life could solve the problem of such nature, he asked from Yudhishthir the following question :—

Whether your (knowledge of) Vedas is successful? Whether your riches are successful? Whether your wife is successful? (5/111)

After listening the above questions king Yudhisthir asked sage Nārad to explain his questions in the following way :—

O god sage! How Veda becomes successful? How riches can become successful? How a wife can be known as successful? And, How the knowledge of Shāstras is (called) successful? (5/112)

Replying these questions sage Nārad said :—

O king! Vedas become successful by fire-sacrifices, by donations and enjoyment the wealth gets success and wife is for getting children and sexual enjoyment and the knowledge of Shāstras is successful by virtues and good conduct. (5/113)

Thereafter Nārad again parried questions to king Yudhishthir : (5/114)

The questions relating to a welfare state are as follows:—

O son! Whether you (patiently) listen to the lessons told by the learned age old economists having the knowledge of duties (law) and economy (arth)? (5/117)

Whether there is a provision for regular help to the Brāhmaṇas (in your government) from the product of agriculture i.e. corn, fruits and the milk and its products obtained from cows for the performance of their religious rites? (5/118)

Whether there is a provision (in your government) for the regular supply of raw material to the artisans and craftsmen (of your state) that which is sufficient at least for four months, O king? (5/119)

It is also necessary to build a nation as welfare state that persons who are ready for social services and actually do that should be rewarded by the king or the government and for that funds should be allotted. Sage Nārad, being conscious about the same asks a question from king Yudhishthir touching such provisions in this way:—

O great king! Do you become aware of the benefaction done by any one? Whether you admire the doer of such benefaction? And becoming grateful to him in the assembly full of pious persons do you welcome him? (5/120)

Whether you have made provisions to protect your nation from the effects of fire, serpents, diseases and evil persons (Rākshas)? (5/124)

Whether you take care of blinds, deafs, disables and orphans having no brethren and ascetics like parent, fully well? (5/125)

Listening patiently parries of question of Nārad king Yudhishthir gave his words to act upon his teachings in the form of questions in this way:—

O godsage! As you have exhorted me (in the question form) I will do accordingly. Hearing your questions my intelligence has increased considerably. Telling so king Yudhisthir behaved like that and that is why he gained the territory spread over to the limit of seacoast. (5/128)

What godsage Nārad exhorted, in question form, to King Yudhishthir in the very beginning of his rule as king of Indraprastha, were the befitting preaching. It was his intention to adjudge the knowledge of economic policy of king Yudhishthir towards his state Kurujāngal, as to whether he was in favour of establishing a welfare state or a dictatorial kingdom. Finding a submissive reply from the king, Nārad became satisfied. As Nārad was considered to be the representative of the learned class or the category of Sages, his satisfaction about the establishment of a welfare state ruled by a righteous king like Yudhishthir carried weight in those days. His questionnaire also brings to light the concept of welfare state, as prevalent, in ancient India, which may be adopted as a guideline in the modern time. At least sages of those days were aware of the concept and the physical shape of a welfare state to which they tried to establish through a righteous king and Yudhishthir was one of them.

■

6

State Planning

The concept of state planning initially crept in the mind of Lord Shiva, when He was living in the state of nature. It was an age when the burning issue of livelihood could, hardly, be solved in that state of affairs. At that time people came to know about the fruits of trees and the cereals which were the products of naturally grown plants in the plain tracts of Himalayan range. In the beginning of Sristi shady trees and caves were available there and the people were bound to surrender to those natural shelters. It was that state of condition that pinched in the mind of goddess Sati, the wife of Lord Shiva. She made a request to her husband Lord Shiva for a house to live in. But initially He was reluctant to accede to her proposal owing to reason, perhaps, that he had a good majority of people (gaṇas) with Him to whom he also wanted to provide houses with Him. A story to this effect finds place in the Vāmanpurāṇa.

Vāmanpurāṇa

The story reads in this way —

In the olden days Goddess Haimvati (i.e. Sati) finding the signals of arrival of summer season told Lord Shankar, who was seated (on a rock of) Mandar mountain: — (1/11)

O God! Summer is approaching, but I see no house, where both of us may live in to save ourselves from the hardness of stormy wind and heat. (1/12)

After listening (the request of) Sati — Lord Shankar said — O Sati I had never any house. I always walked in the forest. (1/13).

O Nārad! When Lord Shankar said so, Goddess Sati passed on the summer with Him (Shankar) anyhow under the shadow of a tree.(1/14)

At the end of the summer there approached wonderful rainy

season which increases the worries by creating darkness due to cloudy sky. (1/15)

Looking at the approaching rainy season, the daughter of Daksha (Sati) said to Lord god head (Shankar) in these words — (1/16)

O great God! The heart tearing wind is blowing. The clouds are making thundering sound. The lightnings are flashing in the dark clouds and peacocks are crying. (1/17)

Pouring rains are continuing pouring from the sky. The cranes are swimming in the ponds, the flowers of Kadamba, Sala, Arjuna, and Ketaka (trees and plants) are falling with the blow of stormy wind. (1/18)

Hearing the thunder of clouds the swans are leaving the tanks and lakes alone as the Yogis leave even their prosperous houses. (1/19)

O Shiva! The herd of deers are taking pleasure (of the season) by bound hither and thither in the forest. O God! Just see lightning are flashing in the dark clouds. It appears that heros are moving from one new healthy tree to other by looking the increasing level of rain water. (1/20)

The velocity of river suddenly increased. O Chandrashekhar (Shiva) ! If a pious woman gets stimulant and comes in the grip of unpious person and her virtue is lost, then what is wonder in it? (1/21)

The sky is covered with the dark clouds. Thus by the flowers of Sala, Kadamba tree by the buds, pumpkin plants by their fruits, rivers by water and lakes by lotus flower and leaves are covered. (1/22)

O Lord Shiva ! In this troublesome, dreadful and wonderful state of affairs, I pray to you that you please get a house built on this great and nice mountain, so that I be carefree by all means, O Shambho! (1/23).

Hearing all these loving words to the ears, Three-eyed Lord Shiva told to Sati — O beloved! I have no means to build a house. I cover my body only with the hide of a deer. (1/24)

O good self! A snake is my sacred thread. The snakes named Padma and Pingal are my earings. The snakes named Kambal and Dhananjaya are the armlets of my two arms. (1/25).

The snakes Ashvatar and Takshak are the bracelets of my right and left hands respectively. Likewise a snake named Neil which is of bluish colour finds place in my waist. (1/26)

Sage Pulastya says — When Sati heard the hard and vigourous words from Lord Shiva being true but appearing to be untrue. She became afraid. Feeling the trouble of her husband pertaining to the residence her breath became warm. Looking at the ground with wrath and shame, she began to say thus. (1/27)

O God of gods! How I shall pass on my rainy season living with trouble under the shadow of a tree? That is why I am requesting you (for a house). (1/28)

Thereafter, Lord Shiva said — O Goddess ! By placing yourself over the layer of clouds you will be able to pass on rainy season. In this way pouring rain will not touch your body. (1/29)

Sage Pulastya (the story teller) says — thereafter, Lord Har (Shiva) rose above very high so as to cross the layer of clouds. Therefrom, Lord Shiva is known as 'Jimutketu or Jimutvāhan' in the heaven. (1/30).

The above story as narrated by sage Pulastya to godsage Nārad is a background of state planning of Lord Shiva. He being godhead could do any thing suo-motto but He avoided to exercise His divine power in the interest of his family only. What tale sage Pulastya narrated pertains to the life style of Lord Shiva when He was performing austerity at Mount Mandar located at the eastern part of the Himalayas. It is known by a few that Lord Shiva had his Ashram at the Mount Mandar before shifting to Kailash in the west, or middle of the Himālayan range.

Shivapurāṇa – 1

After some time Lord Shiva thought it proper to shift to Mount Kailash but with all his gaṇas, that is to say, with all his associates who came into existence at His will at various junctures particularly at the time of destruction of the great and widely known sacrifice of His father-in-law Dakṣha. It would have been a very bad precedence if He did not shift with them. The story pertaining to His shifting to and settling at Kailash finds place in the Shivapurāṇa — Rudrasamhita (Sristi – Volume – 1). It is in the form of a discourse of Lord Brahmā to godsage Nārad. The same runs thus —

Brahmā says — O Nārad! You now listen to the description of shifting of Lord Shiva to the Mount Kailash, the place of austerity of Kuber. (20/1)

After making Kuber as the lord of wealth or riches with his blessings, he returned to his place (of Ashram) and began to think. (20/2)

My body, which came into existence from the eye of Brahmā at His will, known as cause of weaping and is fully destructive by nature, so I shall go to Mount Kailash to reside at, which is the habitation of Guhyakas in the form of Rudras. (20/3)

These Rudras have come out from my heart as my soul. They have no separate entity to cause anything and enjoy power from me and also they be acknowledged by Lords Brahmā and Vishṇu. (20/4)

So, I shall perform austerity residing at the Mount Kailash making friendship with Kuber in the said form. (20/5)

Getting aware of the intention of Lord Shiva, the Rudras enthusiastically began to play with their. Damārus (smallest drum) by making beating sound. (20/6)

That enthusiastic sound of Damarūs (smallest drum like instrument) spread throughout the three worlds. The sound coming out of that Damārū was instigating and serious. (20/7)

Hearing the sound of Damarūs Brahmā, Vishṇu, gods, sages as well as entire Āgamas (Shāstras), Vedas which took the form of persons and also the Siddhas assembled together at that place. (20/8).

All the gods, Rākshasas and Pramathagaṇas reached there

very gladly from the places of their residence. Even Lord gaṇas, who were glorious and being worshipped by the people of the world got incited to go to that place. (20/9)

Almost all of them has equality with Brahmā, Vishṇu and Mahesh and that they were equipped with the Aṇima (an accomplishment of becoming small one) and other accomplishments. Thus brilliant as crores of suns shinning god gaṇas assembled having desire to see Lord Shiva gladly. (20/29).

The entire gods under the headship of Vishṇu and other gaṇa heads having a sight of Lord Shiva came at peace and began to praise Him. (20/30)

Thus Lord Shiva, with the loving association of Vishṇu and other gods as well as gaṇaheads, went to Kailash, the place of great soul Kuber. (20/31).

To have a sight of Lord Shiva's coming to Kailash Kuber with his family (members) worshipped him with regards and devotion by all means. (20/32)

He then with the intention to please Lord Shiva worshipped his gaṇahead and Vishṇu as well as the other gods. (20/33).

Lord Sadāshiva being pleased with Kuber embraced him and after smelling his head (in a token of love), He (Shiva) began to live at Kailash, adjoining to Alakāpuri with his (associates) gaṇas. (20/34)

So far, the above story narrates the process of shifting of Lord Shiva to the Mount Kailash and His arrival there was duly welcomed by the king Kuber. From now the story of His planning to give that place the shape of a capital begins. Lord Shiva became active to invite god engineer Vishwakarmā to make a master plan of the capital and erect the palace and other buildings according to that. The story, pertaining to this as the onward description in the same Purāṇa (Rudrasamhitā – Sristi Volume – 1), is as follows—

Lord Shiva then called for Vishwakarmā and told him to construct residences suitable for the living of gods, all the gaṇaheads and his devotees. (20/35)

O sage ! Getting the orders of Lord Shiva (engineer) Vishwakarmā went to the place (so directed) and got erected residential houses suitable for living them very soon. (20/36)

At the same time Lord Shiva became much pleased with the praise of Hari (Vishṇu). (20/37).

Thus being kind to Kuber Lord Shiva went to Mount Kailash and He entered his palace at a auspicious moment. (20/38)

Hereafter begins the story of Lord Shiva's coronation ceremony as king head not only of the Kingdom, which was yet to be defined, but of other kings also. Before coming to the point, it is imperative to mention here that Lord Shiva, being a austere, liked to be coronated as king of kings including Kuber, who was his great devotee and was installed by Him as king of the concerning region. His intention, perhaps, was to show path to the gods and men in general that governance of a state and its economic as well as other plannings should remain in the hands of a sage or austere. Moreover, in the latter days most of the princes who were coronated as heir apparent of the throne invariably perform austerity to become spiritually sound and to give a righteous rule to their countries or states according to the path shown by Lord Shiva.

As regards state planning, Lord Shiva was the first god head in whose mind concept of a planned state crept up. With this intention he wanted to have the association of other two parallel gods, namely, Lord Brahmā and Lord Vishṇu also. Lord Vishṇu having a divine power connected with worldly things his association was needed most by Lord Shiva. Moreover, the control of wealth being in the hands of Shri Vishṇu, this concept led to be believed that Lakshmi i.e. Wealth, as the goddess is His spouse. It is a well known fact that without wealth no planning of any kind can succeed. So it was essential for Lord Shiva to honour the other two gods of the trinity to find their favour in this regard.

At the time of His coronation as king of Kailash Lord Shiva himself honoured Shri Brahmā and Shri Vishṇu as described in the onward depiction of this Shivapurāṇa in this way—

Thereafter, sages, the Apara power Shri Vishṇu and Siddhas coronated Lord Shiva. (20/39)

In His coronation ceremony his worshipas as well as, was performed his Ārati and other kinds of festives by all. (20/40)

At that time there began rain of flowers from the sky. The Apsaras began to dance joyfully. (20/41)

All the directions then filled with the slogans of victory (Jaya) and benevolence (Namah). It became a festive of joy to all. (20/42)

Shri Vishṇu and other gods as well as Shambhu (Shiva) associated with His gaṇas, being seated on their thrones, were looking glorified. (20/43)

All the gods severally began to praise Lord Shiva in the sweat words. (20/44)

Being pleased with the praise (of gods and others) the Supreme God Shiva blessed all of them with boons according their wishes. (20/45)

O sage Nārad! Thereafter, all of them returned to their places (of residence), happily, taking the permission of Lord Shiva. All were glad to gether with Shri Vishṇu and accomplished with their desires. (20/46)

(Thereafter) Lord Shiva getting me (Brahmā) and Shri Vishṇu seated on the seats (suitable to us) said with love and kindness. (20/47)

O Vishṇu! O Brahman! You both are great among (the society of) gods and are entrusted with the works of creation and protection, so dearer to me. (20/48)

Now, you people go to your places (of residence) with no fear. I will be giving you pleasure always specially after inspection. (20/49)

Listening the words of Lord Shiva we affectionately saluting Him went to our places with His permission. (20/50)

It is, thus, clear that Shri Shiva after getting himself coronated as king of Kailāsh firstly tried to think for the goodness of the other two gods of the trinity of divine powers. Their association was needed in respect of the planning to make His state economically developed and also for the well beings of His gaṇas who came with Him to reside in the territory of Kailāsh which was by then under the political control of king Kuber, though by His own planning, as said earlier. It appears that Lord Shiva was a good political and economic planner because of the fact that firstly, He appointed Kuber His devotee as the King of that region, thereafter, He himself went there to rule as king and got His coronation done by the gods and His gaṇas as well as Shri Vishṇu and Shri Brahmā.

Shivapurāṇa-2

There is another description of state planning finding place in the Shivamahāpurāṇa (Rudra Samhita-War Volume-5). It relates the planning of Maya, son of couple Kashyapa and Danu, called Dānava. This story is also in the form of a discourse of Brahmā to god sage Nārad. In this story the description of austerity of the sons of a Daitya Tārak has been given, who after performing the same, established a kingdom, named Tripur, in a very planned way. It was not only the gods, who came forward with a concept of state planning for the establishment of state as well as for economic growth but also the demons, who were in the same race. The story pertaining to the state planning for the economic growth also begins with the austerity of Tārakāksha, Vidyunmāli and Kamalaksha, the sons of Tārak, jointly. It would be worth to mention here that demons were serious in the joint efforts for the sake of economic progress, while their step brothers, Ādityas (gods, the sons of Aditi) were not so keen.

On being asked by Nārad Shri Brahmā told him the story pertaining to the devastation of Tripur state by Lord Shiva and its cause. Lord Brahmā began to say to tale, as sage Sanat Kumar told to Vedavyas on his request, in the same way.

Sanat Kumar says—O great learned Vyas! You listen the character of Shankar holding the moon, as to how he caused the burning of Tripur by one arrow. (1/6)

When Kārtikeya, son of Shiva killed Tārakāsur then, O great sage! His three Daitya sons began to observe austerity seriously. (1/7)

Among them the name of elder one was Tārakāksha, the name of middle one was Vidyunmāli, the name of younger one was Kamalāksha. All the three were great heroes. (1/8)

They had control over their sense organs were very strengthful, observing Brahmacharya, truthful, strong minded, very brave and also opponenant to gods. (1/9)

All the three went to a cave of Mount Meru leaving away the entire enjoyments good to heart and mind and began to observe hard austerity there. (1/10)

O Sage! Thus being observed austerity by the Daityas when a long period elapsed, then I thought that the sons of Tāraka had gained ability owing to this religious rite. (1/24)

Thereafter, Brahmā, the religious teacher of Suras and Asuras, being satisfied (with their austerity) went there to bless them. (1/25)

At that time grand father Brahmā went with sages, gods, Asuras and other beings and said after pacifying them. (1/26)

O great Daityas! I am glad to you and have come to you for blessing you, so you ask for what desire you have (in your mind). (1/27)

What for you people have observed such a hard austerity? Tell me. I am the giver of consideration of the austerity to all and creation of all, i.e. Brahmā. (1/28)

Listening the words of Brahmā, the Daityas saluted him with joint hands. Thereafter, exchanging their thoughts, they severally began to say politely. (1/29)

O god head! If you are pleased with us and like to bless us then give us such boon that we may not be killed by any living being. (1/30)

Make us immortal in this world and protect us from all hurdles, old age, disease and death etc. which may not ever come to us. (1/31)

O Brahman! We want that we may not get old and do not die. And we shall be capable to kill all other people. (1/32)

We require no ample wealth, great cities, various enjoyments, various places, and glories. (1/33)

Because, if a man has to die, then for him it is useless to get such material of enjoyment for a few days, this we have decided. (1/34)

Becoming aware of their intentions Lord Brahmā remembering His God Shiva told- (1/35)

O Asuras! Nobody in this world is free from death, so you should not request for this and ask for any other boon in which you are interested. (1/36)

O Asuras! There has been none in this world who neither got old, nor died. It is the nature of this world to take birth and pass away. One who took birth he has to die and take rebirth. (1/37)

There is none to violate the nature of the time except Lord Shiva and Lord Vishṇu because these two (gods) are above religion and nonreligion (good and nongood) and express and unexpressed. (1/38)

You people ask for any such boon which though being the cause of death of you people but be based on the quality of truth and try to get yourselves protected from that cause, so that your death may not occur. (1/41)

Listening the words of Brahmā, the Daityas concentrated their mind for a while. Then thought for a moment and thereafter told to Brahmā. (1/42)

O God! Though we are courageous, yet we have no such place in which enemies might not enter and we may live there pleasurely. (1/43)

Therefore, you get three such wonderful cities built and provide to us, which may be full of all kinds of material and cereals and would be unapproachable even by the gods. (1/44)

O God of the world! We shall by the grace of your kindness residing in those three cities move throughout the world. (1/45)

From amongst them the elder one Tārakāksha said— O Brahman! I wish that a city made up of gold built by

Vishwakarmā and that it be impenetrable by the gods be given to me by him. (1/46)

Thereafter, Kamalāksha said—You give me alike city of silver built by Vishwakarmā. (1/47- I part)

Then Vidyunmāli joyfully said—You give a city of iron after getting built which be like that of Vajra. (1/47 – II part)

Then they jointly said— O Brahman! When it be noon and the moment be victorious, moon be of Pushya asterism (Nakshatra) and in the blue sky there be dearth causing cloud be raining at that time we may meet at an interval of our thousand years regularly and that those three cities be situated at one place. Then at the violation of righteousness or religion by us, any such god in whom all the gods would have taken shelter, who be seated on a chariot which be impossible (for men or god) and equipped with war weapons. (1/50-51)

And by one arrow-shot, which can never be possible to penetrate our three cities only then that be destructed, otherwise not, they (Daityas) thought over that there is none else except Shiva. (1/52)

But Lord Shiva is not jealous to anybody. Moreover he is our honourable (god) able to be saluted, why He will destruct our cities like this. This boon those Daityas asked after giving a consideration in the mind. (1/53)

Brahmā, the grandfather of all, listening the words (pertaining to boon) remembering Lord Shiva said— 'be as such'. (1/54)

Thereafter, he called for Maya (an engineer of Dānavas) and ordered to build three cities with gold, silver and iron (separately). (1/55)

Thus giving orders to Maya Brahmā went to his place (from there) while they had an eye at Him. (1/56)

With great labour Maya built a city of gold for Tārkāksha, a city of silver for Kamalāksha and a city of iron for Vidyunmāli and those were given to them (accordingly). (1/57-58)

From among them one was mover in heaven, the other moved

in the sky and the third one moved on the earth, Maya also lived in that city with intent to their well-being. (1/59)

So far Brahmā's discourse pertained to the background as to how three Daityās attained their goal of state planning and the cities according to their desire. From here Brahmā throws light on the virtual position and planning of those cities.

Thus three sons of great hero Tārak after getting the three cities began to enjoy all kinds of things. (1/60)

In those (three) cities there were number of heavenly tree (Kalpa trees) elephants, horses, palaces of various types and also those cities were full of precious stones. (1/61)

Those cities (jointly) were glorifying like the shinning planes as the solar circle shines, and with various ruby stones like moon. (1/62)

There built good looking palaces as high as the peak of Mount Kailāsh in those cities, and also main gates (of each) city. So many divine goddesses, Gandharvas, Siddhas, chāranas were residing in those cities. (1/63)

In every house there was a Shiva temple and (also) a place of sacrificial fire. Well versed Brāhmaṇas in Shāstras as well as devotee of Shiva resided in those cities. (1/64)

Those cities had so many ponds, wells, tanks, small lakes, lawns, gardens, foresty trees of various kinds brought from heaven, rivers having lotus, big rivers as well as wide rivers; as such (those cities) looked pleasent having heaven like qualities. Even the tree planted in those cities were, all the time, bearing flowers and fruits. (1/65-66)

There were various kinds of decorated palanquins, so many elephants in rut, tremulous horses in groups, different kinds of Chariots. (1/67)

There were playgrounds in every direction separately to play according to season or time. Likewise there were schools for the study of Vedas separately. (1/68)

No sinner could see towards those cities even by mind and

speech. Only persons of good conduct and persons of sacred soul could see. (1/69)

Every patch of land was sinless, full of women having fully devoted to their husbands and loyal in their services. (1/70)

In those cities very fortunate, and brave Daityas were residing with their wives, children and Brāhmaṇas. All the Daityas were well versed in the deeds as defined in Shrutis and Smritis and they observed their own religious rites. (1/71)

Whatever laws have been defined in the Vedas and Purāṇas and the laws liked by Lord Shiva, all those were present in the Daityas living in Tripur. (1/75)

Thus all the (three) sons of Tāraka being blessed by Brahmā taking the shelter of great Shaiva Maya were living (in the cities of their choice). (1/76)

Having devotion in Shaivism all the sons of Tāraka entered attacked the great cities of the three worlds and after destructing them began to rule. (1/77)

O sage (Nārad)! By enjoying the pleasure of statism according to their wishes sacred doer passed of a long time. (1/78)

The picture as described by Brahmā about the three cities of the Daitya brothers which they attained as a result of their austerity has the similarity with the modern method of planning of a city. If we go in the depth of the then planning we will find that the planning in question of those cities was in the form of a city-states of ancient Greece and Italy. So it can be said that the Indian people of that age had a clear concept of a city-states and also have the knowledge of the planning thereof. Though in the above story emphasis has been given on the spiritual gains, yet the worldly aspect of their austerity is apparent in this regard. Their sole aim being to avoid death by natural or unnatural means, so Brahmās blessings pertained to materialism having Rājas qualities as regards to economic well-beings of their states.

Matsyapurāṇa

We have seen in the foregoing pages that the sons of Tāraka

were active in the building of three cities, the joint name of which was Tripur. Buṭ in the Mātsyapurāṇa Dānava king Maya has been described as an active person in the building of the city of Tripur. Though at a latter stage the name of Maya has appeared in the above description but as their guardian and not as their king. Therefore, it is imperative to cite the story as narrated in this Purāṇa too, so as to bring to light the difference between the two.

Shri Sūta says, on being asked by the sages, as follows:-

O sages! Listen as to how Lord Shiva destructed Tripur. There was a great illusive Asura named Maya, who was father of various kinds of illusions. (129/3)

He was defeated by gods in a battle; therefore, he began to observe austerity. O Brāhmaṇas! Seeing him performing austerity other Daityas, also followed him to oblige. (129/4)

They were observing hard austerity for the purposes of his cause. Among them one was strengthful Vidyunmāli and the other one was hero Tāraka. (129/5)

Being attracted with the splendour of Maya they were observing austerity being seated behind him. They became so bright with the performance of austerity as if they were the three fires in the worldly forms. (129/6)

Those three Dāṇavas were observing austerity causing distress to the three world. In the winter season they sleep in the pond. In summer they took heat of five fires. (129/7)

In the rainy season they keep themselves standing in the open sky. As such they were causing their dear bodies decay and were only taking roots, fruits, flowers and water. (129/8)

Thus seeing the three Dānavas as the cause of burning the three worlds protector of world the grand father Brahmā appeared before them. Then those (Dānavas) suddenly seeing Brahmā, spoke with great courage and praised Him. (129/12)

Then Brahmā said to those Daityas, who became more brighted with the effect of their austerity, I have come to you (to bless) being satisfied with your austerity. (129/13)

At that time eyes and face of Brahmā were shining with happiness and told them to ask for boon according to their wishes. (129/14-15-I part)

Seeing Brahmā keen to bless, there came brightness in the eyes of Maya with happiness. (129/15-II part and 16-I part)

He then said, 'O god! In the earlier days the Daityas were defeated by gods in the battle of Tārakamaya. (129/16 II part)

They killed some with weapons and some were wounded, by their attack, being enemity with the gods, we ran here and there dreadfully. (129/17)

But, we the refugees could know nothing, as to who would give us shelter. Therefore, I like to make a fort, with the effect of my austerity and at the strength of your devotion, which would be difficult to gods to enter in. O great grandfather (Brahmā)! Give me such boon so that I may build that type of fort comprising of three cities. (129/81-19)

That Tripur be such that even anything made up of earth (soil), water and fire, the curse given by the sages, and also the entrances of gods and their weapons all be ineffective. (129/20)

If it appears good to you then please that Tripur be indestructible by all. Being asked so by Vishwakarmā (Maya, the engineer), the world creator (Brahmā) said. (129/21)

O Daitya king, addressing happily, there is no rule of law for immortality to the people of bad conduct. (129/22)

You build the fort with dry grasses. Listening the words of grandfather (Brahmā), Maya Dānava said. (129/23)

With joint hand he again asked, O creation of Lotus! 'One who can burn my fort with one arrow-shot at only one time and that for other beings we be unkilled, you bless us with this boon'. Brahmā said to Maya, 'it would be so'. (129/24-25)

Therefore, Brahmā disappeared like the wealth obtained in the dream. Then Maya, who was brighting like sun went home and others also did so. (129/26)

It is thus clear from the above that there is a basic difference between the two groups of Dānavas, who are said to have performed the austerity for attaining the knowledge and ability for the construction of three cities i.e. Tripur in the descriptions of the two Purāṇas. In Shivamahapurāṇa the group of Dānavas, who performed austerity comprised of Tārakāksha, Vidyunmāli and Kamalāksha, whereas the description of Mātsyapurāna says that the said group of Dānavas comprised of Maya, Vidyunmāli and Tā rak. Though the figure three is present in both the descriptions, yet the name of main Dānava differs. The earlier descriptions takes the name of Tārakāksha as the main person whereas according to the latter description it was Maya who performed the austerity for himself and that Vidyunmāli and Tārak joined him as associates in his favour. Moreover, in the earlier one all the three have been named as the sons of Tārak. Whereas in the latter one he (Tārak) has been said as an associate of Maya. Thus, Tārak was alive and not dead as said in the earlier description. Further, in the earlier description Maya comes in the picture latter on as the patron of that group, whereas in this one Maya is the architect of whole concept.

The latter part of the chapter of the Mātsyapurnāṇa under study describes as to how Maya planned to build a fort comprising of three cities for himself and his other two associates.

After sometime Maya began to plan the cities in mind, the description of which is as follows—

Those hero Dānavas became glorious with the effect of their austerity and the blessings (of Brahmā). Then great intelligent Dānava Maya (began to think). (129/27)

As to how I should build a fort so that it be a great one and be comprised of such three. (129/28)

And also that none except myself may get entry in that and it could not be penetrated even by only one arrowshot. (129/29)

The gods would he effortful to destroy it but I have to think over that. Among them each city should have an area of one hundred of Yojana. (129/30)

The column of each one should also be of one hundred Yojana. These cities should be built in the asterism of Pushya. (129/31)

In that very asterism of Pushya those three cities will meet in the universe with each other and the person, who would get them meeting each other, only he could destruct them with one arrow-shot. (129/32-33-I part)

From amongst (those three) one built of iron will be on the ground, the second one will be in the space below the sky built of silver, and the third one will be above the silver one, which will be made of Gold. (129/33-II part – 34-I part)

Thus all the three being connected with each other would be called Tripur. Within them there being a column of one thousand Yojana, it would be unapproachable by others. (129/34)

That Tripur would be glorified by palaces, fitted with weapons which could be capable of killing one hundred men at a time, wheel-like weapon, trident (trishul a three pointed weapon), rock or precious stone, flags, large gates like Mounts Mandar and Sumeru, peak-like perkotas. Among that city built of iron would be guarded by Tārak, Maya would guard golden city and the city of silver would be guarded by Vidyaunmāli. All the three would be appointed accordingly. In this condition except that of Lord Shiva none other would be capable to destruct this Tripur. (129/35-36)

The above narration brings to light the planning of king Maya, an engineer of Dānavas, as to how he planned before hand to build a fort comprising of three cities. It was his own planning. He observed austerity to acquire the knowledge of such an engineering so that he could have no difficulty in building that. In the modern time every welfare state makes such a proposal keeping in view all the aspects of the concerning work before taking up its execution. Maya too took up the work of building the fort thereafter.

The story teller Shri Suta says—

O sages! Dānava Maya, thinking so, began the construction of a fort named Tripur by divine means which could have been conducted by his will. (130/1)

He thought that on this path there would be 'Parkota', whether here or there would be main gate of the city. It would be better to keep the door of the big or small palace. (130/2)

Here should be the highway, there should be roads with pedestarians of both the sides and also lanes wherever needed, and there should be platforms also at appropriate places. (130/3)

There should be ladies apartments, that place would be suitable for Shiva temple. He also selected appropriate places for the plantation of banyan tree and the construction of ponds, tanks and lakes. (130/4)

This place would be better for groves, assembly halls, garden and that such places would be better for the exit of Dānavas. (130/5)

In this way an skilled town planner Maya got constructed the divine city of Tripur simply by the desire of mind only. (not physically), I have heard so. (130/5)

The city of iron, which Maya built, he gave to Asura Tārak, who having control over that made it his residence. (130/7)

The second one, which was the city of silver, went under the ownership of Vidyunmāli. It was shining like the full moon. It looked like cloud of lightnings. (130/8)

What the third one Maya built, was the city of gold. Maya kept it for himself and became owner of that. (130/9)

As the city of Tārakasur was located at a distance of one thousand yojana from the city belonging to Vidyunmāli, like that there was a difference of one hundred yojana between the city of Vidyunmāli and of Maya, the great city of Maya looked like Mount Merus. Thus Maya built the city of Tripur in the asterism of Pushya. (130/10-11)

As such Dānava king Maya was not only a man of ordinary prudence, but had a complete knowledge of town planning as well. In the story as narrated by the Shivamahāpurāṇa what knowledge Tārāksha and his brothers acquired about the building of Tripur, was the result of their austerity and the blessing of Lord Brahmā in consideration to the same. Whereas in the description of Matsyapurāṇa the things are more clear. Maya wanted to proceed on his planning with the blessings of Lord Brahmā, so that he be spiritually equipped.

It is generally felt that Dānavas were always against any religious rite whatever kind it would have been. This story nullifies such a feeling. If a king of Dānavas or the sons of a Dānava military general, viz. Tāraka, felt to attain spiritual power by way of observing austerity that too at a place where most of the sages had done concentration, then it cannot be said that all Dānavas were against religious rites.

After getting blessed by Lord Brahmā Maya himself planned by applying his own intelligence, before proceeding with the construction of the three cities in question. Such a description of Mātsyapurāna goes to justify that Maya had a good knowledge of town planning.

Even if it is accepted that Dānava general Tārak's sons performed austerity after his death in a battle, this fact remains unaffected that the Dānavas too took interest in performing austerity to equip themselves spiritually. When they felt weak as well as when desired to attain worldly prosperity. In the context of planning of the construction of joint three cities named Tripur the observance of austerity is relevant only on the point of acquiring a complete knowledge of the same before proceeding with that. When a person or a group of persons attained that knowledge the study comes around him pertaining to his planning for the application of the same. In the case under reference, it is found that the Dānavas succeeded in their mission of construction of three cities in a joint form as well as giving them the shape of the handsome cities with such facilities that could attract the others to plan and proceed on their guidelines. In view of the above description and the conclusion drawn from that it can be said that Maya is the first town-planner who has given a clear picture of the town planning in the modern sense of the terms in the history of state planning.

■

7

Policy of Taxation

Mahābhārat — Shāntiparva – I

It is the general belief that the very idea of taxation initially cropped up in the mind of the ruler, who acquired administrative power when the society turned into a political one. But the Purāṇas narrate a different story in this regard. A description, which finds place in the Mahābhārat Shāntiparva throws light on this subject in the context of origin of Kingship. It says that the proposal for paying tax came from the public which felt the need of a king for the righteous management of a definite territory. The following extract of the said description of Mahābhārat brings to light the Indian viewpoint on the subject under study.

Having no king the people felt great trouble; they together approached Lord Brahmā, the grand father, and narrated the same to Him, thus O God! We are vanishing without a king. You provide us (a king) who be able to rule, nourish us and to whom we may worship. (67/20-21-Ist part)

Thereupon he gave order to Manu for the same, but Manu declined to accept. (67/21-II Part)

Giving reasons of his declination Manu said—

O God! I fear to the sinful acts. It is difficult to govern, especially when the people would be engaged in doing corrupt practices everyday. (67/22)

Then the people collectively said to Manu—

O great one! Do not be so afraid. Sin will have its effect at those, who would do it. We will be giving you one animal per fifty (in number) for the rise of your treasure. When our girls would reach the age of marriage, we would provide to you the one, which would be the most beautiful among them. (67/23-24)

Our chief persons equipped with weapons and vehicles follow you like that of Indra followed by gods. (67/25)

Getting the cooperation of the people you would be strong, unwon and powerful king. As Kuber makes Yakshas and Rākshasas pleasureful by protecting them, so you will protect us and keep pleasureful. (67/26)

You would be receiving one fourth share in the righteous deeds being done by the subjects having been protected by a king like you. (67/27)

O king! Being accomplished with great spiritual gain so pleasurably you protect us from all sides like that of Indra, who protects gods. (67/28).

O Great one ! you make a victory campaign like warm rays of sun. (You) end the proud of enemies, be victorious always. (67/29)

Then shinning Manu came out surrounded with forces of brilliance. (67/30)

As gods get affected to see the glory of Indra, Likewise all the people fearfully began to take interest in their duties. (67/31)

Thereafter, he began to walk around the earth persuading the subjects to take interest in the duties of their own Varna and Āshram as well as keeping the sinners at rest like that of raining clouds. (67/32)

Thus the persons who are desirous of rising glory, they should firstly select a king on this earth for kind blessings. (67/33)

Thereafter, as the disciples devotedly salute a religious teacher and the gods salute Indra rightly like that subjects should make a salute to their king. (67/34)

One, who is welcomed by his own people is honoured by others too and who is neglected by his own (men) is dishonoured by the other in this world. (67/35)

A defeat of king by other is painful for the subjects too. Therefore, it is imperative for the subjects to gift away umbrella, vehicle, clothes, armaments, foods, drinks, sitting material, cots and all other such things to the king. (67/36-37)

It is, thus, apparent from the above that initially source of a king's livelihood was not the compulsory tax levied on the subjects but the voluntary gifts in lieu of his (king's) services rendered to the public of his state.

Mahābhārat — Shāntiparva -2

In the chapter -87 of Mahābhārat, Shāntiparva the policy of taxation has been laid down in detail. Even emergency taxation policy has also been given therein together with the general policy for the sake of prosperity of the nation. What things to be kept in the mind while levying taxes on the people in general and the businessmen as well as agriculturists, in particular, have also been pointed out in the following description—

While levying tax on the businessman purchase and sale of articles, expenses on transportation, wages of employees, welfare of the business itself and savings etc. should be kept in view. (87/13-II part, 14-I part)

Likewise (cost of) production, consumption and the categories of articles pertaining to art and craft be fully investigated before taxing the products and the artisan or craftsman. (87/14-II part, 15-I part)

O Yudhisthir! While taxing a person his capacity to pay be kept in view. A king should tax to such an extent so that the people might not come in trouble. Their work and profit should be considered. (87/15-II part and 16)

If the work and profit both go in vain none would like to take up any work, so a king should find out means as to how he as well as (government) employees get benefited from the work (like agriculture and business). (87/17)

A king should always have an eye while determining taxes on all those things. He should not root out the very means of living to be greedy of taxes. (87/18)

A king should exhibit himself in such a manner which may look affectionate to the people by closing the doors of attachment (of wealth). When a king is known as exploitator his subjects get annoyed from him. (87/19)

How there can be good to a person when all the people have

malice against him? One, who is not affectionate to the people, gets no benefit. A king whose intelligence has not become feeble he should take (tax) from his nation as a calf takes milk of a cow. (87/20)

O Yudhishthir, a scion of Bharat! A cow which is not milked too much her calf becomes healthy and can carry much load. But which one is milked much her calf being weak can carry on no such work. (87/21)

Likewise a nation which is exploited too much gets poor and can take up no heavy projects. A king should himself be ready with kindness for the protection of his nation. (87/22)

It is good to carry on his life on merciful earnings from his nation and that he should take interest in increasing the accumulated wealth of his people for any emergency. By this way he enjoys the fruits thereof. (87/23)

He should consider the same (the accumulated wealth with people) as the treasure of the nation. (87/ 24-I part)

If the citizens and the countrymen presented king through a midman he should be kind to such less wealthy ones according his capacity. (87/24)

The extra-territorial persons perhaps criminals living in the forests etc) should be divided diplomatically for taking money in the interest of nation and also from the middle class persons likewise. By doing this, none of them become angry with him. (87/25)

A king should make a tour in the nation by explaining the need of taking wealth (tax) to the people and by placing before them the instant danger to the same. (87/26)

He should tell the people (thus) – A state of emergency is there on our nation. There is a danger of attack of enemies. As the fruits coming the bamboos cause the destruction of the same, so the enemies for their debacle have risen to attack our nation with many dacoits and put us in trouble. (87/27-28)

I am asking for wealth (as tax) from you people for your protection in such emergency and fearful state of affairs. (87/29)

When such fearfulness would be removed, I would return these wealth to you people. But the wealth which the enemy will rob, he will never return the same. (87/30)

When attacked by the enemy your ladies will firstly come in trouble. Your entire wealth vanish with them. The accumulation of wealth is needed for the protection of ladies and children. (87/31)

As the rise of sons makes the father happy, likewise, I become happy with the prosperity of you people. I will collect wealth from you people according to one's capacity, so that none come in distress and to avoid the instant trouble. (87/32)

As the strong bull carry load even at uneven places, likewise you people should share in this state of emergency on the nation. It would be no good to hide out the wealth at the time of any emergency. (87/33)

A king having knowledge of the activities of time send his employees after persuading them by such sweet words for the collection of wealth from the people. They should also adopt such means. (87/34)

For the construction of boundary walls, for the security of the capital city, for the maintenances of employees and soulders, to remove the danger of attack, for well-being of the nation as well as other necessities may be the reasons for the collection of taxes. (87/35)

The people who are heavily taxed, they leave the country and began to live in the forest. Therefore, a king should have a soft corner towards them. (87/36).

Though the above guideline of the taxation policy finds place in the dialogue went on between king Yudhisthir and prince Bhishma, yet it reflects the views of sage Vedavyas the author on this subject. He being highly connected with the royal family of Hastinapur state, his viewpoint on the subject of a definite and good policy of taxation was immediately needed to king Yudhisthir to rehabilitate the state economy which collapsed during the just ended Kurukeshetra war. Sage Vedavyas being a good advisor of Pāndavas, is expected to have been consulted by king Yudhishthir during his regime, as and when needed, for the economic development of his country.

The guidelines described in the Mahābhārat Shāntiparva have relevancy in the modern time too, while taxes are proposed in the annual budget of a country particularly in the Indian budget. These directive principles of state taxation are never outdated. Such principles have universal and all time value.

Mahābhāarat Shāntiparva - 3

In the foregoing pages where emergency tax policy has been studied, here we are going to study general policy of taxation. King Yudhishthir was curious to know the ways and means that help to increase the national treasure. He asked from Bhishma to throw light on this subject too.

King Yudhishthir questioned Bhishma thus—

O great intelligent grand father ! When a king is completely capable then what would be the ways and means to increase the state treasure, if he likes to do so, please tell me. (88/1)

Replying the question of king Yudhisthir Bhishma said—

O king! A king desirous of righteousness should have an eye on the circumstances of the time and the country and utilizing his intelligence and strength and by keeping himself engaged in the interest or well-being of his subjects should have governance over them. (88/2)

The work which is in the interest of the people as well as in the interest of his own the same should be given publicity in the state. (88/3)

As the black bees take away the juice from the flowers and trees slowly and slowly but does not cut it and that a man takes away milk from a cow giving no trouble to her calf and does not crush the udder. Rightly like this a king should milk the nation without crushing it. (88/4)

As leach suck up the blood of the body slowly and slowly likewise king should collect taxes from the nation. As lioness carries her children by catching them by teeth with no pain, likewise the king should collect taxes with good means or measures. (88/5)

As rat cuts the leg of a man so softly that he simply moves it, having been unaware of the pains. Likewise a king should tax the people in such a way so that they feel no trouble in paying it. (88/6)

Firstly he should levy less tax, thereafter it should be gradually increased and collect that increased one. After that it be increased little by little to suit the time. (88/7)

As a man, who has to carry load on a (new) calf, firstly he effort-fully put a string into the nostrils of the same and gradually goes on increasing the load, like that tax load on the subjects initially be a little and then get it increased gradually. (88/8)

If a person wants to place heavy load on mon (new) calves together after putting the strings into their nostrils, it would be difficult to control them. Therefore, it is proper to put string into their nostrils one by one effortfully and then they should be brought into the use if carrying load. By doing so they would become able to carry full load. (88/9)

Therefore, it is difficult for a king to make effort to control all the people together. So it is proper for him to bring under control by satisfying chieftains by using sympathetic words and only then employ men in general as desired. (88/10)

Thereafter, those, who make consultations interse, should be got divided and that the king then showing sympathy employ them pleasurely with no effort. (88/11)

So it is imperative for a king that he should not levy heavy tax load on the subjects against the time and the circumstances. He should collect taxes by proper means after persuading the people. (88/12)

O king ! I am telling you good means. It is no good for me to let you know the deceitful ways. Those, who do not adopt good measures whimsically and want to bring the horses under control, they make them wrathful. (88/13)

Manu has much earlier made a general law for the entire mankind, except that during emergency, none should ask for anything from anyone. (88/16).

In this way a king has never been free to levy taxes on his subjects whimsically on one pretax or the other or on the grounds of increased administrative expenditure or on account of development. The sages and the authorities on the Shāstras always have an eye on the tax policy of the kings. When needed they tried to bring the kings back on the right path. Such a task is easy in the present time of democracy. A government can be voted out of power, if its tax policy does not appeal to reasons or to the paying capacity of the people. It was the tax policy of the United Kingdom which did not suit the British Americans and that they rose to fight against their own rule and threw it out of power in the freedom fight in the last phase of eighteenth century.

Shukranīti

What part of the income should be taken as tax by a king has been given in the Shukranīti in detail. Every taxable article to be valued first and that the tax be levied thereon after that. Āchārya Shukra is not in favour of flat rate tax on all the householders or articles coming under the taxable limit of income . Where Vedavyas lays down general policy of taxation, Ācharyā Shukra lays down there general rules of taxation to be followed by a king. Moreover, the limit of tax fixed by Shukra is maximum. It is not necessary that a king or government must levy to that extent. The political administration should consider to levy at a minimum level, so that there may have a chance to increase that limit as and when any kind of emergency arises without giving any trouble to the people. The rules propagated by Āchārya Shukra regarding taxation are as follows—

Shukra begins with defining the characteristics of treasure :—

Now I describe under the discussion of treasure the second one in the mixed chapter (of Shukranīti). A group of articles of equal nature is called treasure. That can be several and of more than one kind. (4/2/1)

A king may adopt any means for the collection of wealth. And from that wealth, he should protect the nation, army and sacrificial deeds. (4/2/2)

The treasure which is collected for the sake of protection of the people army and for the performance of sacrifices is pleasureful for the king whether it be this world or that world. It is troublesome, if the collection of treasure is for the different purposes. (4/2/3)

The collection of treasure, for the purposes of well-beings of wife and sons and for his (king's) own use, is the giver of hell because it can never be pleasureful in the next world. (4/2/4)

The wealth, which has been acquired by improper means, is the cause of giving sinful results. The wealth which is acquired from good persons or given to good ones always accretes. (4/2/5)

The person who earns wealth by justified means, and spends for good causes, is called good one. But who does against that is called bad one. When a king takes away that kind of wealth, he is not sinner or guilty of sin. (4/2/6)

A king may take away the wealth of a unrighteous king, either by means of deceitfulness or by force or by the ways of dacoits. Likewise it can be taken away from the enemy nation. (4/2/7)

Those (Kings) who have collected wealth by giving away fair policy that wealth goes in the hands of enemy with the territory. (4/2/8)

Where there is no special emergency, tax, by imposing fine on the subjects, land revenue or increased toll tax and taxes from religious properties of religious places should not be collected by a king for the accretion of his treasures. (4/2/9)

When the need of vanishing enemy is there and the army is to be equipped then especial kind of tax or toll tax may be levied on the subjects for the accretion of wealth. (4/2/10)

In case of any emergent need the king may take away the wealth of rich persons, with a promise to pay interest thereupon, by force. That should be returned, after passing away that emergency, with (the promised) interest accrued thereon to them. (4/2/11)

Otherwise, owing to paucity of wealth, subjects, state, treasure and king (himself) may vanish. More fine or tax is also the cause of decay of state and king like (king) Suratha and others. (4/2/12)

A King should collect taxes to that extent by which maintenance of people as well as of army can be done for a period of twenty years, without imposing fine or revenue or toll tax (additionally). (4/2/13 and 14-I part)

The source of treasure is army and the source of army is treasure and by the protection of both the nation develops and the enemies vanish. By protecting the subjects all the three objects are achieved, i.e. developments of nation and treasure are accomplished as well as enemy vanishes and that heaven is gained (after death). (4/2/14-II part and 16)

The wealth has been created for the performance of sacrifice and sacrifice is performed for the pleasure of heaven and long life and that lack of enemy is the cause of welfare of the army, treasure and the nation all the three. (4/2/16)

It is the policy-skill of the king, who is of forgiving nature, all the above subjects get increased. So full skill of intelligence should be applied for the growth of the above. (4/2/17)

A king, who maintains his subjects like a gardener, and by taking taxes from the enemy by making them taxpayer increases his treasure, is great one. The one who accretes his treasure by means of business or trade, is called middle one, and which one increases his treasure by imposing fine or levying taxes on pilgrimage and temple etc is known as lowest or mean. (4/2/18-19).

A King should protect the subjects, who have less or medium wealth through salaried employee and those who are wealthy should be protected by the king like that of a guarantee holder. (4/2/20)

Because the wealthy people are neither more nor less in comparision to the king. (4/2/21-Ist part)

The wealth which can maintain the family for twelve years is known as mean, which one is able to maintain (the family) for sixteen years is called medium, and that one is sufficient to maintain for twenty years is good one. (4/2/21-II part and 22).

In case of (financial) trouble a king should yearmark such quantity of wealth starting from mean (categpry of wealth) and get it saved (for future). (4/2/23-I part).

The businessmen transact their business with the principal money and donot invest for the accretion thereof. They purchase for collection when the articles are cheap and sell when it costs higher. (4/2/23- II part and 24-I part).

A king should not take away the articles so collected from a business-man without paying their costs. If he does so forcibly his subjects' wrath burn him with his children. (4/2/24- II part and 25- I part)

A king should from time to time collect wealth for his well-being and also for the maintenance of the state for three years. And for glorious people it is proper to have a collection even for more years. (4/2/25- II part and 26).

Only those articles should have been choosen for collection which are ripe, clean, of good quality and well dried, new, having good smell; of good colour and taste, good and stable for years together as well as costly. If of otherwise qualities or so such cereals should not be collected as such. (4/2/27- 28 I part).

The articles which vanish owing to poison, fire and frost, should not be collected (for future use) and should be cousumed till those things do not become useless. (4/2/28-II part and 29- I part).

The king should again put effortfully same quantity and of same quality of articles which are consumed (at the time of new arrival). (4/2/29 II part and 30 I part)

It is also proper for a king to store, herbs, metals, wood, machine, weapons, explosives, utensils, clothes as well as other things which are required for the use of such things as said above because time to time these are required to accomplish the work. (4/2/30 II part, 31 and 32 I part).

The articles so stored should be effortfully protected, because for the collection of these things more pain is taken and four times pain is taken in their protection. (4/2/32 II part and 33 I part)

If neglected even for a moment in protection the articles vanish soon. (4/2/33 II part)

The loss of earned articles causes sorrow to the acquirer and not to the wife or sons and others to so much extent. (4/2/34)

The person who knows to earn only but not no protect it fully, there is none great fool in camparison to him. Because labour of acquisition goes in vain. (4/2/36)

Where Āchārya Shukra emphasizes on acquiring wealth by means of taxation etc. at the same place he forcefully lays down rules and provisions for the storage and protection thereof. He does not forget in expressing his opinion regarding the person who is not keen in protecting the earned wealth or income to the utmost of his capacity. When he says that it is difficult to earn wealth then and there he says it is four time difficult to protect the same. His views are more practical in earning and storage of wealth particularly at the state level.

Shukranīti - 2

Āchārya Shukra is such a policy giver, who, also, lays down norms for taking toll tax on various consumable articles which are transacted in the market by businessmen. According to him rules of taking toll-tax are as follows. Defining the toll-tax he comes on the rules.

A wise man should always specify the value of the articles or things according to the local customs and that what portion (of that value) is taken by the king from sellers and purchasers, is called, 'toll-tax'. (4/2/104)

So far, it is possible toll-tax should be taken only once at the place where it is fixed. Either it should be fixed for taking toll-tax at a place of market path are at the border (of the state or town or capital). (4/2/105)

A king should never take toll-tax deceitfully on a particular article at number of time. He should take only thirty second portion of the cost of article as toll-tax either from seller or from purchaser. (4/2/106).

Or, he should take as toll-tax twentieth or sixteenth part or the profit after deducting the cost of the article and that if seller gets the sale price equal to that of cost price or less than that (in the market) nothing should be taken as toll-tax from him. (4/2/107)

A king should always consider the cost price and the sale price. In the case of more profit is accrued to the purchaser, he should take tax from him. (4/2/108-I part)

Field tax should be taken after getting it measured and also according to its fruitfulness as little, medium or good. (4/2/108-II part)

An agriculturist should be taxed in accordance with the crops of the land and only that much tax be taken from him so that he may not vanish. (4/2/109)

As a gardener plucks only a few flowers from the creepers (plants) likewise taxes be collected (from the agriculturists) and not like that of coal making ones, who do so by cutting, the tree with roots and burning that. The consideration of levying tax be good, medium and worst cropping. (4/2/110)

Throwing light on the cropping position Āchārya Shukra says :-

A good crop is that which yields two times benefit after deducting the land revenue as well as the expenses incurred in taking the crop. The crop which yields lesser profit than that is a troublesome agriculture. (4/2/111)

The fields which are irrigated by the water of pond or well are liable to be taxed to the extent of one-third of the profit, whereas one-fourth tax can be levied at the fields which are irrigated by rain water and that the fields irrigated by the water of river may be taxed to the extent of half of the produce. Likewise one- sixth of the output be taken as tax from the barren fields as well as fields of pebbly character. (4/2/112-113).

A king who receives tax from an agriculturist to the extent of rupees hundred in-silver coins, the (king) should pay him (the agriculturist) the twentieth part of that from his own side. (4/2/114).

Shukrāchārya also throws light at toll-tax to be levied on precious stones and metals as well as wood and grasses etc. as follows:–

After deducting the expenses incurred in taking out from mines half of the quantity of gold, one-third of silver,one-fourth of copper, one-sixth of iron, lead, vang, and from (precious) stones as well as salts half of those things may be taken as tax. Whereas from agriculturist etc. taking into considerations of the profit one-third, one-fifth, one-seventh or one-tenth thereof (produce) be taken (as tax). (4/2/115,116, and 117-I part).

And that from the sellers of wood and grasses etc one-twenteeth (of the profit) should be taken as tax. (4/2/117-II Part).

According to Shukra toll-tax from the sellers of the livestock should also be collected:-

A king can collect tax (from the sellers of) goats, sheep, cows, buffalows, and horses to the extent of one-eighth of their accretion. And one-sixteenth of the milk of cows, sheep, goats and buffalows should be collected as tax by the king. (4/2/118)

Sage Shukra is of the view that even artisans and craftsmen should also be taxed in terms of their labour in accordance with the man-day, as follows:

The carpenters and artists should be asked to work one day in a fortnight with no wage. Those who work in the construction of tanks, ponds, or canals (artificial rivers) and who after tilling the land make it cultivable should be exempt from that taxes. They should be taxed only when they get earnings from the same. (4/2/119-120)

He also directs the people to take their shares without delay together with taxes and toll taxes:-

One should get his land separated, take wages, toll-tax, interest, brokerage and tax immediately with no delay. (4/2/121)

He also frames rules for the collection of land revenue by the king:–

After receiving the land revenue a written receipt with seal (of the state) be given to the agriculturists. Alternatively, a big land holder be asked to pay the entire revenue of all the lands of the village and that he (such payer) be accepted as guranteeholder of the tillers of the land (of the village), who in turn pay tax per month or per season to the king, after collecting it either one-sixteenth, one twelveth, one-tenth or one-eighth which share is to be paid to the king befixed according to the capacity (of the tillers). The king should also appoint (him) as chieftain of the village. (4/2/122 to 124)

The sage also makes a rule of exemption from tax to such articles which are kept separate for the maintence of the family:—

The king should not levy tax on the articles which are stored for the maintence of the family, like milk of cow etc. and that the cereals for personal use and also for the purchase of clothes. (4/2/125)

What share of profit be taken as tax from a businessman and a money lender, Āchārya Shukra does not forget to mention. He says:—

A King should receive tax from a businessman and moneylender one-thirty second share of the profit (over the principal). And he should take tax on the land given for the construction of a house equal to that of agricultural land. (4/2/126)

But he leaves path-tax and shop tax on the reasons of the king of the concerning state saying:–

The king should take tax of land of shopkeepers and path-tax from the travelers for the maintenance of that (roads) and sweeping or cleaning thereof. (4/2/127)

A king after taking tax from all (the people) project (their interest) like that of an employee. Thus a brief discussion on the subject of tax has been narrated. (4/2/128)

Though Āchārya Shukra has said his description as brief one, yet it is in detail in view of his time in which articles to be taxed and the scope of the policy of taxation were very limited. He has mentioned almost all the categories of the properties which were known to him at which tax could be levied either in the form of land revenue, toll-tax or share of profit or accretion etc. of the goods or live-stocks too. Even he has thrown light on the exemption policy.

Apart from Āchārya Shukra, there developed a principle in the states ruled by a king that he received taxes from his subjects in lieu of his services to them. The aim and object of this principle was to have a physical control over the king by learned class of the people. When need they also applied their policy making power, as representative of the people against a king who went against the interest of his subject, to an extent of overthrowing him from the political power as well as from the throne.

Agnipurāṇa

The author of Agnipurāṇa has paid his attention towards the

collection of taxes from their subjects by a king for the maintenance of the state as well as of the taxpayer people. Sage Pushkar who is the teller of the concerning story says in the following words—

A king should collect tax from the shops which are located within his territory and that it should be one-twenteeth part of their income. The consideration should be given to the expenses incurred on the import of goods from the other countries as well as the loss occurred thereon. While leving tax on the articles; the invoice should also be perused. So that he may be earning profit and that only one-twenteeth part be taken (as tax). (223/23 to 24)

If any employee (of the king) collects (tax) more than that (limit) he should be punished. No tax in the form of service charges of (crossing the river by) the boat should be collected from the ladies and ascetics. If any loss is caused by the mistake of boatman, then it should be made good by him.

A king should take one-sixth part of the wheat and the barley etc. kind of cereals, whereas one-eighth of the peas and gram kind of cereals. Likewise fruits and root which are the products of jungle should be taxed according to the time and the country.

Likewise cattles and the gold are to be taxed one-fifth and one-sixth part respectively. Perfumes, herbs, juice, flowers, roots, fruits, leaves, greens, grasses, bamboo, reed, hide, articles made of bamboos, utensils made of stone (rocks), honey, meat and ghee (processed butter) be taxed one-sixth of the income. (223/25 to 29)

A king should collect no tax from the Brāhmaṇa. If a Brāhmaṇa versed in Vedas (Shruti) gets trouble in the state of a king being starved, his state always suffers from diseases, droughts and dacoits. Therefore, being aware of the education of the Brāhmaṇa and his conduct, provisions of suitable livelihood should be made. As a father maintains his own son likewise a king should maintain a learned person and a Brāhmaṇa of good conduct. A Brāhmaṇa, who being maintained by a king performs religious rites, owing to that, a king lives long and his nation and treasure get progress.

An artisan should work one day in a month without any wage,

by accepting meals only for the king (as tax). Others, who also earn their livelihood by manual work (i.e. labour), should work one day in a month for the king (as tax). (223/30 to 34)

The policy and the law of taxation as given by sage Pushkar are on the same pattern as that of other law giver sages on this subject have given which have been described above. Though, there is nothing new in his tax policy yet it reflect the concurrent views of the sages on the said subject and also the survival of the law and the rules framed by sages for long in the same continuity.

Yājyavalkyasmriti

It is a concurrent opinion of the sages that a king gets tax in lieu of his services to the nation and the residents. Sage Yājyavalkya giving emphasis thereon says this—

A king maintaining the subjects justifiably gets one-sixth of their sacred benefits, therefore, maintaining the subjects is greater than any donation. (1/335)

Where Yājyavalkya throws light on the duties of a king against the collection of tax from the people at the same place he expresses his opinion on the subject of non-performance of his duties due to negligence, thus—

Whatever sin the unprotected subjects commit, the half of that goes to the king because he collects tax for their protection. (1/337)

The king, who collects tax from his subjects and increases his treasure by unjustified means, gets vanished with his brethren soon by getting poor. (1/340)

Apparently all the sages and saints of ancient India were against the heavy load of tax on the people. It is also a fact that they had control over the unreasonable and unjustified tax policy of a king. No king could dare to go against the policy of taxation framed by sages and the learned class of the people. Those, who dared to go against their verdict on this subject lost their entity. Sage Yājyavalkya's indication is to towards that.

■

8

War Economy

Bhāgwatpurāna - 1

The Shrimad Bhāgwatpurāṇa brings to light the origin of war economy on the Indian soil. According to this Puraṇa the economy of war began in this country with the establishment of a political rule in the hands of Hiraṇya Kashipu, a son of sage Kashyap with his wife Diti. He had a twin brother named Hiraṇyāksha. The seat of his capital was located at Hiranyapur, perhaps it was named after 'Hiranya' the first part of his name. It is just possible that Hiranyakashipu was a self styled king on the basis of his physical strength as well as owing to the blessings of Lord Brahmā in the form a boon by virtue of his austerity in the young age. The boon blessed on him by Lord Brahmā made him ambitious of establishing a political empire under his reign.

His brother, Hiraṇyāksha, to whom he loved too much, wanted to please him at all occasions. He went on to conquest the world for the satisfaction of his (Hiraṇya Kashipu's) ego. The story in respect to the conquest of Hiraṇyāksha as depicted by the Shrimad Bhagwat runs as follows:-

Fearing death at the hands of none by virtue of a boon blessed by Brahmā, Hiraṇyakashipu was pulled up with pride and brought under his sway by his arms all the three world along with their guardian deities. (3/17/19)

His beloved younger brother, Hiranyāksha, who always tried to please him and was very fond of war, once went up to heaven, with mace in his hand, seeking combat. (3/17/20)

His tempo was difficult to resist. He had anklets of gold tinkling about his feet. Adorned with a Vaijanti (giver of victory) garland, he rested his huge mace on one of his shoulders. (3/17/21)

His strength of mind as well as of body and the boon blessed at him had pulled him up. He had no fear of death at the hands of anybody. As such there was no check on him. The gods, therefore, were seized with fear at his very sight and hide themselves even as snakes hide themselves for fear of Garuḍa. (3/17/22)

The chief of the Daityas saw that they had vanished before his might, and roared aloud on not finding Indra and the gods. (So) he had been intoxicated with power. (3/17/23)

Having returned therefrom, the mighty Daitya, like an elephant in rut, dived into the deep ocean – which was terribly roaring – just for the sake of a game. (3/17/24)

On his entering in the ocean the aquatic creatures forming the host of Varuṇa (the god of waters) were distracted with fear and ran away too far scared by his very splendour without his slaying of a blow. (3/17/25).

Moving about in the ocean for very many years the mighty Hiraṇyaksha smote the gigantic waves tossed by the winds with his iron mace again and again, and reached Vibhāvari, the capital of Varuṇa, O dear Vidur. (3/17/26)

Seeing Pracheta (Varuṇa), the Guardian of Pātāl (bottom) country and the lord of the acquatic creatures, there, he fell at the latter's feet like a low man to make a fun of him and said with a smile, "Give me battle", O Supreme lord! (3/17/27)

You are the guardian of the whole world and a ruler of a wide fame and have crushed the might of arrogant and conceited warriors. Nay, having conquered all the Daityas and Dānavas in the world you once performed a Rājasūya sacrifice, my lord. (3/17/28)

Thus want only mocked by an enemy whose vanity (egotism) knew no bounds, the worshipful lord of waters waxed angry; but he managed to curb the anger that had sprung in him by dint of his reasons and replied — O dear one, we have desisted from warfare. (3/17/29)

I do not see anyone else than the most ancient person (i.e. Lord Vishṇu), who will give satisfaction in battle to you. He is skilled in the ways of war. Therefore, O chief of the Asuras, approach him, to whom even heroes like you mention with praise. (3/17/30)

On reaching Him you will be rid of your pride at once and will lie down on the field of battle, surrounded by dogs. It is in order to exterminate wicked fellows like you and to show his grace to the virtuous, that He assumes various forms. (3/17/31)

Continuing his discourse onward sage Maitreya says—

Hearing the foregoing words of Varuṇa the proud and vain glorious Daitya paid little head to them. And having learnt from Nārad the whereabouts of Hari (Vishṇu), O dear Vidur! He hurriedly be took himself to the depths of the ocean. (3/18/1)

He saw there the all victorious divine boar bearing the earth upwards on the ends of his tusks and robbing the demon of his splendour by his reddish eyes, and laughed – O! an amphibious beast! (3/18/2)

He said, come on! You fool, leave the earth (globe). The Maker of the universe has entrusted her (globe) to us, the inhabitant of 'Rasātal' (i.e. in deep sea). You cannot escape unskcathed with her before my eyes. O vile god disguised as a boar! (3/18/3)

Have you been reared by your enemies for our extermination, as you kill the Asuras by deceptive methods and conquered them remaining yourself invisible. You possess little prowess. The deception (Yogamāyā) is your only strength. By killing you, O fool! I shall wipe the tears of my brethren. (3/18/4)

When you fall dead with your skull smashed by the mace hurled by our arms, the gods and sages, who bear offerings to you, will cease to be like trees without roots. (3/18/5)

Though being pierced by the shaft like abusive words of the enemy (Hiraṇyāksha), the Lord bore the pains, perceiving the earth on the ends of His tusks affrighted, and emerged out of the water like a (male) elephant with a female companion assailed by an alligator. (3/18/6)

The Daitya, who had golden hair and fearful tusks, gave a chase to the Lord while He was rising out of the water, even as an alligator would chase an elephants, and roaring like thunder, said – there is nothing reproachful for shameless wretches. (3/18/7)

The Lord placed the earth on the surface of water within His sight and transferred to her. His own energy in the form of capacity to support herself on the water, while the enemy stood looking on and when Brahmā extolled him, the gods showered flowers on Him. (3/18/8).

The Lord now displaying a terrible rage and spoke laughing at the demon, who was close up on Him, armed with a mighty mace. He was adorned with gold ornaments and protected by a queer armour of gold, and had all along been pinching Him by his abusive words. (3/18/9)

Replying to the abusive words of Hiranyāksha, Lord Boar said as follows—

Indeed we are wild brutes, O wretch! Looking about for dogs like you, Heroes take no notice of your braggadocio, bound as you are with the cords of death. (3/18/10)

Sacred away by your mace, I have stolen the charge of the dwellers in the bottom of ocean. I stand here, casting all shame to the wind. I have to take my stand in the battle field having enimity with a powerful adversary, where can I go? (3/18/11)

Being a leader of leaders of ground (foot) soldiers, take prompt steps to overthrow me giving up all hitch. You wipe the tears of your brethren by slaying me. Because a person does not deserve a seat in an assembly, who fails to redeem his plighted world. (3/18/12)

Continuing the story sage Maitreya told to Vidur— Severely taunted and ridiculed by the Lord in an angry mood, he (the Daitya) waxed violently angry like a serpent which is played with. (3/18/13)

The Daitya whose, (most of the) all sense organs were shaken by wrath, quickly sprang upon Hari (god Boar) and gave Him a blow with his mace. (3/18/14)

The Lord dodged the violent blow of the mace aimed at His breast by the enemy by moving a little aside, just as an accomplished Yogi eludes death. (3/18/15)

Hari being waxed angry rushed to meet the demon (Hiraṇyā

ksha), who began repeatedly to banish it taking up his mace again and biting his lips in rage. (3/18/16)

Then with His mace the Lord struck the enemy on his right eyebrow, but skilled as he was, O gentle Vidur! He intercepted it with his own mace. (3/18/17)

In this way Haryāksha (Hiraṇyāksha) and Hari struck each other with their huge maces in great rage, each of them seeking his own victory. (3/18/18)

There was a keen rivalry between the two combatants. Both of them had sustained injuries on their body from each others blows of pointed maces. They grew more enraged at the smell of blood on their person. In their eagerness of victory they were doing maneuvers of various kinds. Their contest presented a look of an encounter between two bulls for the sake of a cow. (3/18/19)

Brahmā surrounded by sages, came to witness the combat. O Vidur! Hiraṇyāksha and the supreme spirit both of whom bore enimity to each other for the sake of Earth. (3/18/20)

When the worshipful Brahmā, who was followed by thousands of sages and seers, saw that Hiraṇyākshapu was full of manliness and devoid of fear, had returned the blows of the Lord and possessed irresistible prowess, he said to Lord Nārāyana, the earliest Boar. (3/18/21)

Lord Brahma said in the following words—

Having secured a boon from me, my Lord, this demon is proving a constant annoyance and is not only trespassing against, but also causing fear and doing injury to gods. He has sought protection in your feet, as well as to the Brāhmaṇas the cows and other innocent beings. Finding no able rival to contend with him, he goes about the worlds in search of such one. (3/18/22-23).

Do not play with him as a child plays with an enraged serpent. He is skilled in conjuring tricks, arrogant, self-willed and most wicked. (3/18/24)

Managing your own Māyā (divine power or energy) slay this sinful demon. O immortal You Lord! Before he grows formidable with the approach of an hour which is favourable to him. (3/18/25)

The most dreadful hour of twilight, which is ruinous to the world, O my Lord, is fast approaching. O soul of the universe. Be pleased to bring victory to the gods. (3/18/26)

The auspicious period, known by the name of, opportune hour of victory' (Abhijit, meaning so opportune for victory), which commenced at midday, has now passed, therefore, in our interest, I pray you to dispose of the formidable foe quickly. (3/18/27)

Luckly enough for us, this fellow has come of his own accord to you to which his death ordained. Therefore, exhibiting your prowess, kill him in this duel and establish the worlds in peace. (3/18/28)

Sage Maitreya continued to say as follows—

Hearing the words of Brahmā which was sweet as nectar and free from guile, the Lord (Boar) heartily laughed and accepted his prayer with a glance laden with love. (3/19/1).

Thereupon the divine Boar sprang aiming His mace at the chin of His enemy in the form of demon, who was stalking fearlessly before Him. (3/19/2)

But Lord's mace slipped of from his hands being struck by the demon. That looked splendid as it fell down whieling. This was something miraculous. (3/19/3)

Even though he had an opportunity, the demon refused to strike his unarmed foe respecting the law of single combat, there by kindling the fury of the universal Lord. (3/19/4)

As His mace fell and there arose a cry (from the witnessing people), the almighty Lord acknowledged the demons love of righteousness and invoked his wheel Sunabh (Sudarshan). (3/19/5)

Then the wheel began to revolve (in the hand of Lord) and the Lord was contending at close quarters with the chief of His attendants, who had, now, taken birth as Hiranyāksha, there came strange from every direction. The people witnessing the scene from their aerial cars had no knowledge about the reality in the fighting, they said— "You be victorious," dispatch him. (3/19/6)

The demon, who had fearful tusks, stared at Hari, as that he would burn Him. Springing into the air he aimed his mace at Him and exclaimed at the same time— "You are slain". (3/19/8)

The Lord, who had assumed the form of a boar playfully knocked it down by His left foot, as he was representing all the sacrifice, O saint. (3/19/9)

The Lord then said—"Take up your weapon and try again, as you are eager to conquer me". The demon being challenged in these words, aimed his mace once more roaring loudly. (3/19/10)

When the Lord saw it flying towards Him. He stood firm and caught it, with the same ease as Garuḍa seize a serpent. (3/19/11)

The great demon felt humiliated when his valour was thus frustrated. He was then reluctant to take back his mace offered by Hari (Boar). (3/19/12)

He took up a trident (Trisul), which was rapacious as flaming fire, hurled it against the Lord, who is yajya-personified. His act was like one uses spells for a malevolent purpose against a holy Brāhmaṇa. (3/19/13)

Hurled by the mighty Daitya with all his strength, glowing trident, (Trishul) show brighter in the sky. Hari tore it into pieces with His wheel (Sudarshan chakra) in the same way as Indra cut down a wing of Garuḍa dropped by the latter. (3/19/14)

The demon got enraged when his trident was cut into pieces by Hari's wheel Sudarshan, he advanced towards Lord. Roaring loudly he smote Him with his hand first on His broad chest, which bore the mark of 'Shrivatsa (a curl of white hair), and went out of sight. (3/19/15)

Hit in this manner by the demon, O Vidur, the Lord, who appeared as first boar, did not feel the least quacking in any part of His body, any more than an elephant would when struck with a wreath of flowers. (3/19/16)

The Lord, who represented all the sacrifices in His person, then discharged His beloved wheel (Sudarshan), which was capable of dispersing the Māyā (illusionary power) displayed by the demon. (3/19/22)

At that very moment, all of a sudden, a shudder ran through the heart of Diti (Hiranyāksha's mother) as she recalled the words of her Lord (Kashyap), blood flowed from her breasts. (3/19/23)

When he (demon) saw his māyā (magic forces) dispelled, he went into the presence of Keshava (Boar) once more and encompassed Him within his arms being full of rage. He found the Lord standing outside the grip of his arms. (3/19/24)

As he began to strike the Lord with his fists, which was harder than adamant, Lord Adhokshaja (Boar) slapped him at the root of his ear, as Indra hit the demon Vrita (his enemy). (3/19/25)

So struck by the Lord, the conqueror of all, the demon's body began to wheel, the eye-balls bulged out of sockets, he fell down dead like a gigantic tree uprooted by the wind, his arms, legs and hairs on the head broken and scattered. (3/19/26)

In this way Hiranyāksha's victory campaigns for the economic accomplishment of his elder brother's state and colonial expansion as a mark there of-ended with his death. The policy of war economy which has a glorious look in the first phase comes out as a cause of destruction in the last phase.

Bhāgwatpurāṇa-2

Though the victory campaign of demon. Hiraṇyāksha for the well being of his elder brother resulted in his death in the midway as described above, yet it showed a path to his descendants for such a campaign with the aim and object of economic accomplishments. King Bali , who was his brother King Hiraṇya Kashipu's descendant and son of Virochana, also made such a victory campaign over the kingdom of heaven during his rule of Hiraṇyapur state. He was spiritually helped by his chief priest Achārya Shukra, the son of Bhrigu. King Bali surrendered to all the decedants of sage Bhrigu and offered all his belongings to them to obtain their blessings in the said campaign. Being pleased with his offerings and devotion to them the Brāhmaṇas of Bhrigu clan proposed before the king to arrange a sacrifice of called World Victory (Vishvajit). The story pertaining to performance of that sacrifice and his victory campaign runs thus—

Being pleased with the offerings and services (of kind Bali) the Brāhamaṇas of the Bhrigu clan possessing extraordinary power favourably disposed of a World Victory (Vishvajit) sacrifice, as he (Bali) was anxious to conquer heaven. (8/15/4)

While being worshipped by means of sacrificial offering, there arose from the fire a chariot covered all over with gold plates as well as horses of the colour as that of Indra's ones and also a flag adorned with an emblem of a lion came out. (8/15/5)

As well as an ethereal bow plated with gold, a pair of quivers containing inexhaustible stock of arrows and an ethereal coat. His (Bali) grand father (Prahlād) gave him a wrath of never fading flowers and Shukra (his preceptor), a conch. (8/15/6)

Thus equipped with necessaries of war procured (for him) by the Brāhmaṇas and having the auspicious rites performed by them, Bali went round the Brāhmaṇas and having bowed to them he asked leave of Prahlād after saluting him. (8/15/7)

Presently mounting the ethereal chariot bestowed by the descendant of Bhrigu, Bali wore the excellent garland and putting on the armour, he then armed himself with a bow and sword and equipped himself with a quiver. (8/15/8)

Mounted on the Chariot with his arms resplendent with gold armlets and adorned with radiant alligator shaped ear rings, he shone like a fire burning in the sacrificial pit. (8/15/9)

Surrounded by his own retinue in the person of Daitya generals he marched to attack. It so appeared that would swallow away the sky and burn the space with their wrathful eyes. (8/15/10)

King Bali managed to lead his huge army of Daityas according to the rules of warfare and attacked the glorious capital of Lord Indra (i.e., Amarāvati) shaking as it were earth and sky both. (8/15/11)

The city looked charming with splendid orchards and gardens, such as Nandan, crowded with warbling pairs of birds and black bees humming in intoxication. (8/15/12)

There were celestial trees whose boughs were overloaded with leaves, flowers and fruits. There were lotus ponds, abounding within swans, cranes, chakrawākas (ruddy geese) and ducks (Kārandāvas). In which celestial women accompanied by gods enjoy. (8/15/13)

It is hemmed in by the worshipful heavenly Gangā by way of

a moat, as well as by a high fortification wall of gold furnished with clock towers. (8/15/14)

It is built by Vishwakarmā and is provided with entrances whose doors are plated with gold and with city gates made of crystal with roads well-arranged. (8/15/15)

It is rich in public halls, quadrangles and streets and is full of numerous mansions as well as cross roads paved with gems and containing platforms of diamonds and corals at the centre. (8/15/16)

There resides lovely women of everlasting beauty and youth. They are clad in spotless garments and decked with jewels. They shine as fire with flames. (8/15/17)

Every pathway blow breezes wafting the fragrance of fresh wreaths of white water lilies dropped from the locks of celestial ladies in that city. (8/15/18)

The celestial nymphs walk there through the paths covered with yellowish fame coming through windows made of gold which bore the fragrance of (burning) aloe wood. (8/15/19)

There were shades with canopies of pearls, flags with stuffs of gems and gold. Smaller flags of various colours were fixed in the balconies which is resonant with the noise of peacocks, pigeons and black bees and wears a gala appearance due to the sweet songs of celestial ladies. (8/15/20)

The sound of clay tom-toms, conchs, drums and kettledrums, lutes, wooden tom-toms, Riṣṭis (a musical instrument), and flutes, accompanied by cymbals, as well as dances and songs to the accompaniment of musical instruments of demigods delight there the mind of the people. It appears so that it outshines the deity presiding over splendour by its brilliance. (8/15/21)

Those, who are extremely uprighteous, wicked, fraudulent, proud, lustful and greedy and are enemies of created beings, have no entrance there. Only those who are free from such defects find access to it. (8/15/22)

Bali, the commander of his forces, besiezed the aforesaid

city of gods on all sides with his army from outside. He blew his sonorous conch given by his preceptor (Shukra) infusing fear in the ladies of Indra. (8/15/23)

Maghvān Indra, perceiving it to be the supreme effort of Bali, approached the sage Brihaspati (his preceptor) accompanied by all the heavenly hosts and spoke as follows – (8/15/24)

The undertaking of Bali, our old enemy, is great, O worshipful one! I account him irresistible. By what power has he become so strong? (8/15/25)

None is able on any account, whatsoever, to beat him back. It appears that he will swallow away this universe and lick the ten directions, will burn the four quarters with his eyes. He has sprung as the fire of final dissolution. (8/15/26)

(You) point out the cause of such formidableness of my foe. Due to which he regained strength in his organs, mind and body as well as his glory, whence from his such effort has become possible. (8/15/27)

Listening the request and perceiving the anxiety of god king Indra his preceptor sage Brihaspati replied : -

O Indra! I know the reasons of the rise of your enemy. These are the scions of Bhrigu, who being the exponent of Vedas have infused energy into their disciple (Bali). (8/15/28)

Barring the almighty Hari, none like you can stand before him, like that none among the created beings stand before the death. (8/15/29)

Therefore, quit heaven. You all go out of sight. You await a time which may bring a reverse to your enemy. (8/15/30)

Rising more and more by the strength of the Brāhmaṇas (the scions of Bhrigu), he is at the high altitude of power today.

By insulting those very Brāhmaṇas he will perish with his wealth and so on. (8/15/31)

Having been thus offered a wise advice about their timely conduct by the preceptor, who could foresee the things in reality, the gods went out of the heaven (their country). Being capable of assuming any form at their will, they did so. (8/15/32)

After the disappearance of gods (from their country), Bali, the son of Virochan, occupied the city of Amarāvati forth with and brought under his subjection all the three worlds. (8/15/33)

The Brāhmaṇas of Bhrigu clan, then got performed hundred horse-sacrifices from his disciple Bali due to having been affectionate to him and other gods as their disciples. (8/15/34).

Bali now shone like the moon by achieving the glory owing to the effects of those sacrifices and his virtues diffused in the quarters beyond all directions. (8/15/35).

Considering himself as having accomplished all his objects as it were, the high-minded Bali enjoyed the overflowing wealth bestowed on him by the Brāhmaṇas. (8/15/36).

If is, thus, seen that the policy of economic accomplishments by means of waging war in the name of victory-campaign, which was once initiated by his forefather king Hiraṇyakashipu under the leadership of his younger brother Hiraṇyāksha became fruitful during the regime of king Bali; His victory over heaven (the present Tibet) was aimed at to make his own state economically prosperous and to bring the same at par with the heaven economically. King Bali performed hundred horse-sacrifice for equipping himself spiritually to rule heaven and other parts of the world alike Indra. Moreover, performance of hundred horse-sacrifices by a king reflects the economic strength of the kingdom also. A ruler of economically weak state could never perform so many horse-sacrifices even if he was righteous and religious one. He could not even dream of such number of sacrifice, if his state did not earn wealth through war.

Valmīki-Ramāyaṇa—Uttarkāṇd

The war economy was so prevalent in ancient India that even Ram, a king of Ayodhya, adopted that method to establish his family members as kings in various regions of our country. Whatever would have been the cause of attack over the concerning territories is another story. But the fact is that Ayodhyā's political strength during

Ram's rule begins with the attack of his army over the state of Madura, situated at the Bank of Yamunā, under the leadership of Shatrughna. Giving his orders as king of Āyodhyā, Ram said to prince Shatrughna in these words—

Be it so, O Shatrughna! Carryout my order, I shall consecrate you on the holy kingdom of Madhu. Establish the throne, Bhārat (a scion of Bharat), O one of long arms, If you consider, you are brave and proficient, and also have the ability to establish a new city. Founding a city close to Yamunā and many provinces of auspicious fame, one, who having reduced a royal fame is that very city, does not install a king there, indeed goes to hell, you, therefore, kill Lavana the son of Madhu, who had in his mind evil designs. (62/16 to 19)

You rule over the kingdom. If you follow my orders then, O brave one! Carry on the administration righteously, without making any argument or without disobeying me. (62/20)

The elders must be obeyed by youngers, there is no doubt. Please approve of the consecrations, to be performed by me accompanied with the Mantras (Sacred Chants) of the Brāhmaṇas headed by Vasishtha in the prescribed manner. (62/71)

The intention of Ram, as king, is thus, clear that he, on becoming aware of the good opportune, planned to resort to war strengthen his kingdom economically by establishing colonies. The onward portion of the above story is thus:—

After Ram said so, the mighty Shatrughna felt very much ashamed and spoke gently. (63/1)

O king, the descendant of Kukutstha this transaction seems to me as against righteousness, how can a junior be consecrated on the throne superseding the elders? (63/2)

On the other hands your orders must be carried out at any cost as it is impossible to supersede them. (63/3)

O king! The best among persons and delighter of Raghus, I will follow your wishes, but whatever wrongful happens in it from me, you please destroy it. I shall act according to your desire. O bull among men! Please leave out for my sake that which is unlawful, O scion of Kukutstha, descendant of the Raghus! (63/8)

After these words being uttered by the wise and brave Shatrughna, Ram was pleased. He said to Bharat and Lakshaman. (63/9)

Bring forth all the necessaries of consecration, this very day. I shall consecrate the scion of Raghus, the tiger among men (Shatrughna). (63/10)

By my orders, call all of them, the chief priest, citizens, other priests and the councillors. (63/11)

Following the orders of the king, the great warriors, brought the necessary worship material for the consecration, making the chief priest prominent role. (63/12)

The Kings and the Brāhmaṇas entered the Royal palace, thus the consecration of noble Shatrughna went on. (63/13)

(Then) the learned Brāhmaṇas, Kausalya, Sumitrā, Kaikeyi and all other royal damsels performed auspicious acts in the Royal palace. (63/16)

Thereafter the scion of Raghus (Ram) placing Shatrughna on his lap uttered these sweet words enhancing his power. (63/18)

I am giving you this divine arrow, which is unfailing and conquers the cities of foes, O descendant of Raghu, O handsome one, you will kill Lavana with this arrow. (63/19)

This arrow was created, O scion of Kakutstha, when the self born Vishṇu, the unconquerable God, was reclining in the great ocean whom the gods and the demons could not see. (63/20)

Therefore, this one, the best arrows is invisible to all beings, this was created by angry Vishṇu desirous of the two wicked ones, Madhu and Kaitabh, and the creation of three worlds after the two and the other demons were killed with this arrow. (63/21 to 23)

This arrow was not shot by me formerly wishing to kill Ravana, O Shatrughna, because that would caused a great destruction of beings. (63/24)

The great trident, the best among weapons, that was given to Madhu by the almighty three eyed Lord (Shiva) for the purposes of destroying the foes. (63/25)

Placing that honourable (weapon) at home (Lavaṇa) proceeds to all quarters for repeatedly attaining the best of his foods. (63/26)

Whenever, desirous of struggle, any one perchance challenges (him) then Lavaṇa the Rākshas taking hold of this trident reduces him to ashes indeed. (63/27)

So you, O lion among men! Accompanied with this weapon (the arrow), stay at the eastern gate and fight with him. While he is dispossessed of the weapon (trident) and unable to enter the city. (63/28)

O one of the long arms! Challenge him to fight (before) he has entered the residence, then you should kill the Rākshas. (63/29)

If it is not done so, then indeed he would be unassailable. But if it is done so, then O brave one! He (Lavaṇa) will be perished. (63/30)

Thus all has been narrated to you, and also the warding off of the trident, the doings of the dark-throated Shrimat are indeed difficult to overcome. (63/31)

Bearing in mind the instructions so given by king Ram, Shatrughna proceeded to the city of Madhura, situated at the western bank of the river Yamunā. He stayed in the night at the hermitage of sage Chyavan. The onward story is as follows—

The night passed away quickly (while staying at the hermitage of sage Chyavan), because the noble Shatrughna conversing with the sage and other saints, who wished for the holy victory. (67/1)

Then in the morning when it became bright, the said Rākshas, the heroic one, went out of city impelled by the desire of bringing food. (67/2)

In the mean time Shatrughna, the brave one, crossed the Yamunā. (He) stood at the gate of the city of Madhu with bow in his hand. (67/3)

At the midday that Rākshas, the evil doer returned bearing the load of many thousand creatures. (67/4)

The Rākshas saw Shatrughna armed and standing at the gate. He said to him, what will you do with this ? (67/7)

Many thousands of men armed with weapons, O wretched!, have been devoured by me in anger. Death seems to have come nearer to you. (67/6)

O vile one! My food is yet incomplete. How have you come? You enter to my mouth on your own accord. (67/7)

While the Rākshas spoke this and laughed at, the heroic Shatrughna broke into tears with anger. (67/8)

Fiery rays came out from all the limbs of the noble and angry Shatrughna (67/9)

Highly enraged Shatrughna then addressed the demon. Who roamed about thus in the night, O evil one! I wish to enter duel with you. (67/10)

I am the son of Dasharath, and the brother of wise Ram the extirpator of foes. I am Shatrughna by name. I have come with a desire to kill you. (67/11)

So give the duel to me, who desires to fight with you. You are the enemy of all beings with me. You will not be able to escape alive from here. (67/12).

Hearing these words of noble Shatrughna, Lavana became very angry and said wait. (69/1)

Rubbing his hands with each other, and making a rattling sound with his teeth, Lavaṇa challenged the lion Rāghava many a time. (69/2)

Lavaṇa, though with dreadful appearance, yet Shatrughna, the killer of the enemies of gods, said these words. (69/3)

Shatrughna was not born, when you conquered others in the battle. So go to abode of Yama today, after killed by (my) arrow. (69/4)

O sinful one, may the sages too see you killed in the encounter today so also the learned Brāhmaṇas see, as the gods saw Rāvaṇa (killed). (69/5)

Today there will be peace indeed in the city and in the state, as you, the demon, are burnt and slain prostrate by the arrow. (69/6)

Today, the arrow, whose fare-point resembles the thunder bolt, shot by my hand, shall enter your heart, as the ray of the sun enters in the lotus. (69/7)

Being thus spoken, Lavaṇa enraged with anger threw a mightly tree on the breast of Shatrughna, but it was cut in thousand fold (by him with the said arrow). (69/8)

Thus seeing his action fruitless, the powerful Rākshas again took hold of many trees and hurled them at Shatrughna. (69/9)

The brave Shatrughna also tore asunder each one coming upon him, by trees and four arrows of flatterend ends. (69/10)

Shatrughna, who had great might, showered many arrows at the Rākshas, but he was not troubled. (69/11)

Then the powerful Lavaṇa laughed, and uprising a tree attacked the brave one on the head. Shatrughna went into a swoon with the (bodily) joints loosened. (69/12)

So as the brave (Shatrughna) fell, long cries of 'Ha' emanated from the sages, the host of the gods, Gandharvas, and Apasaras. (69/13)

Gaining consciousness in a moment, Shatrughna adored by the sages stood up and waited at the door of the city (with) weapon in their hands. (69/16)

Shatrughna took hold of the arrow, the divine and excelling others, flaming with brilliance and filling the ten directions. (69/17)

All beings witnessed that divine arrow borne by Shatrughna in his hand, like it was the fire broke at the time of destruction. (69/31-32 I part)

Seeing the sky filled with gods, Shatrughna again roared like a lion looking at Lavaṇa. He was again challenged by the noble Shatrughna. (69/32 II part - 33)

Lavaṇa being very angry seemed to give him the fight. He (Shatrughna), the best among archers. (69/34)

Then stretched that bow upto his ear, shot it at the mighty chest of Lavaṇa. That divine arrow desended to the nether-world breaking open his chest. (69/35)

Having gone to the netherworld and being worshipped by the

gods came back quickly to Shatrughna, the descendant of the family of Ikshvāku. (69/35)

Lavaṇa being struck by the arrow of Shatrughna, fell on the ground at once like the mountain struck by the thunderbolt. (69/37)

After the Rākshas Lavaṇa was killed, that mighty divine arrow too came back to the quiver of Rudra which was looked at by the gods. (69/38)

Then the champion of Raghus, after vanishing the terror of three worlds with the shot of one arrow, shone forth as the sun dispels the darkness by thousands of its rays. (69/39)

All gods, sages, Nagās paid homage to him and Apasaras hailed to the fearless victory of the son of king Dasharath, the serpent causing fear laid to rest. (69/40)

After Lavaṇa was killed, the gods together with Indra and Agni as their leader said these sweet words to Shatrughna, the agitator of the foes. (70/1)

O Lion among men, by good fortune, you became victorious and the Rākshas is killed. O of a noble vow ask for a boon. (70/2)

All desirous of your victory are intending to bless you with a boon. We have come (here) and our presence here will not go fruitless. (70/3)

Hearing the words of gods, Shatrughna, the long armed one, disciplined in mind, keeping his joint hands on his head replied thus: (70/4)

Madhura, the city of Madhu, built by gods, may become the capital soon, I desire only this boon. (70/5)

The gods said to Rāghava (scion of Raghu) 'it be so'. This beautiful city will be Shūrasenā by name indeed, there is no doubt. (70/6)

Saying thus, the holy gods ascended to heaven. Shatrughna too, the powerful one, brought back the army. (70/7)

The army came soon hearing the news of death (of Lavaṇa) at the hands of Shatrughna and commenced the establishment (of the capital) by the month of Srāvaṇa (August). (70/8)

That concerning holy state was established as the territory of the Shūrsenas (i.e. of brave soulders) during the course of twelve years, being free from fear. (70/9)

The fields became full of cereals, Indra brought forth rain in time. The warriors protected by Shatrughna were free from diseases. (70/10)

The said city, shaped like half moon, beautified by the banks of Yamunā, was also embellished with the special mansions and quadrangular market place. It was inhabited by the four categories of people and had aboundance of various forms of merchandise. (70/11)

The white (mansion) that was built by Lavaṇa was further beautified by Shatrughna with (the pictures) of various colours. (70/12)

It looked beautiful from all sides with the comforts (Āramas) and walkings (Vihāras) (the places of enjoyment). That city was adorned with human and celestial adornments. (70/13)

The prosperous Shatrughna, the younger brother of Bharat, by seeing the mansion having divine look, full of all forms of merchandise and inhabited by traders coming from various countries, was much glad. (70/14-15)

Then at the commencement of the twelfth year having established the city of Madhura, he thought to see the feet of Ram. (70/16)

After establishing the city which resembled with celestial one, Shatrughna filled it up with men of various kinds, the foremost of Raghus family, considered it necessary to see Raghupati's (Ram's) feet. (70/17)

The chapter-70 of Vālmīki-Rāṁāyana, Uttarkānd makes it clear that the establishment of colony, named Shurasena, under the domain of Ayodhyā was aimed at the prosperity of the concerning state (Ayodhyā). It appears so because of the fact that in those days the said region nourished by the water of Yamunā was fertile one and that it had the trading facilities by boats. It is worth while to mention here that the scion of Diti, the wife of Kashyap liked to settle and establish rule at the fertile places and the concerning territory was one of them. As such the political rule so established by Shatrughna intended to strengthen the state of Ayodhyā economically which became weak during Rama's exile.

Vālmīki-Rāmāyaṇa – Uttarkānd - 2

After establishing a colony of Ayodhyā, named Shūrasen in the plains of Yamunā, the adjoining territory of present Mathura, another proposal came from the maternal uncle of Bharat, the king of Kekaya. Where the earlier proposal came from sages, performing austerity at the banks of Yamunā in the concerning territory, this proposal was from a political power as a safegaurd to his state. King Yudhājit sent, his priest Gārgya, the son of Angirā, to convey to Ram, his proposal to attack over the territory of the Gandharvas which was rich inedible fruits and roots. It was situated at both the sides of river Sindhu and was ruled by the Gandharvas, who were experts in war and had arms. (100/10-11). The wise king Yudhājit of Kekaya wanted to vanish the danger of attack from that corner over his state with no loss of his own.

The proposal, finding place in the Vālmīki-Rāmāyaṇa Uttarkāṇd, is as follows:—

O, scion of Kakutstha, merge the holy city of the Gandharvas in your own kingdom, which none else can do. May it please you. O one of the long arms, I do not say this against your interests. (100/13)

After hearing this, Rāghav (Ram), being pleased with what the sage and his maternal uncle said 'so shall it be' and looked at Bharat. (100/4)

That Rāghav (Bharat) being pleased said with joint hands courteously, O sage among Brāhmaṇas these two brave sons (of Bharat) Taksha and Pushkal will go to that region protected well by my maternal uncle and observe religious rites (there). (100/15-16)

After establishing two such cities and setting his two sons there, this most pious one (Bharat) will again return to me. (100/17).

After saying so to the Brāhmaṇa, he (Ram) gave order to Bharat to (proceed) with his army and attendants, and also consecrated the two sons on an auspicious (day), with the holy star, putting the son of Angira (Gārgya) at their head, Bharat with his army and with his sons proceed (100/19-20).

Then the army went out of the royal city (Ayodhyā) like the army of Indra, followed by Rāghav for a long distance, which was difficult to conquer even by the gods. (100/21).

The flesh eaters and the mighty Rākshasas followed Bharat out of thirst of blood. (101/22)

Hosts of Bhuts (demons), eaters of flesh, the terrible ones, desirous of devouring the flesh of the son of Gandharvas (followed) in thousands. (100/23)

Lions, tigers, bears and the sky roving birds, thousand in number, went heralded the army. (100/24)

Having spent one and half months on the way, the army, hale and healthy bearing happy and well fed men reached Kekaya (country). (100/25)

Yudhajit, the king of Kekaya, when heard the arrival of Bharat as the commander-in-chief of his army, was highly pleased together with Gārgya. (100/1)

He, the lord of Kekaya, and Bharat accompanied with a large army quickly reached the capital of Gandharvas. (101/2)

Bharat and Yudhajit accompanied with rapid action warriers reached the city of Gandharvas with the army and attendants. (101/3)

The great powerful Gandharvas being desirous of war came out shouting war cries everywhere. (101/4)

Then there commenced a great battle enough to cause horripilation for seven nights in terrible form and none came out victorious. (101/5).

River with the streams of blood, having crocodiles in the form of swords, arrows and bows and carrying the corpses of men gushed forth on all sides. (101/6)

Then Bharat, the borther of Ram highly enraged directed the most terrible weapon of death 'Sanivart' (by name) towards the Gandharvas. (101/7)

Struck by the mighty Sanivart, as it bound by the time of death, the Gandharvas, three million (in number) perished in a moment. (101/8)

Even the gods did not remember such a fierce battle in which mighty Gandharvas killed in a moment. (101/9)

When all the Gandharvas were killed, the son of Kaikeyi founded there two great and prosperous cities. He installed Taksha at Takshashilā in the Gandharva region and Pushkal on Pushkalāvat in the region of Gāndhār state. (101/10-11)

Having fully established the two (above named) cities, filled with wealth and gems, beautified by gardens, trying each other to excel through competitive spirit. (101/12)

Both extremely lovely and rich with fresh business, abounding with pleasant groves and carrier vehicles and well-planned with markets. (101/13)

Both the cities, beautifully decorated with mansions and many lovely high palaces (Vimānas). (101/14)

Adorned with attractive temples of worship, made lovely with Tāls, Tāmals and Vakul trees. (101/15)

In the period of five years, Rāghav Bharat, the younger brother of Ram, having long arms, the son of Kaikeyi, returned to Ayodhyā. (101/16)

Though above is the story of Bharat's heroic action of fight with brave Gandharvas, yet the economic reasons are apparent in the said war. It appears that it was the planning of Ram as king of Ayodhyā to settle the sons of his brothers at distant places in his life time to avoid family friction in future, so that his state be kept intact.

Vālmīki - Rāmāyaṇa – Uttarkāṇd – 3

After the coronation of sons of Bharat as kings of two different regions of the territory of Gandharvas after its division king, Ram preferred to establish the sons of prince Lakshmana too with no loss of time to keep up the family hormony and that the economy of the state of Ayodhyā may remain unaffected. The story pertaining his such planning and action is as follows—

Hearing this (i.e. account narrated by Bharat regarding his victory over the territory of Gandharvas.) Ram together with his brothers became glad and said to Lakshmaṇ in these words of wonderful content. (102/1)

O son of Sumitra (Lakshmaṇ)! Your these two sons have knowledge of religion (i.e. law and righteousness) (whose names are) Angad and Chandraketu have firm fortitude (for the protection) of their kingdom. (102/2)

I shall consecrate these two, for which you find out a suitable territory, that may be enjoyable and where they may remain happily without any obstruction. (102/3)

O gracious one, find out that place where there is no king and the hermitage are well protected and we may not be at fault. (102/4)

When Ram said so, in reply Bharat told–The region of Kārupatha is beautiful one and is free from all ills. There the cities for Angad and Chandraketu, the noble ones be established. (102/5-6)

What words Bharat said were agreed to by Rāghav (Ram) and that territory (Kārupatha) after being brought under him, a city for Angad was established. (102/7)

The city that belonged to Angad was beautiful indeed and well protected by Ram unwearied in action. (102/8).

A city known as Chandrakāntā– in Māldā territory was established as the divine city in heaven for the wrestler Chandraketu. (102/9)

Then Ram, Lakshmaṇ and Bharat who were difficult to be conquered in war became very glad. They performed the coronations (of Angad and Chandraketu). (102/10)

Both of them being firm in mind, after being consecrated, Angad was sent to the western region whereas Chandraketu to the northward. (102/11)

Lakshmaṇ the son of Sumitra, followed Angad and Bharat on his part followed Chandraketu as the rear guard. (102/12)

Lakshmaṇ came back to Ayodhyā after staying one year in the city of Angad when his son was fully established and gained strength (politically). (102/13)

Bharat too after spending a year or so, in the same way returned to Ayodhyā and worshipped the feet of Ram. (102/14)

The sons of both Sumitra (Lakshmaṇ) Bharat, the most noble ones ardently attached to the feet of Ram and having deep affection to him, were oblivious of the elapse of time. (102/15)

Thus ten thousand years passed with them starving always to perform tasks of the citizens and always being ready to follow righteousness. (102/16)

Their tuned passed having been fulfilled all desires and establishing in the city of virtue (the economic) properity and the three radiated effulgence like the three great sacrificial fire inflamed by oblation well poured. (102/17)

King Ram of Ayodhyā, thus, showed a new path to the other states of India to follow, where there was possibility of partition of the paternal territory among the different branches in the family to avoid any ruinous stage to come. The economy and prosperity of a state expect unity of the same with firmness in mind of the ruler of the time and the reciprocal affections and regard to each other members of the family and devoted efforts as such. What would have been the political results, thereafter, but Ram succeeded in his policy to enhance the prosperity of the state of Ayodhyā during his rule and settling the next generation of his bothers and make them economically well off by resorting to the war economy.

Mahābhārat —Ādiparva– 1

King Pāndu, the ruler of historic Hastināpur state also resorted to the victory compaign for the sake of economic stability of his kingdom which grew weak during the period when it had no ruler and it was administered by Prince Devavrat Bhishma as a caretaker administrator. After his coronation as king of Hastināpur state he thought it proper to strengthen the same economically within a minimum possible time. So he planned to go on a victory campaign.

The story of his campaign as finds place in the Mahābhārat-Ādiparva is thus—

O Janamejaya king Pāndu, a scion of Kuru after enjoying thirty nights (in the palace) came out of his capital with intent to conquer the entire earth. (112/21)

He bowed his head to the feet of elderly persons like Bhishma and others he saluted scion of Kuru Dhritrashtra and other elder scion of Kuru. Took permission from them and after getting their approval and good wishes he marched with a huge army among which there included, three branches of soldiers namely, riders on elephants, horses and mounter of chariots. (112/22-23)

King Pandu was brilliant like a son of god. With the intention of victory over the earth he attacked on many enemies with (his) strong soldiers. (112/24)

First of all king Pandu, who considered to be the elevator of glory of Kauravas, a hero like lion among men, attacted on Dasharnas and defeated them. They were enemies (of Hastināpur state) from earlier times. (112/25).

Thereafter, Pandu attacked on Magadh. He carried with him an army among which numerous soldiers were the riders of elephants, horses and mounter of chariots and also there were pedestrian soldiers. There, king Dirghā, ruler of Magadh, who had enimity with other kings and proud of his strength, was killed at his (Pandu's) hands. (112/26-27)

After taking from there a huge treasure and conveyance king Pandu attacked on the state of Mithila and defeated the ruler, the scions of Videha (Janak). (112/28)

O great king Janamejaya! Thus that Pandu getting victory over Kashi, Suhya and Pundra states by his own physical strength and heroism began to keep up the glory of his Kuru family. (112/29)

At that time the king Pandu, who was crusher of enemies, appeared to be the burning fire. The arrows collectively were like its flame. Likewise was the appearance of the sword and other weapons. The king's who came to face him, burnt. (112/30)

The kings, who appeared before him in defence, king Pandu vanished them with their soldiers and brought them under his domain and appointed them as his representatives of the concerning territories. (112/31)

All the kings who were defeated by Pandu began to acknowledge him as hero among men on this earth like that of Indra among the gods. (112/32)

(Those, who became aware of heroic fighting of Pandu) came before him with joint hands and bowed down presenting various kinds of wealth and stones. (112/33)

Various kinds of stones, jewels, pearls, corals, gold, silver, cows, horses, chariots, elephants, asses, camels, bufallows, goats, blankets, deer hides, stones, goods made of deer hides etc., which were presented to the king, were accepted by him. (112/34-35)

After taking the presentations (said above) king Pandu returned to the capital of his nation. At that time the horses etc., being used for conveyance were also feeling glad. (112/36)

King Pandu gave new life to the glory of kings Shāntanu and Bharat which was vanished during these period. (112/37)

Those who took away any part of the territory or wealth of Kuru nation, king Pandu made those kings tax-payer of Hastināpur state. (112/38)

The number of kings and the ministers assembled together were discussing like that (as above). The citizens and countrymen were also taking part in the that talks. They were becoming glad heartly as well as hoping for the best. (112/39)

When king Pandu approached the capital then Bishma and other members of the Kuru family came to receive and welcome him. They happly saw that king Pandu and his party (soldiers and others) were coming full of enthusiasm. At that time it appeared so that they were returning back after going a little forward. They were carrying with them loaded on carriers wealth of various kinds, including valuable stones, great elephants, horses, chariots, cows, camels and sheeps etc. When the Kauravas reached there, they saw no end of the wealth being so brought. (112/40 to 42)

Increasing the pleasure (of his mother) Kaushalya king Pandu came nearer to his uncle Bhishma saluted him by touching his feet. He also honoured the citizens and countrymen suitably. (112/43)

Bhishma embracing Pandu, his son (nephew) began to shade tears of happiness, who returned after vanishing his (state's) enemies. (112/44)

With the beat of drum and other fanfare 'Turahi' as well as sounds of hundreds of conch entered the capital city, giving pleasure to the citizens. (112/45)

The story reproduced above makes it clear that king Pandu and his family members were in favour of increasing the state treasure even by means of warfare. Religiously, though, it was not a righteous means of acquiring wealth in which the kings of other states were put in trouble with no apparent fault, yet it was in practice in the political system of ancient India for economic reasons.

Mahābhārat —Ādipurva - 2

To justify the acquisition of wealth by means of warfare, king Pandu tried to appease his elder brother Dhritrashtra, uncle Bhishma, mother, aunt and grandmother as well as his cousin Vidur by giving them their due shares. In the Mahābhārat a description to this effect is thus:—

Vaishāmpayan says— O Janamejaya! After taking permission from his elder brother Dhritrashtra king Pandu presented some parts of the wealth won by his heroic deeds to Bhishma, Satyavati, mothers Ambika and Ambalika. (113/1)

He sent some portion of that wealth to Vidur. Righteous Pandu also presented some portion of the said wealth to the well-wishers. (113/2)

O Bhārat (Janamejaya)! Thereafter Satyavati also presented some portions of so won wealth to Bhishma and Kausalya. Mother Kausalya welcomed by embracing the great brilliant king as Sachi (wife of Indra) welcomes her son Jayant. (113/3-4).

Dhritrashtra performed one hundred great horse sacrifices by using the wealth brought by hero Pandu by his heroic action and that he gave gift of one lac gold coins to the Brāhmaṇas in each sacrifice. (113/5)

It was a general belief in those days in the society of kings that some portions of the wealth acquired by any war compaign should be utilized in sacrifices particularly horse-sacrifices as well as in donations and gifts to the Brāhmaṇas as penance thereof. King Pandu having good knowledge of Shāstras acted according to the directions given by the same. The other side of his action was to establish his state's economic prosperity among the states in ancient India of his time.

But initially policy of accretion of wealth by war was not liked by any reasonable and prudent king. The sons of Diti who initiated such means for accretion of wealth suffered distance in the society. The activities of gods against them centred round such a policy of accretion of wealth or territory and shown their keenness to have a control over that. But on one pretext or the other the policy of accretion of wealth or territory went on rooted deeply amongst the kings. The adoption of such a policy by a king having courage and strength became a status symbol.

If it is said that lord Vishṇu was forced by the circumstances and the policy of peace to take up the form of a dwarf to win Daitya king Bali by asking a donation of three steps land at his sacrificial place. It would not be out of place to mention here that king Bali as a peace lover sacrificer while accepting his request was fully conscious about his political extinction. But he accepted Vāmana's request to avoid bloodshed and with a view to maintain the dignity and value of donation during the performance of sacrifice to the Brāhmaṇas. Here the character of Bali is supreme.

Somehow or the other the kings in ancient India were not in favour of peaceful accretion of wealth at political level. The policy of war based on economic reasons remained in practice. Owing to that the war joined hands with Horse and Rajsuya sacrifices with the march of time.

■

9

Agricultural Economy

In the Rigveda, Book Seven, Sukta sixty four, it has been directed to the king of a state that he should take the help of learned persons for the development of the resources of the earth. So far as the resources of the earth is concerned, it was known to the intelligentia class of the people that the crops of cereals could be taken from the same. The vegetation could only grow in the earth. By their skill of mind they knew that the earth had capacity to produce vegetations in which crops were also included. The sages also arrived at a conclusion in their course of study of the nature that the agriculture at a mass scale could be popularized only with the help of political administration of a given society. With this view point Suktas or Hymns on these subjects were incorporated in the Vedas. The above Regvedic Hymn (7/64), which is aimed at agricultural policy of a state, is reproduced below for the sake of bringing to light the concept of the said Veda on the subject of agricultural policy.

Rigveda - 1

A king should take the help of such learned persons who has the knowledge of the properties of sun rays and the earth and the interse relations of these two (pertaining to the agricultural crops). The king and the people should offer oblation of ghee in the sacrifices happily so that the sun or sun rays (Mitra), Aryamā (the helping or judicial power of God) and Varuṇa (controlling god of water) may shower blessings (in the form of agricultural produce). (1)

O kings! Be a protector of the great righteous path and also of treasure of water of space and of ground as that of Lord. You be active soon in this regard, so that the sun rays (Mitra) and the water (Varuṇa) may together shower rain of cereals for making us glorious soon. (2)

O king and people! You take the help of learned persons (devah) i.e. experts, so that sun rays and the water judicially show you the path of good results (good produce). In this way you both may (or will) be glorious for which they (learned persons) say to you for acting according. (3)

Those kings who offer oblations of ghee (in the sacrifices) aiming of Mitra and Varuṇa (sun rays and god of water or rain) they satisfy the nature to remain potential (in regards to light and water, the necessary elements of good crop) and those people who take these secrets (of crop) by mind and think over the same patiently and act accordingly get prosperous. (4)

O gods of light and water! you both becoming strengthful with our praise like moon and seimen so that we may get light and air to strengthen our intelligence for awarkening it in the righteous or good deeds. You both hearing our praises shower always pious or good things on us to make us glorious. (5)

In the above Mantras (meters) the aim of Hymn, according to sage Vasishtha, who was interested in the progress of worldly life and was the chief priest of the state of Ayodhyā, was to popularize the agricultural economy in his state by giving inspiration to the noble kings of the said state. He was of the opinion that only good rule and the religious activities of the king and the subjects will not make the kingdom glorious. It was thought necessary not only by him but by the entire learned class to explore the proper method and the science of agriculture to make the persons interested in the same be aware of in that regard. He praised dual gods Mitra and Varuṇa, the lords of light and water, so that these primary elements being helpful in causing the crops or vegetation to grow, be favorable to the agriculture. Now it is well known that for the agriculture light, air and water are the essential elements. As such this Sukta may be taken as a guiding one on the Vedic science of agriculture.

Rigveda - 2

The Rigvedic Hymn one hundred one of Book Seven (7/101) throws light on the most valuable and the important element of agriculture that is to say, the water and that too on the rain water. In the present time it is no secret that the large scale agriculture if not totally but mainly depends upon the rains. The god of which is known in the Vedas as Parjanya, the divine power of air to absorb the ground water and convert the same in the form of vapour and thereafter as clouds. It has been explained by giving emphasis that god Parjanya should be worshipped to appease him. So that he may shower rains whenever needed to grow and ripe the plants of cereals which are like herbs for the mankind. The Meters of the said Hymn (7/101), which are in six number, are given below:—

O God! You make the divine powers which are three in number (i.e. powers of space, ground and underground) and are in the form of light, water and earth and soak the juice of the plants or herbal ones and make the same as clouds (as offspring of juice or liquids). By way of this process the clouds so formed rain (on the ground) to energize the herbal plants to produce (the cereal). At the time of raining the clouds make roaring sounds. (1)

God, who generates energy in plants and water to grow, is the god of providing glory in the world or entire universe. He should provide us pleasure in the various or three types shelters to us so that we may enjoy the same in the three reasons. (2)

The clouds rains like a newly begetting cow at the same place the water of rain gets itself converted in the shape of plants. This process goes on in a cycle (chakra), as mother conceives from the (seimen of) father and gives birth to a child after getting it fully developed in the womb. (3)

In whose God this world and the universe are established together with the three worlds and the three kinds of deed are in process as well as three treasures get irrigated, that God may shower all kinds of pleasure. (4)

O God! the rains be showerer of happiness, plants bear good fruits or cereals, and the learned people be able to bring those things in use. Such words should be uttered in respect of the kings, who takes care of their subjects like clouds by the propagators, whose hearty words are like that. (5)

That God is the holder of all kinds of seeds in the form of fluids, provides pleasures (of rains) perennially to the people.

All the movable and immovable beings have taken shelter in that God. That god protects our righteous ways for hundred years. O god! you always protect me (the sacrifice) by good praises or work. (6)

Sage Vasishtha, being one of the two thinkers of this Hymn also, is of the opinion that the output of the crops or the cereal plants being dependant on rain water and the rain water being dependant on the wishes of god, a king should satisfy them by performing sacrifices. The meters pertaining to the praise of god should be uttered in the sacrifices. In other words an agriculturist must have knowledge of interse relations between clouds, plants and also the supreme divine power controlling and energizing those things for the goodness and the welfare of the mankind. He, being spiritually strong, sees the good produce of the crops by the angle of said vision, the agriculturists are also guided by him to adopt agriculture as a sacrifice, though it is a primary means of livelihood.

Rigveda - 3

Another Hymn on the subject of agriculture clearly says that god should be worshipped or praised for the good production of the cereals. The Hymn (7/102) is as follows:—

You sing (song or meter) relating to Parjanya, He may give us green grasses (Yavasam) i.e. root plant of barley, that which is desired, to save gods and sons and gives us pleasure. (1)

That (god) is the womb of herbal plants. He creates the movable rays of light, which is the god (Parjanya) of fluid of mind of men. (Mind floats in a kind of fluid). (2)

You offer oblations aiming to that god in the sacrificial fire, who provides (you) happiness. You worship him, so that He may provide you cereals. (3)

The above short Hymn is clear on the point of production of cereal that an agriculturist, while making efforts for reproduction of cereals in the field, must remember that it is the god of clouds who helps him in getting the produce. He should be fully aware of this fact. The farmers of our country know even to-day that good crop is in the hands of god of rains. This concept includes god of clouds also. The developed science of today could find out no scientific measure which can be used at the time of no rainfall.

Rigveda - 4

There are two meters in a Hymn one hundered one of Book Ten of Rigveda (10/101) in which science of cultivation is described. The same are as follows:—

You people (now) plough the field throughout its measure. In the so prepared field you sow the seeds by throwing process. Sing meters. So that the grains of crop be fully ripe and we (the farmer) may get well ripen grains. (10/101/3)

The learned persons tills the field by ploughs. They place the yoke on the shoulders (of the pair of bullocks). The intelligent persons get pleasure among the gods. (10/101/4)

The above two Richas of the Rigveda describe the scientific method of agriculture in brief. But a detailed description on the method of cultivation is found in the Yajurveda.

Yajurveda

The meters (Mantras 67-73) relating to the method of cultivation of the chapter twelve of the Yajurveda (12/67 to 73) are as follows:—

The intelligent and brilliant god fire to provide spiritual benefits joins the ploughs with bullocks and they carry the yoke separately. (67)

O cultivators! Join the plough with yoke and place that yoke on the shoulders of the bullocks. Thereafter, plough the field. Sow the seeds (in the field) so prepared. The grains after becoming mature should ripe. Then the plants so matured be cut off by sickle and keep the harvested crops in the house, which is adjoining (to the field). (68)

O plough! You have good blade. You plough this field nicely and happily. The bullocks joined with yoke and plough may give no trouble to the ploughman holding the handle of the plough. O Air and Sun! You both irrigate my field with (rain) water and make the herbal plants (crops) good fruit bearing. (69)

By taking permission from Maruts and Vishvedevas the blade of plough lubricated with good ghee i.e. oil. O Blade! Becoming full of grains fulfil (all) the directions with milk, curd and butter (ghee). The herbal plants grown in this field be full of water having nectar qualities and be ripe and strengthened. (70)

This plough with blade he pleasureful and squeezer of soma (plant) while tilling, the field. This plough facilities the way of getting sheep, cows and horses, the carrier of chariot. (71)

O plough! You are the accomplisher of desires. Gods Mitra, Varuṇa, Indra, Pushā and twin Ashvinī Kumārs may accomplish the desires of people and the herbal plants for this enjoyment. (72)

O gods! You are the cause of getting the divine path by deeds. You cause to accomplish the agricultural work for the good of world through the medium of non-violent cows and bullocks etc. Being parted with you (i.e. your soul) now we got rid of the troubles of hunger and thrist by your mercy and gained light like a sacrifice. (73)

The sages of Yajurveda (chapter-12) go in depth to give the agricultural work a shape of sacrifice. A plough, which is an agricultural instrument of tilling the field, has been addressed as a god. Even gods Soma, Mitra, Varuṇa, Indra, Pushā and Ashvinī Kumār brothers have been invoked in a meter for the accomplishment of the agricultural work. In the present materialistic age, though, the concept of sacrificial form of agriculture has disappeared from the mind of the modern agriculturists, yet, the people residing in the villages still hold the view that agriculture is a form of sacrifice. So far the invocation of gods at the time of cultivation is concerned, the Yajurvedic Hymn (72) has named only those gods, who are supposed to have their hands in accomplishing the work and being cause of good produce.

A deep study of the above Hymns brings to light that agriculture in India was never conventional, which developed at the trial and error basis. This work was guided by the sages to the people in general as a form of sacrifice for the purposes of perpetual availability of food grains throughout the year. The use of cereals as oblation in the sacrificial fire brings the agriculture, if not at par with a sacrifice, yet, a preparatory sacrifice through which oblation material are obtained. If the cultivation had no support of the sages in the remote past and agricultural produce were not permitted by them to be used as offerings, the herbs would have been the only material for the same even to-day.

Bhāgwatpurāṇa - 1

There was a king named Prithu in the very ancient time, whose name is taken by the learned persons well-versed in Shastras with great reverence, because of his services towards agricultural improvement in his state. A story, relating to his such services, finds place in various Purāṇas, but the story which finds place in the Bhāgwatpurāṇa, book-4, chapter-47 (4/17) gives a detail account of the some. It is reproduced below:–

Maitreya says, O dear Vidur! When Prithu was crowned and appointed by the Brāhmaṇas as a ruler of the people, his subjects whose body emaciated owing to starvation, the soil being left without any (crop of) grains, approached their king and said. (9)

Oppressed with the gastric fire, even the trees became hollow with burning of fire. We have approached you, today, O king! for our protection. You are fit to protect us and have been made available to us as our lord. You are capable of providing us with the means of livelihood. (10)

You are the protector of the world (country) as well as the bestower of livelihood. Do you endeavour, therefore, to give us food. We are afflicted being hungry. O king of kings! Before we perish for want of (such) provisions, (You do needful). (11)

On hearing the piteous lament of the people, O chief of the Kurus (Vidur)! Prithu thought over for long and percieved the cause (of the disappearance of the food grains). (12)

Having arrived at the above conclusion by force of reasons, he took his bows and in a great indignation fitted an arrow to it, aiming it at the Earth as Lord Shiva aimed his shaff (at Tripur). (13)

Seeing him with an uplifted weapon, the Earth began to tremble and assuming the image of a cow ran in terror like a doe chased by a hunter. (14)

His eyes turned crimson with anger, there upon Vainya (son of Vena, hence the name) followed her, with the arrow fitted to his bow, where-so-ever she ran. (15)

Running towards the various directions and intermediate quarters (between the two directions), as well as towards the heaven and the earth and the region lying between the two, the goddess (Earth) saw him with an uplifted bow wherever she went. (16)

She obtained no shelter against Vainya (king Prithu) even as the created beings find no immunity from death. Then with a sore heart she returned terrified and said to the noble king: O knower of duties (law of righteousness)! Kind to the afflicted, protect me as well, intent as you are on the maintenance of the living beings. (17-18)

Such as you are, where for do you seek to kill me, a meek and innocent creature? How would he, who is acknowledged as a knower of law of duty (Dharma), take the life of a female? (19)

People do not strike the fair sex even though she has committed an offence. Much less would man like you, who is so gracious and fond of the miserable, stoop to such a thing. (20)

Having destroyed me, an undecaying boat on which the whole universe rests, how would you be able to support yourself as well as (all) these created beings on the surface of water? (21)

Thereafter, Prithu replied– O Earth! I shall slay you, who have turned a deaf ear to my commands and take your share in the sacrificial offerings but refuse to yield us crops. (22)

Punishment is not unadvisable in the case of a cow which is so wicked that it feeds on fodder everyday but does not yield the milk of its udders. (23)

Foolishly disregarding me, you refuse to release the food grains, already created by Brahmā, and, which you have concealed within your bosom. (24)

When your bowels are ripped open by my arrows, I shall be able to stop the lamentation of these afflicted ones, seized with hunger, by your fat. (25)

For the rulers of men, to kill the hateful and self conceited soul, who is merciless to the beings, is no killing. (26)

Having torn you, with arrows, into pieces as minute as sesamum seeds. I shall support these created beings by seer dint of my yogic power. (27)

Seized with a tremor and bowing low, Earth spoke with joint hands to the king, who like death bore, a form, which was the very embodiment of wrath. (28)

Hail, hail to the transcendent Person, who evolves diverse forms by dirt of his Māyā and appears as constituted of the three qualities (Guṇas), though He has by realizing essential nature eliminated all identificatious with physieal matter, the embodied spirit and the controller of both and is above all modifications. (29)

The same supreme maker by whom I have been created to the abode of living beings and from whom this creation has proceeded, consisting of three qualities (Guṇas), is ready with uplifted weapon to strike me. Whom else shall I resort to for protection? (30)

He, who evolved at the dawn this world consisting of animate and inanimate beings by dint of his Māyā, which rests on herself and is beyond all speculative reasons, is now out to protect it by the same. How should he seek to kill me, devoted as He is to righteousness? (31)

The Almighty Lord, though one, appears as many by virtue of His Māyā. It is He who evolved Brahmā and caused the universe to be brought about by Him. Surely the deeds of such a Lord cannot be understood by men, whose mind is tossed by his Māyā, which is very hard to conquer. (32)

Hail to the supreme person, the Maker, who brings into play and thereafter withdraws into Himself, His potencies and who bring about the creation, preservation dissolution of this universe by means of His potencies in the shape of the five gross elements, the ten sense organs and the divine powers controlling over them, the faculty of understanding and egotism. (33)

O birthless Lord! It is you, who in order to place on a sound footing the creation brought forth by you and consisting of the five gross elements, the sense organs and the inner sense, lifted me up from the depths of ocean and took me out of water assuming the form of a primaeval Boar. (34)

Appearing in the form of a hero, you once played the role of lifting up the earth, now seek to kill me with your fierce arrows for the sake of milk. You are keen to protect the created beings, who have taken up their abode in me, like that of a boat on the surface of water! (35)

Surely the deeds of a divine personage (like you) cannot be known by the people of my ilk, whose mental horizon is clouded by your Māyā. It brings forth this creation made up of the three qualities (Guṇas). Hail to such personage, who is renowned to heroes themselves. (36)

The discourse seventeen of the Book four (4/17) ends with praises of King Prithu as a Lord Creator of the world and the worldly beings by Earth. The cause of her praise was King Prithvi's readiness to kill her for the misdoings in the form of withdrawal of her potencies which cause the cereal crops to grow. He became angry on goddess Earth, when he was informed by his subjects regarding her apparent sin to keep them in starving condition from the days of his father, King Vena. The most notable in Earth's praise is that she treated King Prithu as an incarnation of God Creator. In His capacity of a supreme Divine power, the economic progress remained in his hands, which should have been exercised keeping her position in the universe intact. What action King Prithu took after hearing the praise of Earth, as goddess, regarding the economic well-being of his state, we have to go through the next chapter (XVIII).

Bhāgwatpurāṇa - 2

The chapter eighteenth of the Book four also begins with the praise of Earth as she was very much frightened from King Prithu. In fact he wanted to cool down his anger by all means, so that what was needed for the progress of agricultural economy should find opportune time to be processed. The stanzas (slokas) are reproduced below:–

Thus goddess Earth glorified Prithu, whose lips were quivering due to anger. She was frightened but she made herself quiet and steady with an effort of her will. She spoke again. (1)

O Lord! You possess power to do anything that you please; kindly control your wrath and consider what I humbly submit to you. Like the bee, a wiseman takes the essence of everything. (2)

Sages, who have realized this truth, have discovered and tested methods for the realization of human ends here as well as hereafter. (3)

Anyone of the later times who follows with faith and reverence those expedients found and taught by the ancient masters easily to achieve the purposes of life. (4)

He, who in his foolishness disregards them and undertakes to accomplish purposes in his own ways, can never be successful in his efforts. His ends are never realized, even though his efforts are renewed every now and then. (5)

O king! I noticed that the herbs and annual plants that had been evolved of by old Brahmā, were being used and enjoyed by those who were unrighteous and had not undertaken any religious vows and observance. (6)

I observed that the herbs and annual plants, finding myself unprotected and uncared for by your predecessors and that a generation of thievish people flourished on earth. I meant to preserve them for sacrificial rites. (7)

It is natural that the plants have got assimilated in me through a long process of time. Now you are the person competent to draw them forth by some expedient known to be effective in this behalf. (8)

O Hero of mighty arms, O Lord sustaining the life of beings, pray, find a calf, a befitting milk pot and one, who can draw the milk, if you want to have nutritious food coveted by living beings. (9-10)

O king of boundless power! Remove my ruggedness and make me level, so that, even when the rains have passed, the water poured down by the god by rain may stand on me. May all be well with you. (11)

From here what the king did, thereafter, to draw milk from goddess. Earth is narrated by the story teller sage Maitreya. The rest of the stanzas (slokas) of this chapter are given below:–

Accepting this agreeable and wholesome advice of goddess Earth, the Emperor made a calf of Swāyambhuva Manu and drew from her in his own hands all species of herbs and (everything) in the form of annual plants. (12)

Likewise all other wise and intelligent persons too took the essence of everything and so after Prithu. Others also drew from Earth, as a cow tamed by him, the objects sought after by them. (13)

The seers and sages. O most righteous one, made a calf of Brihaspati, milked the goddess and got the sacred Veda; for milk their milk pot being the organs of hearing and of speech and the mind, which is the sense of senses. (14)

The gods made a calf of Indra and drew the drink soma, besides mental vigour, ardour of the senses and physical strength for their milk in a vessal of gold. (15)

The Daityas and Dānavas made a calf of Prahlād, the noblest of them all, and obtained wines and distillates for their milk in a bucket of iron. (16)

The Gandharvas and Apsaras made a calf of Vishvāvasu (their king) and derived the sweetness of song and beauty for their milk in a cup of lotus. (17)

The venerable Pitras, made a calf of Aryamā (their king) and drew with reverence what is known a Kavya (offering of cooked food for Pitras) which they held in a sun-dried earthen vessel and which was milk for them. (18)

The Siddhas made a calf of sage Kapil and obtained in the cup of the welkin mysterious powers, the power of will, while the demigods Vidyādharas used the same sage for their calf and the same pot and obtained treading the air. (19)

Others, who were adept in conjuring tricks made a calf of

Māyā and obtained the magic arts relating to those wonderful beings who can disappear by mere wish or thought. (20)

The Yakshas, the Rākshasas, the ghosts, the detestably ugly fiendish creatures known as Pishachas, all of whom feed on raw flesh, made a calf of Rudra, and drew the beer of blood in a skull as a pot. (21)

Even so the serpents with and without hood, the snakes and other poisonous creatures made a call of Taksha (their chief) and drew poison in their mouth as a vessel. (22)

The beasts made a call of the Bull of Lord Shiva and obtained the grasses for milk in the vessel of the woods. (23)

Again, the flesh eating beasts with sharp teeth made use of the lion as the calf and got flesh for milk in the pot of their body. The birds made a calf of Garuḍa (Suparna) and got mobile creatures as well as immobile creatures for milk. (24)

With the Banyan for the calf, the trees got different kinds of saps for milk. The Himalaya was used as the calf of mountains and various minerals, in the basin of their ridges, were obtained. (25)

Earth is a wish-yielding cow. Now that she had been made available for milking by King Prithu, all the species of living beings milked her, each of them with its own chief as the calf and obtained milk in various forms and held it in their own vessel. (26)

In this way, O descendant of Kuru! King Prithu and others, who sought food for themselves to eat milked the cow and got different kinds of milk (juice or so) in the form of their own food with different calves and cups (to hold it). (27)

Thereafter King Prithu became pleased with goddess Earth, who now yielded all the objects of one's desire, and fondly accepted her as a daughter, feeling paternal love for her. (28)

Prithu (Vainya), the ruler of earth and king of kings, crushed the crest of mountains with the pointed ends of his how and levelled the surface of the terrestrial globe. (29)

Vainya (Prithu), who was like a father of his subjects and provided them with the means of subsistence, next planned with due regard to propriety dwellings at different places all over the earth, and he founded villages, towns and cities, built castles and forts of every description, designed abode of cowherds and pens for cattles, contrived camps and cantonments and taught how to dig mines. He provided houses for farmers and cultivators and raised hamlets on hill-sides. (30-31)

King Prithu' Earlier to people had no idea of different kinds of human dwelling, like villages and towns on this globe. Now they began to live comfortably with a sense of security of life and property in every part of the earth. (32)

In this story of milk taking from the earth in the image of cow acknowledging it as a goddess, it has been indicated therein that it (earth) is only means which provides food to all i.e. living and non-living beings in the form in which each of them require. This story is apparently of general nature, yet it particularly aims at human being because of the fact that it were the subjects of King Prithu's kingdom, who made request to him to provide grains as food to them as the crops which were not growing in the earth for long. The earth became angry owing to the bad behaviour of his father against the subjects. The subjects including the sages and the earth as goddess, accepted King Prithu as an incarnation of Lord Vishṇu and expected from him the divinely treatment. It is also indicated in this story that a king should be favourable to his subjects in the matters of providing livelihood, particularly agriculture, because the cereals, as main food stuff, are obtained through cultivation. Moreover, this story also throws light that the dialogue which went on between King Prithu and the Earth was in the nature of divine talks between two divinities. This story provides a guide- line to the modern political system to pay special attention towards the agriculture as the only source of food grains, so that the people may not suffer for want of the same.

Vāyupurāṇa

The above story pertaining to taking milk from the earth, which took the form of a cow, by King Prithu is also there in the Vāyupurāṇa, chapter sixty two, but with some differences, the relevant portions of that different story and being in the context of the present subject are reproduced below:–

Seeing King Prithu, the sages, who were glad told the subjects that Prithu was to provide you means of livelihood and that would be your lord king. (62/151)

After hearing the words of sages, all the people hurriedly came to fortunate King Prithu (Vainya) and began to say, you make arrangements for our livelihood as said by the sages. Thus coming the subjects nearer to himself (he became vigilant). (62/152)

Then he, the great hero, fitted an arrow at his bow and gave trouble to the earth for the welfare of the people. (62/153)

(seeing no remedy, the earth surrendered to the king and said to him) O great among spirituals! You level me from all directions so that my floating milk may spread all over equally. (62/170)

Thereafter, Vainya (Prithu) placed the mountains, spread all over the globe, with the pointed end of his bow at various places, so that at those places the height of mountain increased high. (62/171)

During the past ages (manvantaras) the earth was uneven, somewhere high, somewhere low. In that state of earth, there was no division of villages and cities during the period of last creation. (62/172-172½)

Neither there was production of grains, nor was there cattle tending, nor cultivation. The business etc. was also not in practice. (62/173-173½)

During the age of Chākshushmanvantara, this was the condition of the earth. Those things came into practice during the age of Vaivasvatman- vantara. (62/174)

Wherever the earth was even there they (men) came and settled after building houses. They took flower and fruits as foods and their lives were pulled on with difficulties, we have heard so. But during the period of Prithu's rule every thing began to grow in the world every where. (62/175-176)

He started reproduction of the herbal plants facing lot of trouble which were lost from the earth. Then that glorious Prithu took the bulk of cereals from the earth making Chākshushmanu (head man of history) as a calf by his own hands. From that bulk of cereals, Vainya (Prithu) nourished his subject, and provided means of livelihood to them. (62/177)

The above extract of the chapter sixty two (62) of Vāyupurāṇa brings to light that it was King Prithu, who initiated the agricultural economy in his kingdom, at his own level and made it popular in the people as a means of livelihood perennially. He himself made it a part of the state economy. It was, perhaps, this reason that the earth, that is to say the country, praised him like that of an incarnation of Lord Vishṇu or God.

But at the same time agriculture in India finding a suitable and favourable atmosphere developed by taking its own course naturally. The principle of tending of cow for getting a direct food material in the form of milk facilitated the agricultural economy. The combination of milk and grain was adopted as the main food material by the mass population of ancient India with no hesitation in mind. The vegetarian habit of diet in our country is the outcome of the natural combination of the milk and grain as the food articles. These two food articles when joined hands as the basic source of economy the total philosophy of life style took a turn towards that. Such a philosophy of life-style found favour of the sages engaged in the austerity too, who by then living on the juicy fruits and the like vegetation.

The tending of cows gave birth to calves which were found useful in tilling the land for taking crops of various kinds of cereals which were by then growing naturally, and the people using them as food articles. The natural production of cereals was insufficient to feed all, the major population had to base their life on fruits and roots as well as on leaves of plants grown naturally. The people found three main qualities in the agricultural economy viz., reproduction of cereals in as many quantity as was required at that time, fodder to the cows, bullocks and other tammed animals which were in use in various ways, and developing a total vegetarian life style as a righteous one. The agriculture had played a major role in developing a vegetarian culture in the Indian society. As it facilitated the performance of sacrifices through its products to be used in oblations and offerings, the sages and kings both approved this means of mass production.

As King Prithu associated himself with the development of agricultural economy, he was widely praised by all the sections of society and that his name was projected as the initiator of agriculture. But through his conduct by milking the earth which took the form of a cow before him he also encouraged the economy of cow-keeping. In this way householders began to take interest in the agriculture as well as tending of cow or cows simultaneously.

Further, to add here that the bullock, named Nandi, being the mounting conveyance of Lord Shiva led to believe the Indian people that entire cow race is a means of achieving spiritual and heavenly benefits. One who tends cow and bullocks not only strengthens his economic prosperity, but also strengthens his future or next life.

Even the people believed that a bullock had a divine character being a beloved associate of Lord Shiva, who helped him during destruction of sacrifice of King Daksha in the past, as cited in the foregoing pages. Lord Shiva's bullock Nandi exhibited his divine power to ruin the sacrificial assembly by creating many Rudras after Sati, the wife of Lord Shiva and daughter of Daksha, embraced death by will after becoming aware of her husband's insult there. That scene was witnessed by the learned class as well as by Lord Brahmā and Vishṇu. It revealed and brought to light the inner capacity of a bullock, though exceptional.

The people of those days became aware of the same and began to tend bullocks not only for multi-purpose uses but also for multi-reasons including divine ones. Today it may be treated as a philosophical approach of Brāhmaṇa householders, yet it bore a religious sanctity behind the same. The pair of bullock and cow provided a solid footing to the agriculture economy in India. It led to evolve a theory that the human life could only remain in existence for indefinite period, that is to say till the end of a Kalpa, on the basis of cow-bullock economy. The lives of both the races—cow and human-being mainly dependent upon vegetation, the economy developed on the basis of this pair-proved fruitful.

■

10

Economy of The Tending of Cow

India is a country in which the tending of cattle has been in practice since long as a means of livelihood. It is the manifestation of economic prosperity also. A person who has a good number of cattles, particularly cows, is considered to be economically sound. It elevates the social status even to-day. The Shāstras also emphasize on the tending of cows in as many number as a man can have. It is because a cow supplies a nutritious food material directly in the natural form as milk. It being a balanced diet requires nothing additional to keep the body nourished and healthy. The Creator God initially created milk in the body of women (the mothers) and the cows to keep their newly born baby or calves alive by intaking it. A thing which is nutritious to a just born baby or a calf will always be good for adults also. Such a secret of milk came to light in the mind of yogis and sages in the very early days. They began to tend cows for the sake of milk even when performing austerity in the jungles. It was easy to tend them them, being no problem of fodder etc. With this view the importance of a cow has well been described in the Mahābhārat, Anushāsanparva.

Mahābhārat—Anushāsanparva - 1

The famous discourse of Prince Bhishma throws light on the importance of a cow in the chapter eighty one (81) of the Anushāsanparva of Mahābhārat. Prince Bhishma, who was lying on a bed of arrows in the battlefield of Kurukshetra and counting his days narrated a story to king Yudhishthir in this regard, on being asked by him. The same runs as follows:–

Yudhishthir asks– O grandfather! You describe what is more pious among the pious things in this world and is recommended as such and is really more and more pious. (1)

Replying his question Prince Bishma says— O King! The

cows accomplish great purposes and are more pious. They give relief to the men (from hell or trouble) and protect the lives of the subjects with their milk and processed butter (ghee). (2)

O great Bhārat! There is none the great pious than the cows. They are sacred and pious and also greater than the others in the three worlds. (3)

The cows live in the world which is above the world of gods. Those intelligents and thinkers give cows in donation, get ride of hell and go to heaven. (4)

King Māndhātā, son of (King) Yuuanāshva, Yayāti and Nahusha always gave in donation lacs of cows. With this they achieved such good positions, which were not possible for gods even. (5 and first part of sloka 6)

O Sinless king! I am telling you an old story in this regard. Once upon a time, the great intelligent Shukadeva completing his routine work and becoming pure and pious minded asked his father Krishnadvaipāyan Vyas, who had the knowledge of past and future, saluting him, which one sacrifice is considered greater than other sacrifices? (6-II part to 8).

O Lord! With what deed the thinkers get high position and with what pious deed gods enjoy the heaven? (9)

What is the essence of sacrifice? In which the sacrifice lies? What thing is nice for gods? What greater sacrifice is there than that? (10)

O Father! What is (more) pious among the pious things? Describe to me all these things. Hearing all these questions of Shukadeva, Vyas having knowledge of spiritualism told to him all such things rightly. (11)

O son! The cows are the habitation of all the beings. Cows are the great rest. Cows are sacred and pious and that the wealth of cows makes all pious. (12)

I have heard that in the earlier days cows had no horns. They worshipped immortal God Brahmā for their horns. (13)

God Brahmā after seeing fast unto death being observed by the cows provided with horns to everyone of them.(14)

O son! On getting the boon horns appeared on (the head of) the cows. Every one of them got the desired type of horns, which beautified the cows. (15)

Getting the boon from Brahmā cows became the cause of goods, offerer of oblations, evolver of sacreds, pious, fortunate and blessed with divine bodies and signs. (16)

Cows are divine and great splendour. Their giving in donation is admired. Those righteous persons give cows in donation leaving the jealousy, they are said sacred persons. They are considered to be the donors of all (kinds of) donations. O sinless Shukadeva! They get sacred world of cows (where Lord Vishṇu resides). (17 and 18)

O great Brāhmaṇa! All the trees of the world of cow (Goloka) are the giver of sweet and tasty fruits. Those trees are full of divine flowers and fruits. The flowers of those trees carry very good divine smell. (19)

The soil of that world is full of valuable metals. The sands of that land are mixed with particles of gold even. When that land is touched it gives pleasure. There is no dust or mud. That land ever causes good. (20)

The ponds of that world shine like jungle of lotus and morning sun and glorify like steps having adorned with jewels. (21)

The land of that (world) has so many beautiful lakes. The lakes are full of blue lotuses there. The leaves of those lotuses are like precious jewels and the filaments of such lotuses shines like gold. (22)

O son of Bharat (Yudhishthir)! The sacreddous and glorious persons, who are there, they enjoy their lives and travel (in the space) boarding on wonderful and beautiful planes and feel pleasure. (29)

O king! The beautiful divine girls dance with them. Yudhishthir! By donating cows the persons go in such world. (30)

O king! The powerful sun and brave air who are rulers of such worlds (countries) and king Varuṇa who glorifies that world, the people who give cows in donation go to that. The cows are the holder of age, beautifully bodied, having various form, are in the form of world, and are mothers of all. Shukadeva! The people having control over sense organs should mutter the names of cows everyday as said by Lord Prajapati. (31 & 32)

The man, who serves the cows and follow them by all means, the cows being pleased over him, is blessed with such boons which are difficult to achieve. (33)

One should never be against the cows, should provide pleasure to them, should welcome them properly and worship them with salute. (34)

The person, who having control over sense organs and with happy mood, serves the cows everyday, gets prosperity. A man remain for three days by drinking warm cow urine thereafter for three days by drinking warm cow milk. (35)

After taking warm cow milk he should drink warm ghee for three days. After drinking warm ghee (he) should remain for three days by taking air (only). (36)

The gods too enjoys good and good worlds by taking ghee and with the effect thereof and that which is more pious than other pious things, one should take hold of that ghee. (37)

(One should) offer oblations with the ghee of cow to the fire (sacrificial). He after paying fee (Dakshiṇa) of ghee gets hail from Brāhmaṇas. Take ghee as food and give in donation the ghee of cow. By doing so one gets strength in him and prosperity of cows. (38)

By taking a solution of barley which was extracted from the cow dung for a month as food, a man gets rid of sin of the murder of a Brāhmaṇa. (39)

The gods being defeated by demons observed such a penance and regained their lost divinity and became heroes and great sages (sidhas). (40)

Cows are holy, pious and alike sacred. They are great gods (goddesses). By giving the cows in donation to Brāhmaṇas a man gets pleasure of heaven. (41)

Thus the fortunate cows are the main part of a sacrifice and accomplisher of entire desires. You consider them as Rohini. There is nothing greater than them. (46)

O Yudhishthir! On hearing so from sage Vyās the brilliant Shukdeva resorted to the worship of cows everyday. Therefore, you also perform the worship of the cows. (47)

The above story does not only brings to light the helpfulness of the cows to the mankind for the sake of economic well-being, but also throws light on their divinity and being the means of spiritual benefits.

Mahābhārat — Anushāsanparva - 2

There is another dialogue between goddess Lakshmi and the cows in the next chapter eighty two of the Anushasanparva of the Mahābhārat. It reveals that goddess Lakshmi resides in the cow-dung. As it was known to king Yudhishthir, he wanted to get his knowledge confirmed by prince Bhishma. For this sake he asked a question to Bhishma. The dialogue went on between them on this subject is as under:—

King Yudhishthir asks— O grandfather! I have heard that there resides goddess Lakshmi in the cow-dung but I have a doubt in this regard, so I want to hear reality in this connection. (1)

In his reply Bhishma says — O great Bhārat (king Yudhishthir)! The learned men cites an example of the dialogue went on between the cows and Lakshmi from the history of ancient time. (2)

Once upon a time, goddess Lakshmi adorned beautifully entered the cow-herd. Her form and glory made the cows wandered. (3)

Thereupon the cows asked— O goddess! Who are you and where from you have come. There is no comparison of your beauty on this earth. O fortunate! We wonder (to see) your beauty. (4)

Therefore, we like to know your identity, who are you and where you will go? O excellent woman! You let us know all these things rightly. (5)

In reply goddess Lakshmi gives her identity :—

O cows! It be well to you. I am known in this world with the name Lakshmi. The entire world desires me. I have given away to the demons, therefore, they perished for ever. (6)

Living under my patronage Indra, sun, moon, Vishṇu, god of water (Varuṇa), and fire have been enjoying pleasure for ever. (7)

Gods and sages gets accomplishment by obliging me. O cows! In whose body I do not enter, they perish in toto. (8)

With my association righteousness, wealth and desire get pleasure. Therefore, O cows, the giver of pleasure! You consider me having such effects. (9)

I want to live for ever among you people and for that purpose I am praying by coming to you. By getting my association you people be glorious. (10)

In reply to the request of goddess Lakshmi the cows said —

O goddess ! You are fickle. You never stay at any place. In addition to this you have equal relations to so many, therefore, we doubt to like you. It be good to you. You go wherever you like to reside happily. (11)

We are bodily sound and healthy as well as beautiful. What for we require you? Please go, wherever you like. We are obliged by the grace of your appearance before us. (12)

Then Lakshmi told to the cows —

O cows! What is this! Is it proper to you that you are not welcoming me? I am pious and pure and difficult to achieve. Even then you are not accepting me? (13)

O cows, you vow goodness! The prevalent proverb in the world that visiting a place without invitation, there will surely be disregard, appears to be true. (14)

Gods, Dānavas, Gandharvas, Nagās, Rākshas and men get my blessings by performing hard austerity. (15)

O good natured cows! It is the effect of your (goodness) that I have come to you personally. So, you accept me here. I am not able to be disregarded anywhere in the three world including the movable and immovable beings. (16)

In reply the cows said —

O goddess! We do not dishonour or disregard you. We are only giving away you, that too considering your changeable nature. You stay no where stably. (17)

It is of no use to talk much on this topic? You go wherever you like to go. You sinless? What work we have from you! Our body is handsome and healthy by nature. (18)

Hearing the views of cows, goddess made a last attempt to persuade them to honour Her request in this way —

O cows! You honour others. By your giving away I would be ignored and neglected in the entire world. Hence, you be merciful on me. (19)

You are fortunate and provide refuge to others. I also seek your refuge. I am devotee to you. There is no demerit in me. Hence, you protect me and take me as your own. (20)

O cows! I require your honour. You are the ever doer of well-beings of all, I like to live in any part of your body, whether it be lower or upper or unpious, if it is provided. (21)

O sinless cows! There appears no unpious part in your body. You are great sacred, pious and fortunate. So you give me order, in what part of your body may I reside; you tell me clearly. (22 and the first part of sloka 23)

At this point prince Bhishma adds in this way —

O king! When (goddess) Lakshmi said so, the cows being kind and affectionate as well as of good nature thought over (the request of Lakshmi) interse and then all told to Lakshmi (as follows). (23)

O good and glorious (goddess)! We essentially should honour you. You reside in our dung and urine because our these two things are considered pious. (24)

On hearing the replies of cows in the herd, goddess Lakshmi felt good and told to them thus—

O cows, showerer of pleasure! It is my good luck that you have so been pleased on me by giving your acceptance (to my request). It will be so.(I will reside in your dung and urine). You have honoured me, so it be good to you. (25)

Bhishma then continuing his discourse told to Yudhishthir as his concluding exhortation on this subject—

O scion of Bharat! After so giving a promise to the cows goddess Shri (Lakshmi) disappeared from there, while they had their eyes at her. (26)

O Son! I have told you the importance of the cow dung. Now I am telling you the importance or greatness of cows themselves, listen. (27)

This chapter of the concerned story ends with the said words. In it Bhishma has placed his views regarding the importance of cowdung and cow urine when such things are used as fertilizes in the fields for good yield. The above story throws light at the conventional use of cowdung as good fertilizer. Though, it is a religious faith that the cowdung and her urine are the holy things and are used at the time of worship to any divine power, yet the logic behind it is that these things have honour to provide refuge to goddess Lakshmi. She being the goddess of wealth, the object of using the cowdung in every sort of worship, is to please her for economic well-being or prosperity.

Mahābhārat – Anushāsanparva - 3

Continuing his discourse Bhishma liked to throw light on the subject of greatness of cows, to which Yudhishthir, in fact, wanted to know to give it a shape in the economy of his state as king. Bhishma's discourse to this effect has been fully described in the chapter eighty three (83) of Mahābhārat, Anushāsānparva, which runs as follows––

O Yudhishthir! The man, who always takes the food of left over cereals in a sacrifice and donate cow, enjoys the fruits of performances of sacrifice and the donation of cereals everyday. (1)

No sacrifice is performed without ghee and curd of cow. The merit of sacrifice is gained with these things. Therefore, the cows are said to be the roots of sacrifice. (2)

The donation of cow or cows is known as good against all other donations, therefore, cows are great, pious and holy. (3)

A man should bring into use of that for developing strength in the body and for all kinds of peace from obstructions. Among these milk, curd and ghee (processed butter) are the causes to bring all kinds of sins at rest. (4)

O great king in the scion of Bharat! The cows are considered as brilliant in this world as well as in the other world. There is nothing holy than the cows. (5)

O Yudhishthir! In this regard learned persons cite an example of a dialogue which went on between Indra and Brahmā in the past. (6)

Thereafter, Bhishma began to narrate the said dialogue in this context to bring force in his discourse and make effections in the mind of Yudhishthir.

In the earlier age when the gods defeated the Daityas and Indra became the ruler of three worlds, then all the people with the cooperation of each other began to live pleasurely following the path of truth and rigthteousness. (7)

O son of Kunti! Thereafter, one day when sages, Gandharvas, Kinnaras, Nāgas, Rākshasas, gods, Asuras, Garuḍa and Prajāpatis were present in the court of Brahmā in his services, Nārad, Parvat, Vishwāvasu, Hāhā and Hūhū Gandharvas were worshipping him by singing songs and playing with the musical instruments, wind was blowing taking in it the good smell of flowers, various seasons were presenting, separately, flowers which were vested with good and pleasant smell, the society of gods was also present there, all the beings were getting together, the sound of divine musical instruments was being enjoyed, the divine dancing girls and admirer were also seated there, at this (good) junctions, god king (Devarāja) Indra after saluting god head Brahmā asked (as follows)- (8 to 12)

O grandfather god! Why the world of cows is above the world of gods and the rulers of all directions? I want to know the reason thereof? (13)

What austerity the cows have performed here and Brahmacharya observed on account of which leaving the Rajas qualities are they, pleasurely, enjoying the place which is located above the gods'one. (14)

Then Brahmā told to the brave Indra—O Indra! You are the devastator of Balāsura (name of an Asura), you have always disregarded the cows. O Lord ! Therefore, you do not know the greatness of cows. O great god! I am telling you their effects and greatness, listen. (15 to 16)

O Indra! The cows are said to be the part of sacrifice as well as expressed form of sacrifice, because without their ghee, milk and curd no sacrifice can be performed by other means.(17)

They (cows) nurish the people with their milk and ghee. Their sons i.e. bullocks work in fields for the purposes of cultivation. (18)

The bullocks cause the production of cereals (by their labour) which are used in the performance of sacrifices and also in the oblation of offerings. (19)

O king of gods! From those cows milk, ghee and curd are obtained. Cows are very pious. The bullocks carry loads keeping themselves hungry and thirsty. (20)

Thus the cows nurish the sages and the people by their own deeds. O Indra! In their behaviour there is no place of Māyā or diplomatic action. They are engaged always in truthful acts. (21)

Due to these reasons the cows reside in the world which is above ours. Indra! I have told this (in reply) to your question, as to why the cows reside at a place above the (place of) gods. O Indra! In addition to this the cows have been blessed with the boons and have the power to give boon to those with whom they please. (22-23)

The Surabhi kind of cows are sacred doers, holy and have good signs. They have gone on the earth with (certain) objects.(24)

I am telling you that object, (you) listen. O son! When in the righteous age (Satyayuga) god head was ruling (the worlds) and that Aditi was performing difficult and hard austerity standing on one leg with a desire to get a son and being pleased with her austerity

Lord Vishṇu was to come in her womb, at that time, the daughter of Daksha, named Surabhi, seeing goddess head (Aditi) performing austerity also began to perform it gladly. (25-28)

She observed yoga by standing on one leg for eleven thousand years at the very beautiful top of the Mount Kailāsh, where gods and Gandharvas reside. By her austerity gods, sages and great Nāgas became afflicted. (29-30)

They all went to goddess Surabhi (cow) with me and stood close to that female ascetic; then I asked her. (31)

O goddess ascetic! What for you are observing such a hard austerity? O good and lucky! I am satisfied with your austerity. You ask for your desired boon. O Indra ! Thus I inspired cow Surabhi to ask for boon. (32-33).

Being inspired by Lord Brahmā the cow named Surabhi said to him in this way—

O god! Sinless grandfather! I need not ask for any boon. Your pleasure at me today is the greater boon for me. (34)

O god head! god king! Husband of Shachi! When Surabhi said so, then what I said her, you listen. (35)

O good faced goddess! You have given away desire and covetousness. I am very much pleased with your this desire-free austerity. So, I bless you with immortality. (36)

With my blessings you will reside above the three worlds and your place of residence would be known 'Goloka' (world of cow) by name. (37)

O lucky goddess! Your all the good children will reside in the human world (i.e. on the earth) doing reasonable deeds. (38)

O good goddess! Whatever you will desire in your mind whether it be divine or human or it be heavenly pleasure all would be coming to you automatically. (39)

O thousand eyed god! In that 'Goloka' (cow world) the entire desires of all get accomplished. The death and old age never approach. Even the fire has no approach there. (40)

O Indra! Neither there is any misfortune nor any nongood. There is availability of divine jungles, and divine residences. Even very handsome and comfortable planes which move according to will (of the person boarded at) are also available there. (41 and first part of 42)

O lotus eyed Indra! Brahmacharya, austerity efforts, control of sense organs, donation of various kind, sacredness, pilgrimage, great labour and with performance of very many good deeds, the world of cow 'Goloka' is accomplished. (II part of 42, 43 and 44, I part)

O Indra! As you asked for, I have narrated all thing accordingly. Now you should never dishonour the cows (44-II part-45)

Thereafter, Bhishma said to king Yudhishthir as follows—

O Yudhishthir! Indra on hearing the sayings of Lord Brahmā began to worship cows everyday. He expressed all kinds of honour to them. (46)

O great soul! All these qualities of cows relating to their holiness, pious nature and very good greatness, have been told to you by me. (47)

It is, thus, clear that the worship of cows and tending them as a mark of respect and honour to them in India do not depend, merely, on faith but there are logical reasons of their qualities and divine character also for the same. In addition to that they are very helpful in gaining the economic prosperity.

Atharvaveda - 1

Wherein the description of Mahābhārat it has clearly been stated that the cows gained divinity in them by means of hard austerity in early ages, the Vedas too throw light on the qualities of the said animal. The Atharvaveda adds a very peculiar quality of a cow belonging to Brāhmaṇa. Due to these qualities a cow is such a property of a Brāhmaṇa which is not to be taken away by the Kshatriyas or others. The Sukta five of Kāndika (Book) twelve of this Veda exclusively narrates the worldly as well as heavenly qualities of the cows as follows:—

Created by austerity and having taken shelter in Parbrahma i.e. the supreme spirit the Brāhmaṇas gained the cows with hard labour (in the form of austerity). (12/5(1)/1)

It is full of truth, property and eternal fame. (12/5(1)/2)

It is deprived of cakes to be offered to maines protected and cosecrated in religious ceremony and that place with sacrifices. Looking at her is like death to Kshatrias. (12/5(1)/3)

One gets the seat of Brahmā through the cow. The owner of the cow is the Brāhmaṇa only. (12/5(1)/4)

One who takes away such a cow (or cows) of Brāhmaṇa and a Kshatriya who afflicts a Brāhmaṇa, they suffer loss of wealth, strength and weat speech. (12/5 (1) 5&6)

In the above Hymn (12/5(1)) the divine characteristic of a cow, perhaps Surabhi one has been described and her ownership has been said to be vested in the Brāhmaṇas only. Even Kshatriyas i.e. the rulers have been prohibited from taking away the cow or cows of a Brāhmaṇa in any way. But the Indian society could not remain refrained from tending the cows. The tending of cows in the latter days became the general means of livelihood of every caste. Not only this, most of the rulers were honoured by the sages for giving good number of cows to them in donation.

Atharvaveda - 2

All the meters of this Sukta (12/5(2)) are in the continuance of Sukta (12/5(1)) :—

Bodily strength, brilliance, force, speech, sense organs, wealth (Lakshmi), and religion, (7) Veda, field, nation, Vaishyas, light, fame, power, wealth (8) age, form, name, fame, inhale, exhale, ear, eye, (9) milk, juice, cereal, fire, righteous path, truth, spiritual desire, act of pious liberality, sons (people or subject) (10) vanish of those Kshatriyas who take away the cow of a Brāhmaṇa and also get their lives shortened. (11)

In the above Sukta all the meters are in one seritum intending at if a king takes away even a single cow from a Brāhmaṇa then he loses all he possessed, so he should not act as such at any cost. At present it aims that a state should not take away the properties of a learned person. According to the Vedas forfeiture of estate of a learned person should be avoided even if found guilty of any serious offence.

Atharvaveda - 3

It is the inherent quality of a cow belonging to Brāhmaṇa that she herself punishes the wrong doer either against her or her owner. In the Hymn (12/5(3)) this quality of the cow has been described.

The cow of a Brāhmaṇa is dreadful enough. She becomes poisonous like the poison of sin hidden by a hide. (12/5(3)12)

In that all the dreadfulness and causes of death are present. (12/5(3)/13).

All the fruits of wrong deeds and the killing property to a man (i.e. wrongdoer) are present in her. (12/5(3)/14)

This cow causes death to a person, who takes away her from a Brāhma ṇa by force. (12/5(3)/15)

She becomes a deadly weapon to a man who is the cause of shortening the life of a Brāhmaṇa. (12/5(3)16)

Therefore, learned person should know the cow, which belongs to a Brāhmaṇa, in said form. (12/5(3)/17)

She rises upward like (the flame of) fire and runs like Vajra (a wheel like weapon of Indra). (12/5(3)/18).

She becomes like a weapon of Lord Shiva making sound of her hoobs. (12/5(3)/19)

When she roars while sounding there she becomes like sharp Vajra. (12/5(3)/20)

The cow making a sound 'Hi' becomes like the death and turning round her tail she looks like extremist. (12/5(3)/21)

By all means shortening the life the cow turns round her ear and urinating she becomes the generater of tuberclosis (a chest disease). (12/5(3)/22)

When being milked then she takes the shape of a deadly weapon and after milked she turns headache. (12/5(3)/23)

When handled she fights and standing nearby she hits or tears out. (12/5(3)/24)

When beaten she is troublesome and her mouth is covered she perishes. (2/5(3)/25)

While siting she is of less understanding and when seated she generates fatal diseases. (12/5(3)/26)

The cow belonging to a Brāhmaṇa while following the person is taking away her from such owner takes away the life of that one. (12/5(3)/27)

The above Atharvavedic sukta is aimed at protection of the cow of Brāhmaṇas, so that he may not be deprived of his means of livelihood, while resorting to austerity in jungle. Moreover, its aim is to make such deterent Vedic provisions so that the same would be effective. Perhaps it has come out for the protection of Kapila (red) cow which is, particularly, considered as the only belonging of a sage and his livelihood.

Atharvaveda - 4

This sukta (12/5(4)) is also in the continuation of the above ones and finds place for the same purposes. It is as follows—

The cow of a Brāhmaṇa so taken away is the cause of partition in the decendants and the disruptions. (12/5(4)/28)

While she is taken away she is like a weapon and when took away she causes decay of bodily strength. (12/5(4)/29)

She creates cruelty being the form of sin. (12/5(4)/30)

When she is taken as food she is like poison and who took (as food) she puts the life in danger. (12/5(4)/31)

During digestion it is toxication and when digested causes bad dreams. (12/5(4)/32)

When getting angry she soutes out and while wrath causes decay. (12/5(4)/33)

On being excited she causes sorrow and when excited she becomes like poisonous snake then her smell takes away the awakenness. (12/5(4)/34)

On being offered as offering in a sacrifice she causes defeat and when offered then becomes non-existent. (12/5(4)35)

When being made ready (for a sacrifice) she is like the

angry Shiva and when made into pieces she comes in the condition of a hide or skin. (12/5(4)/36)

When it is taken as food the cow causes poverty and when took as food she takes the form of goddess Niruti to cause bad consequences. (12/5(4)37)

Causing harm to a cow belonged to a Brāhmaṇa that one deprives (a man) from this and next worlds both. (12/5(4)/38)

This hymn throws light on such cases in which a cow belonging to a Brāhmaṇa is taken away for the purposes of offering in a sacrifice. The bad consequences of the same has been described in it. So one should keep himself away from such acts even for religious purposes. It is directed by the Vedas that a person should adopt or create own means of livelihood than getting prosper by taking away the means of others.

Mahābhārat – Anushāsanparva - 4

The importance and value of a cow, particularly red cow, to a Brāhmaṇa can well be known by a dialogue went on between king Nahusha and sage Chyavan. It is a part of the story pertaining to sage Chyavan's coming out of a river in a fishing net, while the fishermen were taking out fishes, nearby the capital of king Nahush. It may be recalled here that sage Chyavan was performing austerity there in the water. He was caught hold of in the net by fishermen. When it became known to the fishermen that he was sage Chyavan, they frightenedly informed the real position to the king, who in turn came to the sage to honour him. This story is described in the Mahābhārat, Anushāsanparva, which is as follows:—

Bhishma says to King Yudhishtir during his discourse —

O scion of Bharat (Yudhishthir)! By getting aware of sage Chyavan's coming (out) near his capital King Nahush reached there with his priest and ministers. (51/1)

He told (to the sage) —O great Brāhmaṇa! Tell me, what good should I do for you! O god! I will get your order accomplished, whether it be a very difficult work. (51/4)

Then sage Chyavan gave an order to him in this way—

O king! You pay off the cost of fishes and also the cost of mine to the fishermen. (51/5)

Thereafter, a long discussions went on between the king, his ministers and also with the sage in the end another sage informed him that the cost of a Brāhmaṇa is nothing but a cow. He said like this—

O lion king! There can be no value (in terms of money) to cow and the Brāhmaṇa who is greater than other Varṇas. Therefore, you give him a cow as his cost. (51/22)

In this context Bhishma continuing his discourse says—

O king (Yudhisthir)! Listening the words of that sage King Nahush became glad with his ministers and priest. (51/23)

O king (Yudhishthir)! He went to sage Chyavan, who was performing hard vow, and spoke by satisfying him. (51/24)

King Nahush said thus—

O great Brāhmaṇa sage ! O son of Bhrigu! I am purchasing you by giving a cow. It is your proper cost to my mind, so you get up, get up. (51/25)

Thereafter sage Chyavan being satisfied told to king Nahush in this way—

O sinless king of kings! Now, I get up. You have purchased me by paying proper cost. O king! You never betrayed your idealness. I donot see any thing equal to the cows.(51/26)

O brave king! Muttering the name of cows and singing their qualities, hearing that and giving them in donation as well as visiting them, these deeds have been admired in the Shāstras. These deeds extinguishing the effects of sins cause well-being to the doers. (51/27)

The cows are always the root cause of wealth (or goddess Lakshmi). There is even no particle of sin in them. It is the cow that provides always cereals and offerings to the gods. (51/28)

They keep nectar in them and when milked they provide nectar (an auspicious liquor). They are the base of nectar. The whole world bow before them. (51/30)

As such sage Chyavan is also of the opinion that the cows are not only the primary source of an individual economy but also a regular source of economy to the entire human society. The dairy farming in the present days has elevated the milk business to the form of an industry.

The tending of cows evolved in the society of mankind as a source of wealth directly. It was the mental skill of the Indian sages, who while living in the jungles adopted the work of tending the cows for getting the milk as primary food easily. They thought it proper, while living in the state of nature, that cow would be of a great help even in the matters of fuel by using dung. Its tending in forest was easy than in the plains. Perhaps, its tending came into practices firstly in the society of sages, thereafter, it became popular among society of householders too, when sage Chyavan fixed his person's price as a cow only to the king; his intention was to justify and popularize the values of cow or cows in the society.

In the natural life style non-violent animal were the good friends of men. Among them the cow was considered as the best one, for the man. So this animal was given the status of a diving creature and that it was recommended and approved for worship as a goddess in general, when the knowledge of science advanced further cows milk was accepted equal to that of a mother's milk. Keeping in view this reason cow was given the status of a mother. Going a step further sage Chyavan tried to explain with his conduct that the value of a cow was greater than a man or the wealth. He refused to accept any amount of wealth in face of a cow as a cost of his person.

In this materialistic world, where everything is valued in terms of physical wealth, refusal of wealth by Chyavan was meaningful. Though his logic was based on Vedic principles, yet it carried weight when it was viewed with other angle. His basic needs was likely to be fulfilled by the cow, he asked for the same as well as its maintenances for him was problem-free. That notion was widely acknowledge in those days.

Vālmīki-Rāmāyana — Bālkānd

There appears a story in the Vālmīki-Rāmāyaṇa pertaining to fight between sage Vasishtha and king Vishwāmitra, son of Kushik, (later on sage) for taking away of the earlier one's cow, named Shabalā. This story throws light as to why the sages and seers of olden time kept a cow to fulfil their economic needs. It would also throw light about valuation of the body of sage Chyavana in terms of a single cow as discussed earlier. The story runs thus—

The highly glorious King Vishwāmitra, who carried on his administration and ruled over the earth for many thousand years, (one day) collecting an army and accompanied by an Akshauhini (a division consisting of 21,870 elephants, an equal number of chariots, 65,610 horses and 1,09,350 on foot forces) once went round the globe. (51/20-21)

Marching successfully across cities and states rivers and great mountains as well as hermitage, the king , it is said, came to the site of the hermitage of Vasishtha, which was rich in flower, creepers, trees of various kinds, infested with hordes of wild animals of every description and frequented by Siddhas and Chārṇas. (51/22-23)

It was graced by (the presence of) gods, demons, Gandharvas and Kinnaras, abounded by in most peaceful deer and was resorted to by flocks of birds. (51/24)

It was crowded with multitude of Brahmarishis visited by Devarishis, Siddhas engaged in austerities who were resplendent as fire adorned with all sides with exalted souls. (51/25)

The presence of other sages called Vaikhānasas glorified the hermitage of Vasishtha. The mighty Vishwāmitra, the foremost of the victorious, held the site of his Āshram looking like a second Brahmaloka. (51/28)

The very hero Vishwāmitra bowed low to the celebrated Vasishtha, out of modesty, the foremost of those engaged in muttering prayers.(52/1)

He was greeted by the sage Vasishtha in these words— "Welcome to you (in this hermitage)", and offered him (Vishwāmitra) a seat. (52/4)

After taking his seat, the great sage (Vasishtha) placed before Vishwāmitra fruits and roots according to the rules of propriety. (52/3)

Accepting the hospitality from Vasishtha, the king enquired about the well-being of the sage and about his austerity as well as Agnihotra and his pupil. (52/4)

The king also equired about the condition of his (Vasishtha's) plants (the means of their sustenances). In reply Vasishtha told Vishwāmitra saying that every thing was going well. (52/5)

The great ascetic Vasishtha, son of Brahmā, asked the king, when he took his seat comfortably—(52/6)

Is every thing well with you; O monarch? Do you rule over the people, O pious king! According to the course of conduct prescribed for a king, delighting them with your righteousness? (52/7)

Are servants duly maintained by you and do they stand at your beak and call? Have all your enemies been fully conquered. O destroyer of foes? (52/8)

Is all well with your forces, treasures and allies. O destroyer of foes! No less than your sons and grandsons, O tiger among men! Divorced from sin as you are? (52/9)

In reply, the glorious king Vishwāmitra told Vasishtha, the noblest one, about his all round welfare. (52/10)

Having carried on all such talks for a very long time with supreme joy, the two celebrated and most pious souls felt pleased with each other. (52/11)

At the end of dialogue, O scion of Raghu, the almighty Vasishtha said to Vishwāmitra laughing heartly, as follows—(52/12)

I wish to offer hospitality to this army as well as to your own unfathomable self, according to your dignity, O mighty king! Please accept it for me. (52/13)

You receive my honour, O king, as you are the worthiest of my guests and deserve to be zealously honoured. (52/14)

You have duly entertained in every way, with fruits and roots that are available in your hermitage and water for washing our feet and rinsing our mouth with your very sight. (52/16)

O enlighted soul! I shall depart. Let my salutation be to you. Regard me with friendly eye. (52/17)

The pious and liberal –minded Vasishtha (then) actually invited the king ones more, even though he went on saying like that again and gain. (52/18)

Thereupon, Vishwāmitra, replied to Vasishtha- All right, let it be as it pleases your self, O jewel among sages!(52/19)

When addressed thus, the glorious Vasishtha felt fully delighted and called his cow, Shabalā washed and clean of mud. (52/20)

Come along, come soon, O Shabalā and hear to my words. I am determined to entertain with a sumptious this royal sage (Vishwāmitra) along with his army. Get every thing ready for me. (52/21)

O celestial cow! Yield every thing in six varieties of dishes in desired quantities, that may be pleasing to a particular individual for my sake. (52/22)

O Shabalā! Look sharp! Produce in plenty all kinds of food accompanied by sweetmeats, drinks, and dishes that can be licked or sucked. (52/23)

Instructed, thus, by Vasishtha, O destroyer of foes, Shabalā, a cow of yielding, yielded all the luxurous things as desired by each individual (of Vishvāmitra's camp). (53/1)

Sugar cane, honeys, fried grains of paddy, maireya (a kind of liquor) and excellent spirituous liquors, as well as other costly drinks and foods of various kinds also. (53/2)

There could be seen mountain high heaps of rice, varieties of sweet rice boiled in milk, pulses boiled in the liquid form mixed with salt, streams of curds, and also silver plates in thousands, brimful with delicious fruit juices of various kinds as well as with sweetmeats. (53/3-4)

Fully entertained by Vasishtha, O Ram! The entire army of Vishwāmitra wholly composed of joyous and well fed men, felt highly gratified. (53/5)

Being fully entertained along with his in mates and Brāhmaṇas including his family priests, ministers, counselors and dependants, King Vishwāmitra, a sage king, felt rejoiced and strong. Being delighted, he said to Vasishtha as follows:—(53/6-7)

I have been honoured and sumptuously entertained by you and you also deserve for the same, O holy one! I shall prefer a request, O master of expression; listen. (53/8)

Shabalā may be handed over to me in exchange of a hundred thousand cows, as she is a jawel and a king is the person who ought to receive jewel. (53/9)

Therefore, make over Shabalā to me, she is rightfully mine, O holy Brāhmaṇa! Thus addressed by Vishwāmitra, the almighty Vasishtha, a fore- most ascetic, whose mind was given to piety replied to the king– I shall never part with Shabalā in exchange of a thousand million cows, what to talk of one hundred thousand, even not for heaps of silver (coins). She does not deserve to be away from my presence, O subduer of foes! (53/10-12)

Shabalā is inalienable for me, as glory is inalienable from a man practicing Rajyoga. Moreover, an offering made to the gods and to the manes, as well as the sustenance of my life depends upon her. (53/13)

Agnihotra, as well as Bali (daily offerings to the fire and a portion of meal to the creatures daily), so to Vaishwādeva sacrifices, so to the various Mantras (meters). (53/14)

All these no doubt rests on this cow, O Royal sage! She is my all as also the source of my delight, I say on oath. (53/15)

For (these) numerous reasons, I shall not give Shabalā to you. Thus addressed by Vasishtha, Vishwāmitra then said thus. (53/16)

An expert in making out the meaning of words, Vishwāmitra replied- I offer to you fourteen thousand elephants equipped with girths and chains of gold and decked with goads of gold. I, further, offer to you eight hundred gold chariots driven by four white horses each and decorated with small bells.(53/17-18)

I shall (also) give you, O sage of noble vows, eleven thousand highly spirited horses of excellent breed and born in territories noted for such horses. (53/19)

I shall give one crore young cows distinguished by their different colours. Let Shabalā be given (in lieu of those things). (53/20)

I shall give you without reservation as many jewels and as much gold as you want, O'jewel among the twice born! Let Shabalā be given to me. (53/21)

Even, though, solicited thus by the talented Vishwāmitra, the almighty Vasishtha answered— I shall on no account part with Shabalā, O king! (53/22)

She is indeed the only jewel in my possession. She is my only wealth. She is alone my everything. She is alone my very life. (53/23)

She is alone my half monthly sacrifies performed on the new moon as well as that is performed on the day of full moon, sacrificial performances concluded with gifts and even so ritual acts of various kinds, O king! (53/24)

All my religious rites, no doubt, are rooted in her, O king! What is to be gained by prattling a good deal? (53/25)

When sage Vasishtha did not part with his wish yielding cow, O Ram, Vishwāmitra thereupon proceeded to take Shabalā away by force. (54/1)

On being taken away by the mighty king, Shabalā on her part felt afflicted and distracted with grief and fell weeping. (54/2)

She reflected – Have I been deserted by the high souled Vasishtha, that I am being taken away in this wretched condition by the king's retainers, sore distressed as I am? (54/3)

What wrong has been done by me to this eminent seer of pure mind. What caused him to abandon me when I remained devoted to the pious soul (Vasishtha). (54/4)

Deeply pondering thus and sighing again and again, she on her part ran to the supremely powerful Vasishtha forthwith. (54/5)

Shaking off the aforesaid retainers numbering many hundred,

O destroyer of foes (Ram), she atonce swiftly ran as the wind to the soles of feet of that exalted soul. (54/6)

Shedding tears, the celebrated Shabalā submitted to Vasishth standing before him in a voice sonorous as the numbling of clouds, weeping and wailing as follows—(54/7)

Have I been forsaken by you, O almighty son of Brahmā, that the king's servants are taking me away in your presence? (54/8)

Questioned thus, Vasishtha whose heart was tormented with grief, on his part replied to Shabalā, as to an afflicted sister, in this way. (54/9)

I am not abandoning you, O Shabalā, nor you have caused me any wrong. Intoxicated with power this mighty king is taking you away. (54/10)

My strength is not equal to him. Even the king is particularly strong today. The king is a Kshatriya and ruler of the earth to boot. (54/11)

Here is his army, full one strong Akshauhiṇi, equipped with elephants, horses, chariots and crowded with the best of elephants. In this respect he is mighter. (54/12)

Thus told by Vasishtha, Shabalā, who could correctly understand the sense of other's speech, replied like a meek lady to the Brāhmaṇa seer of matchless plendour as follows. (54/13).

The wise (men) declare the strength of Kshātriyas as nought. The Brāhmaṇas are stronger. The strength of a Brāhmaṇa, O holy one, is spiritual and is superior to that of a Kshatriya. (54/14)

Your strength is immeasureable being very powerful. Vishwāmitra is not stronger in comparison to you. Your glory is unassailable. (54/15)

You, who fostered (me) by your Brāhmaṇical (spiritual) strength. You command me, O glorious sage and put an end to the pride, strength and endeavour of that wretched. (54/16)

As she urged, O Ram, the illustrious Vasishtha said forthwith, create a force capable of destroying the army of enemy. (54/17)

Listening the command of sage Vasishtha, the wish yielding cow produced a number of warriors forth with, O king. (54/18)

(The so created hundreds of Pahalvas) began to destroy the whole army before the eyes of Vishwāmitra. Highly enraged and his eyes dilated with anger, King Vishwāmitra too made short work. (54/19)

Vishwāmitra began to destroy Pahlavas by means of his weapons of various kinds, seeing the Pahlavas killed in hundreds by Vishwāmitra, Shabalā immediately produced the other terrible Shakas, akin to the Yauanas, who flooded over the land. (54/20-21)

They being brilliant and powerful resembled the filaments of the Champak flowers in colour, carried sharp edged swords and Pattishas (a kind of spear) on their person and were clad in yellow. (54/22)

They killed the entire army of Vishwāmitra like that of blazing fire. Thereupon the highly glorious Vishwāmitra discharged missiles (in numbers), which put the Yauanas and Kāmbojas as well as the Bārbaras into confusion. (54/23)

Seeing the warriors created by Shabalā stupefied by the missiles of Vishwakarmā and that they are fleeing hither and thither, Vasishtha asked Shabalā to evolve more warriors, as she is the wish yielding cow, by dint of your yogic power. (55/1)

(Thereupon) from her roar sprang up the Kāmbojas, brilliant as the sun. And again from her udders, the Bārbaras carrying weapons in their hands were produced. (55/2)

The Yavanas came forth from her genitals, the Shakas were issued from her anus and that from her skin there evolved Mlechhas, Hāritās and Kirātās. (55/3)

They together wiped out the entire army of Vishwāmitra instantly including the foot soldiers, and soldiers mounted on elephants, horses and chariots, O scion of Raghu (Ram)! (55/4)

Looking at the extermination of his army by mighty Vasishtha (with the help of forces generated by the divine cow), the hundred sons of Vishwāmitra rushed very furiously towards Vasishtha carrying weapons of various kinds. The great sage, however, reduced them to ashes by his roar. (55/5-6)

As such the sons of Vishwāmitra were reduced to ashes instantly with their horses, chariots and foot soldiers by mighty Vasishtha. (55/7)

The illustrious Vishwāmitra seeing the annihilation of army (as well as of his sons), Vishwāmitra filled with anxiety mixed with shame forth- with. (55/8)

He resembled the ocean that has lost its fury and the snakes whose franqs have been broken and suddenly became lusterless like the elipsed sun. (55/9)

Having lost his sons and army, he felt miserable like a bird whose wings were clipped. His strength and spirit were shattered. He reached a state of despondency. (55/10)

He retired to the forest instructing his only (surving) son in these words—rule the earth according to the moral code prescribed for a Kshatriya in order to carry on the administration. (55/11)

The above story of a struggle between a sage or holy Brāhmaṇa and a pious Kshatriya for the sake of a cow which was a worldly beast in the modern sense of the term (cow) throws light on the inner power of a divinely created cow.

Though no one in the modern society would like to think on the line that an animal like a cow could develop such an strength which resembles divine one, yet the people of India had a faith in that regard in the past which is effective even today. Our countryman do believe in the divinity of cow.

Moreover, what divine character of a cow has been narrated by the various Suktas of Rigved, reproduced above, is fully seen in the above episode, even if it is considered to be an imaginery story included by the author of the epic Rāmāyaṇa. It also throws light on the worldly character of cow which when comes in a mood to show her loyalty towards her master develops self strength to save her entity and that the entity of her keeper, when commanded to do so.

It is an unique precedence that our Shāstras depict about a cow. That was the reason why sage Chyavan wanted that a Brāhmaṇa should be valued in terms of a cow rather than in terms of money or other valuable things as discussed above in this chapter. Further, it is also true that we have lost our battle in the foreign attacks only on account of protection of the cows, but at the same time it is also true that our survival on the map of the world rests in the worship of cow and stronghold of agricultural economy based on cow scions, which cannot be measured in the years and the centuries to day. Cows as the natural source of livelihood is not only a matter of faith but is practically established in the above story. Though a wish-yielding cow might have been rare in the past too, yet it was available and Shabalā cow of sage Vasishtha was one of the same.

It was that episode which developed a faith in the remote past that a king should protect cows and Brāhmaṇa both. He should never go against them in any circumstances. Further, it may be added here that cow was the source of livelihood of Brāhmaṇas living in the forest, who were observing austerity there for the welfare of the king and the country, so a duty pertaining to the protection of cow and the Brāhmana was attached to the political administration. Vishwāmitra while taking retirement from political power after his defeat at the hands of a Brahmaṇa and a cow gave definite instructions to his only son to take his place and run the administration according to the rules of law prescribed for the purpose by the Shastras, because of the fact that he himself experienced the result of his negligence in that regard.

Agnipuraṇa

During the course of a dialogue went on between physician Dhanvantari and his pupil Sushrut such a matter also arose for their discussion in the past. Placing has viewpoint Dhanvantari says as follows—

O Sushrut! A king should maintain cows and Brāhmaṇas both. Now I proceed to describe the means of 'cow peace' . The cows are holy and the cause of well-being. The entire world is established in the cows. The cow-dung and the urine are the means of the destroyer of poverty. To pat their body and placing the hand at their horn as well as cause them to drink water remove the poverty. A mixture of urine, dung, milk, curd processed butter of cow and water touching kusha (a kind of grass) is a good drink and (its use) dispels the bad dreams. The gorochan destroys poison and the Rāksasas. A giver of food to the cows gets heaven. In whose house cows are troubled, he gets hell. One, who provides food to the cows (even) belonging to others, gets heaven; whereas, who is always ready for their welfare gets the world of Brahmā. By the donation of cow, by the description of the greatness of cows and by cow-protection a person causes salvation of his manes. This earth becomes pious by the breath of cows. By their touch sins decay. By taking one day the mixture of cow-dung, cow-urine, cow ghee, milk and curd with the water (contacting) kusha (a kind of grass) and keeps fast that day even a bad man becomes pure. In the olden days even gods observed such rites for the destruction of their sins. (292/1to7)

From the above description of the greatness of cows it is clear that a thorough study regarding the practical way of living and an economy based on tending of cow was conducted in the remote past. On the basis of that study the religious and social philosophy behind the cow tending was propagated by the learned scholars of those days. Their study, when transformed into practice placed the philosophical approach at the solid ground.

Leaving apart the divine character of cows a saint taking shelter in a jungle for performing the austerity, it was necessary for him to keep a cow for his proper nourishment in such lone place with no problem of her maintenance. On these grounds there developed an economy of tending the cows on the Indian soild, when the people were forced by the circumstances to live in the state of nature for long. It was an independent economy suited to the mankind even in the absence of other physical wealth and the consumable goods. It was this reason that the Brāhmaṇas where more attached to the cows. As the time passed on a tendency of tending cow developed in the other classes of society too.

The tendency of tending cow accelerated when the people

came to know her divine character, even though as exceptional one. The role of Shabalā cow belonging to sage Vasistha in the episode of her kidnapping by king Vishwāmitra by force in the protection of herself and that of the sage inspired the general people to have a cow for economic, divine and worldly reasons. It is also clear from the concerning story cited in the foregoing pages that sage Vasishtha's life was totally dependant upon his cow named Shabala. When he expressed this aspect to Vishwāmitra he in turn offered to accept a huge quantity of wealth in lieu thereof. A man of ordinary prudence could have transferred his cow in the consideration of that huge wealth.

It was Vasishtha, who did not favour to assess the divine value of a cow in terms of the physical wealth. On this account he requested his cow Shabalā to use her divine power for the protection of her person and also the person of her master. He also showed his divinity which he achieved by performing austerity, but thereafter.

The people of India even today believe that a cow in the form of wealth and as a means of living bear a divine character and a person having a cow can never become pauper and through her services can attain salvation. If we go deep, we will find that the entire ancient economy of our country rested on the cows at the one hand and on the bullocks at the other hand. Movables go to the cow side and the immovable go to the bullocks side in the form of agriculture and plantations as well as in the form of shelter. The bullocks played important roles in the development of those things even in the recent past. It was the pivot of cow and bullock around which the whole of Indian economy revolved for long.

■

11
Business Policy

According to the Shāstras business is the third means of livelihood which is called triad or 'Vārtā' profession. The other two ones are agriculture and cattle tending, especially cow tending, which have already been discussed in the foregoing pages. Though the Vedas are considered to be in favour of the natural way of life and the earlier two means being natural ones have been given preference, yet business joined hands with the earlier two means of livelihood at a stage when other two were firmly rooted and therefrom it constituted a triad called 'Vārtā' profession. The word Vāṇijya i.e. Business finds place in the Vedas too having the present meaning relating to the trading transactions.

Atharvaveda

The Sukta fifteen of Atharvaveda, Kāndika three pertains to business. Indra and fire, being the twin gods of this Sukta, have been prayed for the progress of the business of the sacrificer or worshipper. The meters of this Sukta are thus—

I praise Indra in the capacity of a businessman. That Indra (may) like to come here and those, who place hinderances in the business being inimical, places obstruction as a robber, and extinguishing to lions etc., march ahead. He may provide me wealth in the form of income in my business.(1)

The path of the countries with which I have trade reaction should be able so as to provide me milk and ghee, so that I may bring the principal money with profits to my place of residence which I get from sale and purchase. (2)

O Fire! I offer oblation to you, so that my desire to earn profit in the business be accomplished and also strength to walk on foot be gained, for which i praise you also. (3)

O Fire! You forgive my sin, which is the result of loss of my fast etc., due to long journey. You give me strength to bear the trouble in this distant country. Sale and purchase both be profitable and pleasureful. You accept my offerings, O gods! The earnings on principal make me pleasureful. (4)

O Fire! You return those gods who place obstruction in my profit making them satisfied with that oblation. O gods! The money with which I want to increase my wealth that may increase regularly with your blessing. (5)

Indra, Savitā, Moon, Prajapati and Fire may inspire my mind towards that wealth. I desire money through the means of business. (6)

O carrier of oblation to god! I praise you with the oblation. You be vigilant for the protection of my sons and grandsons. (7)

O knower of all beings came into being! I offer you oblation as grass is offered to the horses every day. I, in your service, be prosperous with wealth and cereals. (8)

This Suklā is especially included in the Atharvaveda as a guideline to the persons who like to adopt business as a means of livelihood. How a business can be carried on, it is indicated therein. The sacrificer has foreseen the obstacles which come in the way of a business and to over- come them gods Fire and Indra have been prayed.

Shukranīti - 1

It is not only the sacrifice which should be performed for a good and beneficial business. Āchārya Shukra who has been honoured as a good policy advisor to the King Bali has given some guidelines for a man entering the business profession for his livelihood, which are as follows:—

A man having knowledge; before initiating a business firstly studies as to what type of that business is? What are the means to do that ? How much money to be invested? What is the position of use (i.e. Consumption) of the (concerning) things? Such a person only then takes it up. Otherwise he does not take up even a small one. (3/264 I part-265 II part)

A person having good knowledge should not take up such business in which more investment is needed and comparatively profit is lesser. He should take up such business in which profit is more. And the cost of the goods to be sold and also its weight or number is to be kept in mind.(3/365 and 366).

Thus according to the Shukranīti, a person, who has to adopt business, must bear in mind all the aspects relating to the same. A new comer in the field of business who does not carefully consider these aspects generally suffers loss.

Shukranīti - 2

Āchārya Shukra has also given directions to the partners, that is to say, the partnership business as follows:—

I shall share nothing, saying so and share half of the amount to be invested (as capital) with such an agreement the (partnership) business be started. (4/5/315)

A partnership business may have any other kind of agreement between the partners. In the above stanza (sloka) Āchārya Shukra has given his opinion considering only two partners which can be increased and the conditions he agreed upon accordingly.

Shukranīti - 3

Those who start partnership business pertaining to gold, cereals and juicy fruits or alike, in that the partners get their share in the benefit, according to each ones work and the share in the capital investment, that is to say, if equal , less or more, then their share in(the profit) is according to that.(4/5/307 II part-308)

Shukrāchārya is of the opinion that a partnership business has many problems and if two or more persons join hands in such business they should be properly guided by the state in respect of their shares in the profit. Otherwise they will have to face several problems which may damage the business itself. Thus it would be causing harm to the economic growth of the country. As a policy giver Āchārya Shukra has given proper attention towards the problems of business which might crop up even in future. It would have been so that such problems would have cropped up in his tenure as chief priest of Danāvas and that he was forced to think over such matters by the circumstances of the time. Whatever would have been the pressure of the time Āchārya Shukra is very clear in the policies and rules of law while expressing his views on any subject of business or trade.

Yajyavalkya Smrīti

As all the smrīti-Law-givers have with one voice recommended for the implementation of law of Varṇas in the ancient period business exclusively went in the hands of Vaishyavarṇa. But this Varṇa was again divided into professionwise or according to the means of livelihood. This was the reason why castism came into existence and that a separate caste pertaining to the business evolved in the Vaishya varṇa. This caste too was given the name Vaishya. Presently this community, though with certain exceptions mainly adopts business as the means of livelihood. In this regard the Yajyavalkya smrīti says thus—

For Vaishyas increase in wealth by using money, agriculture, business and cattle tending are the means of livelihood. (1/119)

The author of Mitākshara commentary sage Vijyāneshvar says- Accretion of wealth by using money and sale and purchase for gains are called business while commenting on the above sloka. Accordingly, trade including accretion of wealth by the use of money as well as sale and purchage of goods, whether it be agricultural or industrial products come under the category of business.

Relaxing the law of Varṇas on the subject of livelihood sage Yajyavalkya says—

(The means of livelihood of) Shudras is to serve twice born people, (finding it insufficient) business can be taken up as means of living. (1/120-I part)

The commentator Vijyaneshvara commenting on the above sloka says—

If it is not possible to pull on life by the services of twice born persons then live with the profession of business.

In the context of living when Shudras have been recommended to take up business as the means of livelihood the twice born communities may also take it up in the absence of their Varṇa's means.

Mahābhārat - Anushāsanparva - 1

It has been described in the Mahābhārat Anushāsanparva that Vaishyas are the most important class of the society. In fact it is only this class of society which is said as the category of hourseholders. Because this category includes the agriculturists, the cattletenders and the traders under the consolidated name of Vārtā kind of profession, therefore, generally it becomes difficult to distinguish the conducts and rules of law applicable exclusively to the business class and to the trade. A description relating to the 'Vārta' profession i.e. a triad of agriculture, cattle tending and business is as follows:—

The Vaishyas came into being from abdomen, therefore, they should adopt the profession of 'Vārtā' (agriculture, cattle tending and business) for the maintenance of stomach and to carry on the life. (numberless sloka at p. 5918 (part I))

The following is an extract of Maheshwar Shiva and His wife goddess Uma's dialogue which finds place in the chapter -141 of the Anushāsanparva of Mahābhārat.

Maheshwar Shiva says—

O goddess! Likewise Vaishyas have also been recognized as helpful in the journey of world. The people of other Varṇas (castes) carry on their life on their support because they produce the result directly. If the Vaishyas do not exist the people of other Varṇas will also exist not. (chapter-14, p. 5921)

The ancient duties of Vaishyas are thus– Cattle tending, agriculture, business, fire worship, donation, study (particularly of Vedas), taking the path of truth, observance of good conduct, to welcome visitors, renouncing the worldly things and control of sense organs, to welcome Brāhmaṇas, and sacrifices (or abondment) (141/54-55)

A righteous businessman should not do trade of sesamum, sandalwood and juicy material and also give respect to the triad as far as possible. (141/56-57 first part)

Lord Maheshwar Shiva also narrates to His wife Uma the general rules of conduct to be observed by the householders including the business class.

But one thing worth to be noted here that it is only the business class for which such rules were propagated far general interest. Those rules are as follows:—

There are some rules prescribed by the Shāstras for taking an active part in the worldly affairs for the householders. Those (rules) are well and good for all the human beings. I shall describe them now. (141/76)

A person who is interested in self should give in donation according to his capacity, should perform sacrifice always and also should do healthy works all the time. (141/77)

A man should earn wealth by righteous means. He should then divide that wealth into three parts and thereafter effortfully begin deeds which are righteous. (141/78)

Those who are desirous of their progress, they should utilize one of the three part in the accomplishment of religious rites and the wealth and that second part to used for enjoyment and the third one (to be invested) to increase itself. (141/79)

Such good conducts, though, recommended by Lord Shiva, in general to all the householders, yet, these rules mostly apply to the business community. It is this community which is expected to divide its income in such a way so as to make a good provision for the future investment and effortfully increase the same in a regular way. Increasing money by investing it, is the exclusive profession of a businessman. In the past too, it was tried and the result came in affirmative. One thing more has been given prominence in the above discourse and that is the righteous path in the transaction of the business as well.

Lord Shiva has also prohibited the Brāhmaṇas to sell juice (i.e. Juicy fruits) and cereals. He says thus:—

It is condemnable to the Brāhmaṇas to sell juice and cereals. (chapter14, page 5919-I part)

The things which are prohibited to be sold by a Brāhmaṇa, it may be inferred therefrom that those things are the subjects of sale by the business class exclusively.

Skandapurāṇa - Revākhand

A story, though pertaining to the truth of godism, yet has a relevancy regarding the transaction of business with the countries situated at distant places. It is in the form of a discourses of Shri Suta to sage Shaunaka and others. This story finds place in the Skandapurāṇa, Revākhand (volume), and runs as follows:—

At one time a seminar was arranged by the sages at the beautiful place of Naimishāraṇya, who were interested in the peoples welfare and that it was pleasurely to all. (1/1)

There came Shri Suta, a disciple of brilliant Vyās, with his followers muttering the name of god Hari, at the same time. (1/2)

The great sages Shaunaka and others got up seeing Shri Suta coming, who was well versed in Shastras. (1/3)

Being fully versed in all the religions (Vedic and Shastric Suta and great Vaishnava saint (Shaunaka) suddenly saluted each other by laying on the ground. (1/4)

(Thereafter) very intelligent Suta took his seat as provided by sages Shaunaka and others. (1/5)

Then Shaunaka and other sages, saluting Suta who was sitting there, by joint hands, said. (1/6)

O great sage! O Suta knowing all! What are the means to resort to devotion to Hari by the mankind in this Kaliyuga. (1/7)

O god (Suta)! Tell us. Because in the Kali age all the human beings would take interest in the sinful acts and (being) ignorant of Vedas. Then what would be the means of their welfare? (1/8)

In the Kali age the men though alive, yet would be of short span of life, poor and troubled in many ways. (1/9)

As the sacred acts are done by a great labour that is why people would not do sacred deeds in Kali age. (1/10)

And due to loss of sacred work all would be doing sinful deeds.

The people having a little knowledge vanish with their decendants. (1/11)

O Suta! Tell us as to how with less labour, wealth and time sacred deed could be performed. (1/12)

From whose exhortation a man does good or bad deeds, he becomes sharer of the same. (1/13)

Those, who exhortate sacred work, are kind, having no deceitful intention, are sinless and have no opponent. These fair kinds of persons are like God Nārāyaṇa. (1/14)

Though having good knowledge in the world, yet do not deliver it to others, great God, in the form of knowledge, do not get pleased. (1/15)

The persons, who satisfy others by the wealth of knowledge, they are God Nārāyaṇa in the form of men. (1/16)

O great intelligent! What is that fast, the observance of which desired result is obtained. We are interested in listening that one. (1/17)

O great sage! You have knowledge of Vedas with their parts. We see no other orator like you because you are the disciple of Vyas. (1/18)

In reply to the request of the sage Shaunaka and others Suta said:—

O great saints! You thankful, you are to be counted first among the Vaishnavas, because of the reason that you people like well-beings of others. (1/19)

O Shaunaka! Listen, I shall tell you that nice fast which was asked by Nārad from Lord Vishṇu, the husband of Kamalā (the goddess Lakshmi), in the same form in which he told to him (Nārad). O sages! Listen that carefully. (1/20)

The first chapter of the concerning story which ends here, is like that of preface. Even then it brings to light as to what knowledge the story listener wanted to be delivered by Suta. A person having no knowledge of the background of spiritualism of Indian soil may get himself ready to understand what is going to be exhorted to him about the worldly acts regarding the livelihood, particularly observance of righteousness in business transaction.

The second chapter begins with the discourse of Shri Suta in this way:—

Once upon a time Yogi Nārad travelling in the various planets came over this planet which causes death, with the intention of doing good to the people. (2/1)

Here he saw all the beings getting various troubles and by taking birth in the different races are suffering from pains of their sinful acts. (2/2)

Seeing this he thought over the means of relief from the trouble in his mind and proceeded to the world of Vishṇu. (2/3)

There he saw Nārāyaṇa, whose body was of fair colour, having four hands, and holding counch and wheel as well as wearing sacred garland in his neck. (2/4)

Seeing that Godhead, he began to praise him. (2/5)

Nārad said, (O god!) you are not to be described by the mind and words, you are also not able to be held, you have such power which has no origin, nor middle or end have no worldly qualities. (2/6)

O God! You are the creator and vanisher of troubles to your devotees. Hearing the praise of Nārad Vishṇu said. (2/7)

O Nārad! What for you have come to me ? What is in your mind? I shall tell you what is asked. (2/8)

Nārad said, all the people of death world after taking birth in various races are getting trouble by their own sinful acts. (2/9)

I want to know from you any short means by the observance of which their trouble may end. (2/10)

God (Vishṇu) said, you have asked a very good question being kind to the people. (You listen) I am telling you that means by the observances of which the mankind would get rid of attachments. (2/11).

O Brāhmaṇa! I am bringing to light that fast which is difficult to get in the three worlds, on being asked by you. (2/12)

That fast is of True God (Satya Nārāyaṇa), which if performed with all the rites one gets pleasure in this world and salvation in the other world. (2/13)

Listening the words of God, Nārad said again. (2/14)

Nārad asked, what is the result of that fast and who performed that one. You tell me in detail about that fast. (2/15)

Shri God said, it ends sorrow and trouble (of the doer) and increases the wealth as well as causes (the birth of) decendants and comes out with victory all over. (2/16)

For this fast the man, with full devotion and faith at any day in the evening, perform the worship of True God (Satya Nārāyaṇa). (2/17)

He may take Bhoga of nice sweets (weighing about one and a quarter kg.) together with his brethren and Brāhmaṇas. (2/18)

May take banana, ghee, milk and flour of wheat. In the absence of flour of wheat, flour of rice (may be taken), country made sugar or guḍa may be mixed in the same. (2/19)

The 'Prasad' so prepared be given to all who heard the story (of Satya Nārāyana) and also to the brethren and also the Dakshina (fee) be given to the priest and Brāhmaṇa. (2/20)

After taking the 'Prasad' with the brethren, may arrange (religious) songs and dance. (2/21)

Thereafter, all the audience remembering God Satya Nārāyaṇa should go to their places. By observing the fast in this way desired results are gained. (2/22)

There is no other means, on this world, greater than this, particularly in the Kali age. O Nārad! Now listen the story of the person, who performed this first. (2/23)

In the city Kashi (Vārānasi), there was a poor Brāhmaṇa named Shatānaṇd, who begged door to door being troubled with thirst and hunger. (2/24)

Brāhmaṇa-lover god Nārāyaṇa seeing the (said) troubled Brāhmaṇa, taking the form of an old Brāhmaṇa, asked him with honour.

O Brāhmaṇa! What for you move round on the earth every day. I want to hear the reason thereof. If you like, tell me. (2/26)

The Brāhmaṇa said, I am very poor, I walk on the earth for the sake of alms. If you know about this, please tell me. (2/27)

The old Brāhmaṇas (i.e. God Vishṇu) said, 'O great Brāhmaṇa! You observe the good fast of True Nārāyaṇa. That accomplishes all the desires. (2/28)

Doing that a man get rid of all the troubles, you do that observing the rites effortfully. (2/29)

The old Brāhmaṇa, that is, God True Nārāyaṇa disappeared, thereafter (the begger Brāhmaṇa) decided in the mind to observe the fast in the next morning. (2/30)

Being worried about that he could not sleep in the night. Getting up early in the morning, he took a vow to perform the fast and worship. (2/31)

With this determination he went for begging. This day he got the material more than ever. (2/32)

He performed the ceremony of Satya nārāyaṇa fast with his brethren using the said material. He became prosperous and got rid of all the troubles with the effect of the fast and worship. (2/33)

He got then recognition of all over the city by the effect of that fast. Thereafter, he began to perform the worship (of Satyanārāyana) keeping fast every month. (2/34)

God said, what for Shatānand (the Brāhmaṇa) observed and worship performed, knowing this. (2/35)

Any person, who does so (keep the fast), he, after getting rid of all the sin, gets salvation. (2/36)

The men, who would keep this fast and perform worship their troubles would surely vanish. (2/37)

As the fast of Satyanārāyana came into practice by the discourse of Lord Vishṇu with the aim and object of prosperity it can be said that a divine power always remains active to help a righteous man. A business which stands on honesty and integrity expects righteous path even if there is lesser profit. God will come out for the rescue of such righteous businessman likewise.

Continuing his discourse in the chapter-3 Shri Suta said:—

O Shaunaka! As said by Nārāyaṇa to Nārad, I told you, if you have to know anything more you ask me. (3/1)

Shaunaka said: O Suta! Who observed that fast after that Brāhmaṇa on this earth with reverences? I would like to hear that. (3/2)

Suta said; O sages! Who thereafter observed that fast you listen, when with own religious rite. (3/3)

The Brāhmaṇa got himself ready with his brethren to observe that fast, there came a woodman at the same time. (3/4)

He, being thirsty and hungry and placing the bundle of wood at outside, went inside the house of Brāhmaṇa and saw performing him the fast and worship. (3/5)

He humbly saluting him with joint hands asked, what are you doing? What result come out by doing this. Tell me in detail. (3/6)

The Brāhmaṇa said, 'It is the fast of Satyanārāyaṇa (True God), which accomplishes all the desires and ends the trouble and sorrow. (3/7)

It is his gift that this wealth is achieved. Hearing this the woodman became glad. (3/8)

He took the 'Prasād'and drank water and went home concentrating in mind the name of Satyanārāyaṇa. (3/9)

He decided in his mind that what money he would get by selling his wood with that he would perform the worship of Satyanārāyaṇa after keeping fast. (3/10)

Thinking so in mind he went to the town of richmen placing the bundle of wood on his head. (3/11)

On that day he got two times the cost of his wood. Becoming glad he purchased banana. (3/12)

And sugar, ghee, milk, wheat flour also he purchased. With these things he went to his house. (3/13)

He then invited his brethren, kept fast and religiously performed the worship of Satyanārāyaṇa. He got wealth and sons with the effect of that fast. (3/14)

Enjoying the pleasure in this world, in the end he went to the World of Truth. O sages! I am, further, telling the story, which you listen. (3/15)

Now begins the fourth chapter. This is a story pertaining to a king. He usually performed the worship of Satyanārāyaṇa to remain prosperous as well as for the sake of the prosperity of his state. It is as follows—

Shri Suta said—There was a king named Ulkāmukha who had control over his sense organs. He always visited to the temple of god. (4/1)

He used to donate money and movables to Brāhmaṇas every day to get them satisfied. He had a wife who always remain smiling and that her facial appearance was lotus like. (4/2)

He observed fast of God of Truth at the bank of river Bhadrashielā with his wife. (One day when he was performing the worship) there came a businessman. (4/3)

He anchored his boat at the bank of the river, which was filled with tradeable material. Then he alighted from the boat. (4/4)

Seeing the king performing the fast (and worship), he humbly asked from the king. (4/5)

Sadhu (perhaps his name) asked- O king! This you are doing what? It is my desire to hear. Tell me with devotion. (4/6)

In reply the king said—O Sadhu! This is the fast and worship of great brilliant Vishṇu, which is performed with the desire of sons and other thing together with brethren. (4/7)

Then that businessman saluting him spoke—O king! Tell me about this fast. I shall also perform this. (4/8)

Because, I have also no issue. Performing this fast, I shall get that. Being aware of the method of performing this fast. He came to his house and narrated about this son-giving fast to his wife. (4/9)

And he took a vow as to when he would be blessed with son then he would perform the fast of Satyanārāyan̦a surely. (4/10)

After some time his wife Lilāvati gladly came in the family way. (4/11)

In the tenth month she gave birth to a daughter. She began to grow like the moon of lighted fortnight. (4/12)

The businessman performed her birth-sacrament with his wife and put her name Kalāvati. (4/13)

One day Lilavāti told her husband with sweet words, why not you perform the fast according to your earlier vow? (4/14)

Sadhu said- O beloved! I will perform that fast at the time of her marriage surely saying so he went out of city. (4/15)

Here the growth of Kalāvati continued in her father's house. (4/16)

One day righteous Sadhu, the business, saw her daughter playing with her friends and found her age marriageable. Then called for his employees and said. (4/17)

You search out a suitable bridegroom for her and bring him. On getting the order his employees went to Kānchannagar. (4/18)

From that town they brought son of a business man to Sadhu. He saw that handsome and able boy. (4/19)

According to the religious rites he celebrated the marriage of his daughter with that boy, the son of a businessman, in pleasing mood and that his brethren also participated in it. (4/20)

Unfortunately, he forgot to perform the worship with fast of God Satyanārāyana. Then He became angry. (4/21)

After some time that businessman being skilled in his trade went out with his son-in-law for transacting business. (4/22).

He went to a town situated at the see coast the name of which was Ratnasār and started business there. (4/23).

At the same time God Sātyanārāyaṇa cursed him for violation of his own vow saying that he would be put in trouble. (4/24-25)

On the same day the thieves stole all the wealth of the king (of that area) and ran towards the direction of Sadhu (the businessman). (4/26)

The thieves, seeing the watchmen of the king to follow on them, kept the wealth (nearby) Sadhu hiding out themselves. (4/27)

When the watchmen of the king saw the belonging of.their king lying there, then they tied the businessman with his son-in- law and brought them to the king. (4/28)

Presenting them before the king, they (watchmen) said to the king, these are the two thieves. (Please) give order accordingly having a look at them. (4/29)

The king looking at them gave his orders (accordingly). Then the watchmen after tying them strongly put them in the prison. (4/30)

Though in the above story two separate characters of king and businessmen are there, yet the conduct of the businessman violative of his own vow pertaining to the performance of religious rites, importance has been given to it. In this story it is noticed that to make the business beneficial one should be religious minded and follow the divine rules without any hitch. Business being a risky transaction always depend upon the wishes of God, so a businessman should in no way displease God or Goddess Lakshmi to avoid such kinds of divine sufferings.

In the fifth chapter the divine power of God Sātyanārāyaṇa through which his blessing or the curse becomes effective in this world. Suta in his discourse makes it clear and gives emphasis that he should never be ignored in the transaction of business. If the businessman wants to avoid the market risk.

In continuance of the story Suta said-

Due to this illusion (Māyā) of Satyadeva king Chandraketu did not hear anything about the two businessman and took away their all properties. (5/1)

Because of the curse of Sātyanārāyaṇa the ladies, at the house of Sadhu and his son-in-law, were also put in trouble. The thieves stole away the wealth of their house. (5/2)

Being troubled by the diseases and other causes as well as thirsty and hungry Lilāvati used to go door to door for the sake of cereals. (5/3).

And so also the girl Kalāvati began to go door to door for the said purpose). One day Kalāvati went to the house of a Brāhmaṇa being troubled by remaining hungry in the previous night. (5/4)

There she heard the story of Sātyanārāyaṇa fast and asked blessing for the accomplishment of her desire. (5/5)

She took the Prasād and came home late in the night. Then Lilāvati began to condemn her daughter. (5/6)

O daughter where you were till later night ? What is in your mind? Then the girl tell her mother what the truth was. (5/7)

O Mother ! I have seen the fast and worship of Sātyanārāyaṇa in the house of a Brāhmaṇa which accomplishes all the desire (of a man). Listening the words of her daughter Kalāvati, Lilāvati began the preparation of the fast and worship of Sātyanārāyaṇa (5/8)

The pious wife of Sadhu (the businessman) performed the fast and worship of Sātyanārāyaṇa together with her family members. (5/9)

She asked a divine blessings that her husband and son-in-law may return home soon. (5/10)

My husband and son-in-law have the quality to be foregiven, therefore they be pardoned. Sātyanārāyaṇa became satisfied by her prayer. (5/11)

And told to king Chandhraketu in a dream in the night, O king! You let of both the businessmen who are of good conduct. (5/12)

Also give the wealth which you have taken away. Otherwise, your properties, sons and kingdom would be vanished. (5/13)

Telling so to the king God Sātyanārāyaṇa disappeared. Then in the morning when the king took his seat in the assembly hall conveyed the subject matter of his night dream to his council of ministers and gave an order to acquit both the businessmen. (5/14-15)

Listening the order of King the concerning employees let them off from the prison and presented them before the king humbly saying. (5/16)

Both the businessmen after letting off have been brought before you. Now what is you order. (5/17)

They both after saluting the king and remembering the earlier happenings the businessmen said nothing to the king. Seeing the sons of businessmen the king said with honour. (5/18)

Unfortunately you people met with great trouble, how you donot be afraid. Then their hand culfs were removed and their shving and hair cutting was got done (by the king). (5/19)

Then their clothes and ornaments etc. were handed over to them to their full satisfaction. (5/20)

What amount of wealth was seized by the state, in return twice the amount was given to them, thereafter they were ordered to go home. (5/21)

Both the businessmen after saluting the king said we are going home on your mercy. (5/22)

This chapter brings to light that without the blessings of God nothing could be achieved even in age of righteousness. It is the Kali era, a businessman must be cautious about the factor of risk in the transaction. In this context it can well be said that the business class of India do not forget taking the name of God while transacting any business.

The sixth chapter of the story begins with the prayer of well-being to God and departure of the said two businessmen to their house. Shri Suta describing the events says—

Sadhu, worshipped god with the prayer of well-being and donated wealth to the Brāhmaṇas and proceeded to his town. (6/1)

When He covered some distance, God Sātyanārāyaṇa with the intention to know what he had in his mind, asked what had he in his boat? (6/2)

The proudy businessman smilingly said, O sage! Why you are asking this? Whether you want to take it away? (6/3)

There are creepers and papers in my boat. Then the saint said be your words true. (6/4)

Saying so he sat at the sea coast. (6/5)

When the saint went away, he did his routine morning work, thereafter he watched his boat wonderfully that it became light. (6/6)

Seeing his boat filled with grasses he lost his senses and fell on the ground. When he regained his senses, he became worried for that. (6/7)

The son-in-law of the businessman said, what for you worry that saint had cursed you. (6/8)

He could do every thing, there was no doubt in that. Therefore, they should go in his shelter, because their desire could be accomplished by him. (6/9)

Sadhu, listening to the words of his son-in-law, went to that saint and after saluting him, saw him with devotion and humbly told him. (6/10)

Kindly forgive my sin in respect of the words I told you, saying so, he saluted him many a time and became sorrowful. (6/11)

Then the Dandi saint told seeing him weeping, do not weap, listen my words you always turn your face from my worship. (6/12)

O badminded man! You are getting trouble at my will all the time (due to that). Listening the words of God, Sadhu (the businessman) began to praise. (6/13)

Sadhu said – O Lord! Due to being confused by the effect of your divine power (Māyā) even Brahmā and the other gods fail to know your wonderful qualities and form. (6/14)

Being confused by the effect of your such power (Māyā) how I, the less intelligent man, would be able to know you, so you be please on me. I shall perform your worship with detail. (6/15)

I am under your shelter. Kindly give my all the previous wealth. God became satisfied hearing his devoted words. (6/16)

After giving desired blessing God disappeared from there. Looking the boat filled up with the wealth (like earlier), he boarded at the same. (6/17)

He narrated the story to his brethren that his desire

accomplished with the mercy of God of Truth and also performed the worship methodically. (6/18)

He became glad by the mercy of God, the Truth. Then arranging the goods loaded on the boat he proceeded to his country. (6/19)

Approaching his town Sadhu began to say his son-in-law, look at my wealth-city. (may be name of the city Ratnāpuri) and send his employee (watchman) to that place. (6/20)

The messanger went to the town and told to his wife after seeing and saluting. (6/21)

The businessman is approaching the town with his friends and others as well as with the multiple of wealth. (6/22)

Hearing this news from the mouth of the messenger she became glad and performed the worship of God Truth and told to her daughter. (6/23)

I am going, you come after completing the worship. Her daughter after hearing her words, soon completing the worship. (6/24)

And for getting to take the Prasād she went to see her husband. Being angry with this God Truth drowned the boat of her husband in the water (of river). The girl Kalāvati not seeing her husband. (6/25-26)

She began to weep sorrowfully and fell on the ground. Sadhu seeing his daughter in sorrowful state. (6/27)

With dreadful mind, he said, this has happened what? The sailors also became worried. (6/28)

Then Lilāvati seeing her daughter in sorrowful condition, surprisingly began to weep and said to her husband. (6/29)

How he (son-in-law) disappeared at this moment? Who knows as the dishonour of which god the boat is not seen in the water (of river). (6/30)

Who can know the greatness of God Truth? Saying so, and weaping with her kins. (6/31)

Took her daughter in the lap and that Kalāvati not finding her husband there her trouble increased. (6/32)

(Kalāvati) taking the wooden sandal of her husband became ready to burn herself. Looking upon this character of his daughter, the religious businessman, Sadhu with his wife. (6/33)

Became very sad and began to think—I have been deceited all the time by the Māyā of God, the Truth. (6/34)

Now, I will perform the worship of Sātyanārāyaṇa methodically. Calling all. He began to say like this. (6/35)

He saluted lying straight on the ground. On this, God Sātyanārāyaṇa the maintainer of poors became satisfied. (6/36)

With the mercy of God Satyadeva, the lover of devotees, there was heard words coming from the sky, 'your daughter came to see her husband giving up the Prasād.' (6/37)

That is the reason why her husband disappeared. She should go home and take the Prasād. (6/38)

Only then she would get her husband undoubtedly. The girl after hearing the words coming from sky— (6/39)

She went home, took the Prasād and saw her husband. (6/40)

Then Kalāwati being satisfied told her father to come to house soon without delay. (6/41)

Listening the words of his daughter Sadhu with his son-in-law beiṇg satisfied went to his house with wealth and his associates. (6/42)

From that date he regularly began to worship God Sātyanārāyaṇa every month and on Sanskranti, methodically. Thus getting pleasure, he went to the world of Satyadeva. (6/43)

Then Suta told – O sages! I tell you another story also. (6/44)

This chapter ends with the good effects of the worship of God. But it throws light at hazards of non-performance of determined worship timely. A king and his subject trader bearing in mind the righteous persons by words and action as such.

The seventh and the last chapter narrates a story of dishonour done by a king to the Prasādam of God Sātyanārāyaṇa and the effects thereof.

Suta says— There was a king named Tungadhvaja who was engaged in the care of subjects, who was put in the great trouble by dishonoring the Prasād of Satyadeva. (7/1)

From here the actual story begins —

One day he went to the jungle and killed many animals and while returning he saw the ceremony of the worship of God Sātyanārāyaṇa under the shadow of a banyan tree. (7/2)

Which was being performed by milkmen and their brethren with cool mind. Owing to proudness, the king neither went there nor saluted (to God). (7/3)

When those milkmen offered him Prasādam then he did not take it. Then they placed it there and returned back. The king thus dishoured the 'Prasādam'. (7/4)

Such dishonour of 'Prasādam' caused him great trouble. There were one hundred sons to the king, all those died and also his wealth vanished. (7/5)

Then he thought over in his mind that Lord Satyadeva had caused the end of his wealth. Therefore, he should go to the same place where the worship was being performed. (7/6)

Thinking so he went there and performed the worship of Satyadeva methodically together with the milkmen and others with devotion and belief, then he regained his lost properties and sons etc. (7/7-8)

He after enjoying the pleasure of this world in the end proceeded to the Satya-world. The persons who perfrom the worship of Satyadeva which is very difficult to do. (7/9)

And also hear the story devotedly with pious mind, they get multiple of wealth in the form of Prasādam of Satyadeva. (7/10)

Poor get wealth, prisoner gets acquital, dreadful becomes fearless, with no doubt in it. (7/11)

By keeping this sacred fast and performing worship men always get pleasure and in the end go to Satya-world. I have said the story of Sātyanārāyaṇa fast to you Brāhmaṇa. (7/12)

By performing this men get relief from all the troubles. The story of Satyadeva bears fruits in Kali age. (7/13)

To whom, one will say Time, or Truth or supreme God, or Sātyanārāyaṇa or Satyadeva. (7/14)

Lord Vishṇu in the form of Satya i.e. Truth in the ancient Kali age will take many forms to provide the desired result to all. (7/15)

The person who either reads or hear this story his entire sin vanishes by the grace of Satyadeva, undoubtedly. (7/16)

The story under study ends with a teaching that a businessman and a king both should be more cautious about his dealings even in day to day life. The grocer, about whose business conduct the story relates, appears to be insincere in his determination as well as his words to be spoken. He has taken everything lightly. With the result that he had to face loss of the wealth every now and then. In a business transaction honesty in the words should utmost be maintained with a feeling in mind that Almighty God is looking everything. This story particularly emphasises on this point too. Even a king should not dishonour the things or a ceremony related to the supreme divine power. If he does so he would have to bear the consequences thereof. In India a king and a grocer have always kept this aspect in mind.

Mahābhārat – Shantipārva

According to Bhishma, the government should be lanient towards the businessmen. They should not be put in trouble by the king, rather he should always keep in the mind their well-beings. His views are as follows :—

O son of Kunti (Yudhisthir)! (A King) should pacify them, protect them, help them with money, make efforts again and again to strengthen their position (economically) make provisions of necessary things and do such works which are in their interests. (87/37)

O Bhārat (scion of Bharat)! Businessmen should always be given the considerations of their labour, because they are the cause of progress of the nation with their dealings in business and agriculture. (87/38)

Therefore, an intelligent king should always be affectionate to them (businessmen). Having been cautious be kind to them while imposing tax on them. (87/39)

O Yudhishthir! such arrangements should be made so that they (businessmen) may move throughout the country safely. There can be no other greater work (for a king). (87/40)

Thus it is clear that during the Krishna's period business was fully developed and even a sage like Vedavyās was aware of the problems being faced by the business class at that time. That was the reason why he described such matters in the Mahābhārat.

Agnipuraṇa

In the Agnipurāṇa light has been thrown on the subject of fair dealings in the transaction of the business, which is as follows:-

A businessman who does not deliver the article sold after taking the cost thereof to the customer, it should be got delivered to him. If the customer belongs to the foreign country he should be got delivered in his country with the same profit which he should have earned by selling there, by the king. If the earlier customer does not take it feeling any kind of doubt then that sold article may beresold to any other. If the delivery is given by the seller and the customer does not take it and that article vanishes by the Act of God or the king, then that loss is to be borne by the customer and not by the seller. When the seller does not give the delivery of the goods sold on demand by the customer and that goods vanishes by the Act of God or the king that loss is to be borne by the seller. (258/44 to 46)

Now the story teller (Agni) comes on the issue of penalty to be imposed on the seller or purchaser whoever avoids to take the delivery or to give the delivery as the case may be on one pretex or the other. Such rules of law are as follows—

A businessman, who resells the goods sold to some one else or sells a bad quality article saying to be of good quality, the king should fine him twice the cost of the article.

Knowing (the consequences) fully well, if the cost of the goods sold increases or decreases and the customer is ignorant of its loss or profit he should not avoid to take (delivery of) that article. So the seller should also not avoid the delivery thereof. But if the customer notices loss in the transaction then he may object to take delivery of the goods purchased. Likewise the seller may stop the delivery of the goods sold if he notices loss in selling it on the (agreed) price. If the circumstances (as said above) do not warrant for such objection even then it is done so by the seller or the purchaser. Then one-sixth of the cost should be imposed as penalty for that (on the concerning party). (258/47-48)

From the above provisions of law, as depicted by the Agnipurāṇa, it is clear that the business in India was transacted on the principles of natural justice and that law and the rules on this subject were expressly defined in the Purāṇas also, a king or the parties to the business transactions were not free to deal according to their whim, or arbitrarily, any sale or purchase.

Yājyavalkya Smrīti

Sage Yajyavalkya placing the time limit within which a customer may return the article purchased if found below the standard quality at which it was dealt with. He says–

Seeds (of cereal), iron, bull (carrier of load) cattle, precious stones, maid servant, milky cattle, male servants after being examined may be returned with in a period of ten, one, five days, one week, three days or a fortnight respectively. (2/177)

As such it is apparent that a law giver like sage Yājyavalkya studied the practical business deal in depth and then frammed rules there on or on the subject of period of limitation for the return of the sold article in the case of any disquality or defect.

Business as a means of economic well-being came into practice at a very late stage that too when rural economy based on the tending of cows or other animals and agriculture became stable. With the creation and initiation of Kingship the urban culture placed its feet on the earth. The seat of king when turned into the capital of the country business oriented economy came into the existence to fulfil the requirements of the people residing there. To attract the individuals in this newly evolved field of economy the king had to provide such facilities which were needed initially. Hence the root of business in India lies in the ancient capital cities.

It is also seen in the stories pertaining to the policy of business as cited above that the political administration and the business class are closely related to each other. As the chances of loss are apparent in the trade or transaction, businessmen needed help from the king. The views of Vedāvyas referred to above reflect such a state of affairs. He is impartial in his direction to a king to be ready to extend his help to the needy businessman.

Vālmīki - Rāmāyaṇa -Yuddhakāṇd

It is generally believed that in India there developed only an economy which can be termed in the modern age as rural one, that is to say, an agricultural economy. But indications are available in our Shāstras which throw light that our country was not against the development of the urban economy through business. In the Rāmāyaṇa of Valmīki it has been depicted that wind-god Marut presented to king Ram of Ayodhyā a golden garland at the time of his coronation ceremony after return from he exile at the instance of Indra in the following words—

Inspired by Indra, the wind-god presented to Rām a golden garland consisting of hundred lotuses and casting a splendour with his body. He also presented to Ram a necklace of pearls interspersed with jewels of every variety and enriched with gems. (128/69 to 71-I part)

As both the above presentations were made up of gold and that godking Indra was behind the same, it can be inferred that the wind-god, named Marut followed the directions of his king (Indra). An inference can also be drawn that Marut, the wind –god was engaged in the business of jewellery in the state of godking Indra. He was Indra's subject. So the concept of jewellery and the trade thereof initially originated on the land of gods ruled by Indra. It can, further, be said that a trader-subject of a state had to follow the orders or directions of his ruler.

Moreover, the concept of urban economy in the very ancient India found place, firstly, in the society of gods and with the passage of time it placed its step on the society of mankind. The desired personality of gods and the godkings as described in the Purāṇas also go to throw light that it was the concept of urban economy which inspired the learned scholars to think over their splendiferous body in the narration of stories pertaining to them.

Vālmiki - Rāmāyaṇa —Balkāṇd

In the description of the city of Ayodhyā, the capital of Ram's state it has been clearly said that traders were also residing there during the reign of king Dhashrath. The concerning narration is as follows-

It is thronged with crowds of feudatory princes that flock from all sides on the mission of paying their tribute and is graced with (the presence of) traders who were the resident of different countries.(5/13)

Through it is a brief mention on the issue pertaining to the presence of foreign traders, who were living in the city of Ayodhyā for the purposes of trade and business, yet it brings to light the city developed in those days as a trading centre. The city was attracting the businessmen from the then world for the sake of business. It is another issue that what kind of business they were doing in Ayodhyā during the reign of king Dashrath.

The question before us is whether there was any policy of business in the states of ancient India in the remote past? Our reply would be in affirmative on the ground of aforesaid narration of Vālmīki-Rāmāyaṇa. It also goes to establish that our urban economy was not in the initial stage but it had taken the shape of foreign trade. Our viewpoint is corroborated by the following narration of the Rāmāyaṇa :—

The Kshatriyas follow the lead of the Brāhmaṇas, the Vaishyas are devoted to the Kshatriyas and the Shudras take delight in their own work while serving the other three Varṇas. (6/19)

The above is the description of the prosperity of the inhabitants of Ayodhyā during the reign of king Dhashrath. It exhibits the very condition of Ayodhyā that even the members of business community residing in that city were freely doing their work, but within the framework of the rules of law laid down by the political administration of those days.

Vālmiki - Rāmāyana — Ayodhyākānd

Further, it may be added here that Ayodhyā, the capital city of Avadh state, was inhabited by merchants also, who had their own business as citizens. This fact comes to light by a description as regards to the condition of the city after the departure of Ram to the forest. It runs as follows—

The life of those citizens who had returned dejected and despirited in this way after meeting Ram and felt sore affilicted became extinct. They were full of grief and there eyes were overflowing tears. (48/1-2)

Reaching each his own abode and surrounded by their sons and wife, all were shedding tears, their face were covered with the same. (48/3)

People neither made merry, nor did they rejoice, merchants did not display their merchandise, nor did they place salable good at the proper place, nor the same were looking charming. Nor the house holders cook their food. (48/4)

The people of Ayodhyā did not rejoice to recover their lost property or to receive a large fortune. Nor did the mother rejoice to meet her first born male issue. (48/5)

Stricken with sorrow and shedding tears women in every house sharply reproached their husband returned home (without Ram) even as the drivers of elephants would prick them with goads. (48/6)

Such was the condition of the city of Ayodhyā after Rām's departure to the exile. In that state of affairs the business transaction came to a stop in the city is clear from the following description—

The celebrated city of Ayodhyā — in which singing, rejoicing, dancing and the instrumental music had been completely set at rest, whose delight had fled forever and the rise of whose trade had been hampered — looked at that time like an ocean whose water had dried up. (48/37)

The meaning of the above description is clear. A city looks glorified only when the local business is on. It looks deserted when the businessmen stops to display the salable goods and merchandise for sale. In the other words, the city of Ayodhyā must have developed its glory through the business transaction and not only due to being a seat of political administration. It reflected a look of urban civilization during the reign of king Dashrath. Even King Dashrath would have favoured the urban civilization to grow up. That would have been the practical aspect of economical growth of his time.

As sage Vasishtha was his priest, his (Vasishth's) approval, would have been there, though through his silence on this particular issue. It can well be said here that India was not against the urban economy even in the days of Ram or his father Dashrath. There would be no exaggeration if it is said that the roots of urban economy lies in the capital cities of states of ancient India. The very idea of urban economy placed its feet firstly on Indian soil, for which the business was the only means.

■

12

Developmental Work and Salvation

Emphasis has also been given in the Shāstras for taking up of the developmental works by the kings in their states by the name 'performance of the pious deeds' like digging wells, ponds, tanks, or canals, planting groves or other like works. In Sanskrit such works are called "Ishtapurta". Whether or not such works provide spiritual benefits to the doer king, yet these works are valueable in the development of a given country. In the earlier ages when the country was facing the problems of drinking water and the living beings had to depend upon to natural water resources or rain water, the utility of the works mentioned above, was too much. The author of Shāstras categorised such works as pious ones and sources of getting heaven after death. So was the need of firmness in the observance of the rightousness and good conducts through the development of the places of worship.

Nāradpurāṇa - 1

There appears a dialogue between king Bhagirath, a scion of Ikshwākru, as well as the king of Ayodhya and Dharmarāj the eternal judge, regarding the religious utility of the digging of wells and ponds etc by a king, in the Nāradpurāṇa, Chapter - 12. The story pertaining to their dialogue is as follows:-

While discoursing to sage Nārad sage Sanak told to him-

O great Brāhmaṇa ! A person, who does not do good to others is like dead one. Those, who do not do good to others by wealth, mind and words, they are considered to be sinner. I am telling you a story on this subject, you listen to it, O Nārad! (12/26-27)

In that a description of greatness of Gangā has also come up in its context, which is the destroyer of all the sins and narrates the signs of donations etc. (12/28)

This story is connected with the dialogue went on between Bhagirath and the creator of sacred (deeds) Dharma (Dharmaraj an eternal judge). There was a king born in the scion of Sagar, named Bhagirath. (12/29).

He ruled over the earth expanded to the extent of seven oceans. He was engaged in performance of religious rites every day and was truthful as well as brillient. (12/30)

That king was handsome like Kāmadeva, was patient like of Himalaya, and in the righteousness he was like that of Dharma (rāj) himself. He was learned and performed several sacrifices. (12/31)

O sage! He was full of all (good) signs and well versed in all the Shāstras; full of all the glories and he was to give pleasure to all. (12/32)

The king kept himself busy in giving the special attention to welcoming the visitors, was hero, full of merits, taking advice from his ministers always, helper of troubled ones, intelligent and that he performed worship of Vāsudeva always. (12/33)

Hearing the fame of such king Bhagirath, Dharmarāj himself came to see him at any time. (12/34)

The lord of land (king) welcomed Dharmarāj, who came as visitor, according to the rules of Shāstras. Dharmarāj became pleased with the rules of his welcome. (12/35)

Dharmarāj said- O king ! Great among learned! You are renowned in the world. Hearing your deeds, I have come to see you. Being pleased with your great merits even gods like to see you, who are followers of right path as well as ready in the well-being of all the living beings, and the lover of truth. (12/36-37)

O lord of land! Where there is deed (good one), properties with good manner, there lies all the merits and men of good nature also reside. (12/38)

Oh King ! O fortunate one! Your character is good looking one. Your merits in the maintenance of the living beings are not found even in gods. (12/39)

So told by Dharmarāj king Bhagirath touched his feet and benevolently said. (12/40)

O Gòd! Having knowledge of all the righteousness, see equally (to all)! God head! Kindly let me know what I ask from you. (12/41)

How many kinds of righteousness are there? What country the doer of righteousness gets? How many kinds of penal of hell are there? To whom the troubles of penal are given? (12/42)

On whom you have equal feelings and to whom you give penalty? O fortunate one! You (please) explain the same in detail. (12/43)

Replying to his questions Lord Dharmarāj, the eternal judge, began to explain thus—

O great intelligent! You are lucky one. Lucky one, because you have obtained pure mind. I am defining the righteousness and unrighteousness in reality. You listen to it attentively. (12/44)

The religions which impart sacred world are said of many kinds. Likewise penal of hell are also numerous. (12/45)

It is not possible to narrate on these subjects for hundreds of thousands of year in detail. That is why, I am giving an account of them in brief. (12/46)

It is said as sacred giving to donate any thing for the living of Brāhmaṇas. Likewise, whatever is given in donation to the persons having spiritual knowledge . (12/47)

You listen, what sacred results come out, if anyone makes provision for the livelihood of the persons well versed in Shāstras. (12/48)

He gets pleasure till the end of a Kalpa (creation) and goes to the world of Vishṇu with his crores of ancestors of paternal and maternal families. (12/49)

The particles of sand and drops of rain can be counted but the results of the provisions made to Brāhmaṇas cannot be counted even by Brahmā. (12/50)

The Brāhmaṇa is set to be the form of all the gods (jointly).

Who can count the fruits of the provisions made by a man to a Brāhmaṇa? (12/51)

The person, who does well-beings to a Brāhmaṇa always seems to have performed all (kinds) of scarifices took bath in all the pilgrims and also did entire austerities. (12/52)

He, who inspires to others to donate something to the Brāhmaṇas gets the result of the donation. (12/53)

From here the eternal judge Dharmarāj begins to say about the eternal result of digging ponds etc, that is the construction of water reservoirs -

He says— What can be said more on this subject? He who himself makes a pond or gets it made by others, his sacreds cannot be counted even after completing the age of hundred years. (12/54)

Even if one person will take water from that pond, then the sins of its maker will be wiped out, there is no doubt in it. (12/55)

The man, who makes (a land) for the storage of water even for a day gets rid of his sins and lives in the heaven of one hundred years. (12/56)

A person, who contributes in the construction of a pond to the extent of his capacity also gets the result equal to that of getting a pond constructed, and that getting inspired of seeing his work also obtains the same result, so also who becomes happy with that. (12/57)

He, who throws some soil from the pond (under construction), gets rid of his crores of sins and lives in the heaven for hundred years. (12/58)

The construction of a tank is done only by a man at whom a perceptor or gods become pleased, such is the law of Vedas, as heard. (12/59)

Narrating the above spiritual benefits, Lord Dharmarāj (eternal judge), he comes at the main point. It is natural that a person or king takes up only such works which are eternally beneficial in a country like India, where the roots of every work has in spiritualism.

In that context even the developmental works have also been so shaped and have been made the subjects of discourses of the eternal judge to a king like Bhagirath. Perhaps, the roots of king Bhagirath's glorious works would have gone so deep in his public utility projects which would have attracted Dharmarāj as said above.

O great King! I am telling you an old story on this subject listening to which man becomes free from sin undoubtedly. (12/60)

There was a king in the country of Gauḍa who was much brilliant, learned and worshipper of Brāhmaṇas and his name was Virbhadra. (12/61)

That king was versed in Vedas and Shāstras and the family conducts as well as maker of friends. He had a queen named, Champak Manjari, the great fortunate one. (12/62)

The said King had also good ministers, who discussed the good and non-good duties of the king and gave their decisions judiciously and according to Shāstras. (12/63)

The penances, treatments and decisions relating to the astronomy which are not according to the Shāstras, are said to killer of Brahmā. (12/64)

Determining so in the mind, he always heard from the Āchāryās about the views of Manu and others. (12/65)

Maintaining the subjects righteously none did injustice in the country of that king and their was none mean. (12/66)

His state was being counted in the category of good giver of heaven. That king one day went to the forest for hunting deers. (12/67)

There he moved here and there with his ministers in the noon, Per chance, getting no hunting animal, he became tired with his followers. (12/68)

At the same time he saw a pond, but dry, seeing it dry, he began to think, who constructed it at such a high land. (12/69)

How could that king got water from that pond to quench his thurst and remain alive. (12/70)

O great king! Then and there an idea to dig it came in his

mind. Thereafter, when it was dug about one and a half feet, then the water came out. (12/71)

The king became satisfied by drinking that water. O lord of the land! His minister named Buddhisāgar also got satisfied by drinking that water. (12/72)

That Buddhisāgar, versed in the elements of religion said to the king – O king ! This pond was full of rain water earlier. (12/73)

To day I wish to make nice bund around it, O god! Give me order therefor, approving it. (12/74)

That truthful king became glad to hear the words of his minister and became ready to construct it by his own. (12/75)

He appointed that minister in that good work. That sacredful minister Buddhisāgar became glad. (12/76)

And became ready to make it a lake from the of pond and got lake constructed when extended to fifty bows in length and so much in breadth. (12/77)

Then making a bund around that with stone (bolders and rocks) got it filled with deep water. Thereupon, he said to the king. (12/78)

From then all the thirsty persons of the forest and travellers began to drink that clean water. (12/79)

After some time the life of that minister Buddhisāgar came to an end, owing to being short in the age and came to my world, which governs other worlds. (12/80)

Then I asked the religious writer Lord Chitragupta about him. He told me — (12/81)

He himself preached the king to do righteous work, so he deserves to board on the religious plane with the effect of this sacred work. (12/82)

Telling so by Chitragupta, I gave an order to board him on the plane named Dharma. (12/83)

O king! After the lapse of some time that king also came to my world after death and was presented before me gladly. (12/84)

O king! I asked his account pertaining to the duties. Chitragupta told me his sacred works relating to that lake. (12/85)

At that time, what I told to that king (Virbhadra) you listen to that perfectly. Earlier, a killer bird dug one finger hole with its beak. Thereafter, a pig (boar) dug a hand deep pit with his mussle. (12/86-87)

Then at one time this Kali increased it by two hands (deep). (12/88)

The water accumulated in that pit, the thursty beasts of the forest and other beings used to drink for two months. (12/89)

O good vowed (King)! After the lapse of three years this elephant had increased it by digging to the extent of three hands (deep) so more water accumulated therein. (12/90)

By using that much water beasts residing in the forest quenched their thirst for three months. You came over there when it dried up. (12/91)

O king! It was dug one hand deep at that time and from that water the thrust of your employees was quenched after hearing the discourses of that minister. (12/92)

O King! thereafter, you got it constructed (dug) fifty bows in length and so much in width, which turned it into a lake. By making a bund with rocks again, it took the form of a great water storage. And also trees were planted at its banks in the interest of all the beings. (12/93)

By the sacred works of their own all the beings have boarded on the plane of religion. You also board on that plane. (12/94)

Hearing my these words, that king (Virbhadra) also boarded on the plane of religion, who was rightful of taking sixth part of their sacred works. (12/95)

I have told you (O King!) what is the fruits of constructing a pond by means of this story. Listening this narration man gets rid of sins that cause the bondage of birth and death.(12/97)

The man, who reads this story with full devotion he too gets the same result which comes out by the construction of a lake. (12/98)

The above story ends with the exhortation and inspiration to take interest in the public utility projects especially in the construction of water storage ones. As the agriculture is wholly dependant on the irrigation, water storage projects are of great importance to increase the production of cereals in this age of population growth. Though, for the purposes of drinking water facilities, artificial syntex tanks are being built, yet the importance of construction of underground tanks cannot be ruled out.

It cannot be said, as such, that life in the ancient India was totally dependant upon the natural resources of water. There can be no exaggeration if it is said that for this our countrymen received divine inspiration regarding that. The above story which was narrated by the eternal judge called Dharmarāj to the king Bhagirath, who brought the holy river Ganga on the earth, is self exampilary and explanatory on this subject. The Lord of eternal judgment himself gave several examples to inculcate in the mind of king Bhagirath of Ayodhyā to become active for making canals or other perennial water resources for the irrigation and drinking facilities being capable to do so.

Vālmīki - Rāmāyaṇa — Balkāṇda

The king Bhāgirath after listening the discourses of Dharmarāj decided to practice austerity for bringing down Gangā on the earth as a perennial water source, which may not dry in the summer. To get success in this great task he took a decision to go to Mount Gokarṇa for the said purposes. The story related to his austerity and the success thereof is as follows :—

Emperor Bhagirath, a pious royal sage, was issueless and as such desirous of progeny, O Rāghava! entrusted the administration to the people, as well as to his ministers. As intended in the descent of Ganga, he practised prolonged austerity on the Mount Gokarṇa, O delight Ragha (Ram)! (42/11-12)

With uplifted arms and keeping the sense organs under fully control, he exposed himself to five fires and partook of food once a mouths. He remained in the practice of severe asceticism for one thousand years. (42/13)

O mighty armed one! The almighty Brahmā, the lord and ruler of all the created beings, got much pleased with that high souled king. (42/14)

He (Brahmā) called on the high souled Bhagirath with hosts of gods, who had been practising austerities. Brahmā, thereupon, spoke to him forthwith : —(42/15)

I am pleased with the austerity duly practised by you, O great King! the ruler of the people. You ask for a boon from me, O king of noble vows! (42/16)

Standing with joint hands the exceptionally glorious and mighty - armed Bhagirath submitted to Brahmā. (42/17)

O Lord! If you are pleased with me and if there is any reward for my asceticism let all the sons of Sagar receive libation of water from me. (42/18)

When the ashes of these princes of gigantic body get soaked with the waters of the Gangā all my grand- uncles bid fair to attain the everlasting heaven. (42/19)

O glorious one! Born in the line of Ikshwāku, I ask for a (male) progeny, so that our race many not get extinct. Let it be another boon, O Lord! (42/20)

Brahmā thereupon, answered the king, who had uttered the prayer in the following benignant and agreeable speech, full of sweet expressions. (42/21)

O Bhagirath ! Your ambition is great, a great car-warrior ! May it be realized ! May success attend to you, O promoter of Ikshwāku race! (42/22)

Here is the river Gangā, the elder daughter of Himvān (the deity presiding over the Himālayas), which emanates from Himālayas. Let Lord Shiva alone be invoked to support the Gangā, when it descends on the earth, O king! (42/23)

O Monarch! The earth will not be able to sustain the fall of Gangā. And I do not perceive anyone else other than Lord Shiva, capable of sustaining it, O king! (42/24)

Having thus told to the aforesaid king and instructed Gangā,

Brahmā rose to his heaven with all the gods including the wind-gods (forty nine in number). (42/25)

O Ram! When the celebrated Brahmā had left, Bhagirath waited upon Lord Shiva for a year remaining standing at the tip of one of his great toes stamped on the ground. (43/1)

When one year completed, Lord Shiva, the Protector of the living beings, the adored of all the worlds, addressed in the following words to the king forthwith. (43/2)

O jewel among men! I am pleased with you and shall do that which is pleasing to you, I shall receive the Gangā on my head. (43/3)

Swelling into the form of a very mighty stream and acquiring a formidable force, the Gangā, the adored of all the worlds, thereupon, descended forthwith, from the heavens on the blessed head of Lord Shiva, O Ram! so as the tradition goes, the said Gangā, which is all-glorious and most difficult to sustain, thought. (43/4-5)

Floating Lord Shānkar, along with my (water) stream, I might as well enter the Pātāl. Enraged to perceive her arrogances, the three eyed Lord Shankar for this part forthwith made up his mind to conceal her. Fallen on the holy head of Lord Shiva. (43/6-7)

O Ram! Thick with coils of matted moor and resembling the Himālayas that sacred river could in no way reach the earth even it made every effort. (8)

Revolving in the coils of His matted locks it did not find an exit for reaching its end. The divine stream continued to meander on His head alone for several rounds of years. (43/9)

Bhagirath saw it there and took it to supreme asceticism once more, Lord Shiva felt extremely pleased with that, O Rāghava (Ram)! (43/10)

Thereupon Lord Shiva let fall Gangā in the Bindusar (a Lake in Himālayas). While the river was being released it split up into seven streams. (43/11)

Three of the blessed streams of the Gangā consisting of delightful waters, viz. Hlādini, Pavanī and Nalinī, ran in the easterly directions. (43/12)

Suchakshu, Sitā and the great river Sindhu, these three consisting of blessed water, flowed in the westerly directions. (43/13)

The seventh of them (the Gangā) followed the chariot of Bhagirath, who was mounted on a beautiful chariot. The royal sage Bhagirath, vested with unique splendour, marched ahead. (43/14)

The river descending from the heaven to the head of Lord Shiva, came down from there to the earth. (43/15)

There the water (of Gangā) meandered along with a terrific noise. The earth looked exceptionally charming with fishes, tortoises and multitude of sea-elephants falling and (already) fallen. (43/16)

At that time, seized with bewilderment those celestial sages, Gandharvas and Yakshas as well as Siddhas. (43/17)

The gods stationed there behold from their aerial cars, as big as cities, as well as their horses and excellent elephants, the Gangā descended on the earth from the heaven. (43/18)

Eager to see this celebrated, wonderful and superb descent of the Gangā on the mortal plane multitude of gods with infinite strength collected (in the heaven). (43/19)

With the hosts of gods coming down with great speed and with the brilliance of their jewels the cloudless firmament looked as if irradiated by hundreds of sun. (43-20-21 Ist part)

Scattered on that occasion with multitude of sea-elephants and snakes as well as with throbbing fished the sky appeared covered with streaks of lightning. (43/21- II part and 22 Ist part)

With the volumes of white foam that were being tossed about in numberless particles the vault of heavens looked as if over east with autumnal clouds and crowded with flying swans. (43/22-II part and 23- I part)

The Gangā now flowed very swiftly, now fortuously, it broadened out and narrowed down. It was tossed high and now it glided. (43/23 II part and 24).

Buffeted by the same water indeed, the water spouted upwards once more and dashed to the ground again. (43/25-I Part)

Fallen on the head of Lord Shiva and again dropped on the surface of earth, the limpid water, which rids those who come in the contact with it of (all) sin, shone bright on that occasion. On that spot hosts of Rishis and Gandharvas as well as the inhabitants of the globe touched the water fell from the person of Shiva as purifying. Those who had fallen from the heaven to the terestrial plane through a curse were rid of their sin by bathing in it. (43/ 25 II part to 27)

Having been rid of their sin through that water and further invested with merit, they ascended once more to the heaven. (43/28)

Returned to their respective realms, delighted with that sparkling water and getting rid of their sins. (43/29)

Having taken bath in the Gangā, people rejoiced. The Royal sage Bhagirath mounted on a charming car. (43/30)

He drove ahead while the Gangā followed at his heels as well as gods including Rishis, all Daityas, Dānavas and Rākshasas (followed). (43/31)

The foremost among Gandharvas, Yakshas, Kinnaras, great Nāgas, serpents, Apsarasas followed Bhagirath, O Ram! (43/32)

The Gangā, the foremost of all the rivers, capable of eradicating sins followed Bhagirath in whatever direction he drove. (43/33)

Proceeding from there, the Gangā actually inundated the sacrificial ground of the high souled sage Jahnu the doer of miracles and performing a sacrifice. (43/34)

Jahnu felt enraged to perceive the pride of Gangā O Rāghav. (43/35)

(He) drank up all the water of Gangā which was a supreme miracle indeed. The gods including the Gandharvas and Rishis became highly astonished. (43/36)

They worshipped the high-souled Jahnu, the great among men, and reduced the Gangā to the position of a daughter of that exalted soul. (43/37)

Pleased at that, the powerful sage, who was vested with

exceptional glory discharged the Gangā through his ears. Hence Gangā is said as the daughter of Jahnu and called Jāhnavi. (43/38)

The Gangā once more followed the chariot of Bhagirath and reached the place of excavation made by Sagar's sons. (43/39)

Then that foremost river forced its way into Rāsatal for consummating the feet of Bhagirath. He lead the Gangā with efforts. (43/40)

The Royal sage, Bhagirath beheld his great grand - uncles reduced to ashes and fainted. The most sacred water of the Gangā submerged in the heap of their ashes and purged of their sins. Sagars's sons (then) ascended to heaven, O Rāghav. (43/41)

Though the above story describes the salvation of king Sagar's sons by touching the holy water of Gangā which came down to the earth from the heaven yet, it has the economical value. The plains of river Gangā are more fertile part of the land in our country. Had the king Bhagirath done no so much efforts to bring down this river as well as river 'Sindhu' as a branch of the same this part of the country would have remained barren and question of its fertility never arose. Such a developmental task of Bhagirath was indeed a courageous one. The river Gangā is called Bhāgirathi after the name of king Bhagirath owing to his aforesaid difficult task.

Whatever the spiritual shape the Shāstras have given to the severe austerity and the physical as well as financial works of king Bhagirath of Ayodhyā in causing a great river to flow on the surface of earth in the northern India, such a description brings to light the policy of economical development of capable states or kings. Even certain gods like Dharmarāj, Chitragupta, Brahmā and Shiva are seen active to make their contributions in such tasks of people's interest. Where the eternal judge inspires king Bhagirath, Brahmā, the creator of all the beings, advises him to take the shelter of Shiva for getting the Gangā stopped from going to the bottom of the ocean named "Rasātal" as was its intention while falling from the heaven. It was the physical or Yogic contribution of Lord Shiva as the emperor of that region (as referred to in the first chapter) which stopped the Gangā on the surface of earth and follow the path shown by king Bhagirath.

Such textual information should be taken into consideration as the guidelines in persuing the study further to obtain the a concrete result pertaining to the developmental projects. The ancient kings or states in the early India under- took for the economic progress and prosperitiy, with fullzeal. From the description of falling of the Gangā from heaven and its flow to the different directions of the earth, it comes to light that the river Sindhu is one of the branches of Gangā and that it had no existence on the surface of earth prior to the coming down of the Gangā on the earth.

When the present project of digging the lost river Sarswati to cause it to flow again, as it was flowing in the Vedic period, would be complete, then the great task of the king Bhagirath, which appears, so far as an illusionary one, would take the shape of a physical work on the ground.

Nāradpurāṇa -2

Dharmarāj, the eternal judge also told to king Bhagirath about the heavenly gains of getting the temples etc. constructed in the state. Through temples are the places of worship, yet these have been the means of economic development of the country, from a very ancient time. As the development of cities and business places had always been connected with the pilgrimage in our country Dharmarāj's exhortation during the course of discourses to Bhagirath is valuable in the sense that it was given recognitions even by divine powers from the time immemorial. The discourses of Dharmarāj are as follows : —

Dharmarāj said — the man who constructs or gets constructed a temple of Shiva or Vishṇu, what sacred results he gets, listen to it. (13/1)

That man resides in the country of Vishṇu for three Kalpas with his lacs of ascendants of paternal and maternal families, there is no doubt about it. (13/2)

He, who gets, the god - temple, constructed only with clay, I am telling you the sacred results come out of that, listen. (13/3)

That person taking the divine form and boarding on a nice plane resides in the country of Vishṇu. There is no doubt in it. (13/4)

After enjoying the pleasure of the said country what the sacred results he gets by constructing the god-temple, listen. (13/15)

With taking that divine form after enjoying the sacred fruits of the country of Vishṇu, he goes to the country of Brahmā. (13/6)

Residing there for two Kalpas (Span of creation), he again returns back to the heaven and resides here for one Kalpa. Thereafter he takes birth— in this dying would (on the earth) in the family of Yogis. (13/7)

After passing away this life, he gets Vaishṇava Yoga and through that he attains the imperishable salvation. But who makes a god-temple using wood gets the sacred result two times than that. (13/8)

Those, who construct with bricks get three times sacred results and those who constructs with stone rocks get four time results and those who construct by using the crystal stones get ten time results. (13/9)

Who constructs with copper plates gets hundred time results and who construct with gold gets one crore time results. Those who (simply) maintains the constructed ponds, temples or village or gets reconstruction thereof are benefited with one hundred time than that of the person who erected the same. (13/10-11-I part).

Those, who cleans the god-temple devotedly and are in its service get unended sacred results. But those, who do such works according to their will, they being the great ones on the earth get sacred results of the country of Vishṇu. (13/11- 2nd part to 13-Ist part)

O king! Those who construct small pound that person gets half of its (big pond's) sacred result, by constructing well gets one forth of that and constructing a tank gets sacred result equal to that of a lake. (13/13-II part and 14-Ist part).

O king ! Maker of a trench gets one hundred time more results than that of one who makes a large circular well. (13/14-II part)

It is told by Brahmā himself that a rich man who constructs the pond together pucca banks with stone rocks and that a poor man construct that of clay (kutcha) both get equal sacred result. (13/15)

Giving an example of words of learned persons having good knowledge of Vedas Dharmarāj says –

Where a rich man donates a city and a poor man donates only one hand (one and a half feet) land, even though, both get the equal result. (13/16)

Likewise what result receives a rich man by constructing a pond the same result is received by a poor man by constructing a well. (13/17)

He, who constructs any thing for the welfare of several persons righteously, goes to the country of Brahmā with his three ascendants. (13/18)

Perhaps the above sloka pertains to the plantation of tree or trees because the slokas here inafter reproduced describe about taking shelter under its or their shadow. It says thus:-

The cows or Brāhmaṇa of whatever category they be who take shelter under its shadow cause the getting of planter the heaven. (13/19)

O King! The planter of groves, the constructer of god-temple, and establisher of a village are worshipped with Vishṇu. (13/20)

(Now) you listen to the sacred results which are received by a person, who plants a garden of flowery plants for the worship of gods or for the well-beings of all. (13/21)

From here Dharmarāj narrates the sacred results of the flowery plants which are planted in a garden, perhaps, adjoining to a temple with the object of availability of flowers to be used in the worship of god or deity of the temple.

(The planter) resides to the extent of that much years in the heaven pleasurely as much leaves and flowers are there in that garden of flowers. (13/22)

He, who constructs boundry walls around that garden or get

fenced with thorny plants, such a protector resides in the country of Brahmā for seventy-one Yugas. (13/23)

The Lord of maines (Yamarāj) now begins to tell to king Bhagirath about the results of plantation of Tulasi plants —

O lord of men! He who plants the plant of Tulasi, I am telling you (now) the sacred result of that. (13/24)

O king! Such a person resides in the country of Nārāyaṇa for one hundred Kalpas together with the seven crore ascendants of paternal and maternal families. (13/25).

(Then Lord of eternal justice) said about the results of using soils of that or of Chitrakoot or of the Gangā or Gopi sandal or with the soil of roots of Tulasi plants or a lotus, saying to listen it. (13/26)

That one boarding at a great plane hearing his praises by the Gandharvas and the Apsarasas enjoys the pleasures of the country of Vishṇu. (13/27)

His so much sins of hunting of Brāhmaṇas vanish as much leaves fell down from the roots of Tulasi plant. (13/28)

He, who irrigates the root of Tulasi (plant) even by the handful of water resides with Vishṇu, the resident of milk-sea. (13/29)

He, who provides to the Brāhmaṇas the tender leaves of Tulasi, resides in the country of Brahmā with his three ascendants. (13/30)

He, who offers Tulasi leaves on the idol of Shalgram (stone), resides in the country of Vishṇu till the end of the Kalpa. (13/31)

He, who makes fencing around that (Tulasi plant) either pucca or by thorny plants resides in the country (temple) of Vishṇu with his twenty-one ascendants.

He, who worships the lotus like feet of God with the tender leaves of Tulasi, O king! has not to return from the country of Vishṇu again. (13/33).

The above discourses of Lord Dharmarāj, Chitragupta by name, are like the rules of eternal law on the subject of good and divinely conducts of mankind. King Bhagirath may be treated as a medium to whom his words aim at,but practically such works are the causes of the country's development in the form of vegetation.

It is a well known fact that in India plantation of trees in the form of garden, especially the trees of juicy fruits and digging of the well and tank were considered as the means of spiritual gains till the world war two. Even the heads of middle class families were keen in the plantation of mango trees and digging of well if there economic conditions so permitted. Such a traditional faith, perhaps, found its root in the discourse of Dharmarāj as cited above. It was also believed in general that there were eternal matrimonial relationship between a garden and a well, that is to say, that the well was considered to be the wife of garden because watering to the plants or trees, so it can be said that the interse relationship between the two, though imaginary one, yet, was based on the sound footing. No plant grows without watering. The maintenance of a garden being totally dependant on water, digging a well or tank was thought necessary adjoining to it, for the proper growth of the trees so planted till the recent past, such a faith based on scientific reasons, helped in taking up of developmental projects of like nature by the kings and landlords with the equal spirits.

Agnipurāṇa

There is a description of scientific plantations in the Agnipurāṇa (Chapter-242). In throws light in which description a particular plant may be planted around a dwelling house. A mention is also there that every garden should have a pond. Though the purpose in not mentioned, yet it is clear that when there exist a pond it facilitates watering.

The description about these things is thus—

Physician Dhanvantari says to his pupil Sushrut—O Sushrut! Now I shall describe to you the code of medicine pertaining to plants. In the north of a house (the plantation of) a Pakar tree, in the east Bargad tree, in the south mango tree and in the west Peepal tree are considered to be good, the thorny plants which grow in the south of a house are also good. A garden be made nearby the dwelling house or it should be beautified by flowery sesamum plants alround. (242/1 -2)

The trees should be planted after worshipping the moon and the Brahmanas. For the plantation of the trees asters like uttarā, swāti, Hasti, Rohini, Shravana, and mool are praised. In the garden a pond be dug and led a canal of river flow in that. For opening of a pond asters like Hasti, Magha, Anurādha, Pushya, Jyestha, Shatbishā, Uttarāshādha, Uttarā-Bhārapada and Uttara-Phalguni are useful. (241/3-5)

What the Agnipurana means to say is that people must develop a habit to reside adjoining to the vegetation which is good for the health, physically and mentally as well. If a house has been recommended to keep green surroundings, it leads the path that a village or city should also have green surroundings for healthy environment. In the present time an idea to make a city green has develop which is good sign. But one should not think that it is a new idea that has been given by modern architects, such an idea of garden or park planning attached to a dwelling house was conceived of much earlier by the ancient Indian planners.

Vrihadāranyakopnishad

It is a scientific question as to why human life and the life of vegetation should remain close to each other? The great sage Yājyavalkya has replied this question at length in the Vrihadāranyakopnishad, which is as under :—

Vegetation is like that of a tree, a man is also like that, it is quite true. There are leaves in the tree whereas in the human body there are hairs; there is skin in the human body with this similarity there is bark at the outer part of a tree. Blood comes out from the skin of a man, whereas, a kind of juice comes out from the bark of tree also. Due to the reason of this similarity when hit juices comes out of tree, likewise a cut blow cause blood to come out of human body. There are flesh in the body of man, whereas pulp is there in tree. There are nerves in the body of man and that there are vessels which are stable like that of nerves. As there lies bones within the net of nerves, likewise there is wood surrounded by vessels and that fat is present in the both. But when a tree is cut then it grows in a new form again from its root. Likewise if man is cut by death from what root he will born? He takes birth from semen, donot tell like this because it is found in a living man. Tree grows from seed. But a tree born from seed when cut it again germinates and develop, it is seen practically. But if a tree is rooted out, it will never grow again, likewise if death takes the life of man from what root he will take birth? If it is said that man is born so it takes no birth again in such a condition who will cause his rebirth after death? (Yājyavalkya himself replies to this question) science is the delight Brahmā. He is the ultimate goal of the donor and is the ultimate shelter of the knower of Brahma and Brahma loyalist. (3/9/28)

In this way sage Yājyavalkya established the similarity between the man and the vegetation which is a very deep issue in this scientific age. Man is a movable creature whereas vegetation is stable and rooted in the earth. He proved the similarity between the two by the logic of science which sages generally avoid. His words that science is delight Brahma means and explains that the man must try to understand the similarity between himself and the plant. The scientific reasoning of which will delight him and inspire to bring him closure to the vegetation.

Not only this for taking up of the developmental projects, whether it be state or any private individual, consideration should be given to the environmental values and that atmospheric equilibrium should be maintained with all efforts. But in the modern time while proposing a project such aspect of the environment is not deeply studied. The pollution problem of the modern age has come up due to such carelessness.

Sage Yājyavalkya is also of the opinion that if one has to lead delighted life he has to advance his knowledge about the birth and death cycle through rebirth. The principle of rebirth should never be sighted of. A soul carrying pollution infection may take rebirth with deformed body after death. If the principle of similarity between man and plant as discussed by Yājyavalkya is studied by various angles his viewpoint will be clear to the modern scientists.

Bhāgwatpurāṇa—

So far development through plantation is concerned a story regarding the same is there in the Book four of Bhāgwatpurāṇa. It is a story of life style of Prachetas (ten in number), the sons of king Pārchin Barhi, who were performing austerity for a very long period. During the period of their austerity there grew good many tall trees in their state covering the whole land, perhaps, cultivable, causing damage to the output of cereals. When they became free from the austerity they became worried about such a state of affairs in the territory. The onward story is as follows :—

(After getting the boon from Hari i.e. Vishṇu) Prachetas came out of sea and saw that the entire country is covered with the tall trees as if they grew tall for stopping the path of heaven. Seeing this they became angry over the trees. (4/30/44)

Then they breathed out fire and wind through their mouths in rage, O king, like Kālāgnirudra at the time of dissolution of the three worlds, in order to strip the land of all vegetation. (4/30/45)

Seeing the trees being reduced to ashes Brahmā arrived and pacified the sons of Barhishman (Prachetās) by the words of wisdom. (4/30/46)

Being full of terror, the trees, so survived bestowed their daughter upon the Prachetās under the advice of Brahmā. (4/30/47)

Bowing the commands of Brahmā the Prachetās married with Mārishā (the daughter of the trees) through whom Daksh, the son of Brahmā took rebirth, who was killed by Lord Shiva (during the destruction of his sacrifice, earlier). (4/30/48)

The above description regarding the decision of the Prachetā s to reduce the trees to ashes, the growth of which was treated as unnecessary can be said as the need of the hour. The developmental work either private or public should conform to the need of the time. If any such work is considered to be superfluous should be abandoned forthwith. It places a guideline before the people and the government that economic development should always be balanced, so that the economy of the state may not collapse.

The story of marriage of Mārishā, the daughter of trees with the Prachetās goes to suggest that the vegetation is the backbone of a nation and it should not be destroyed in toto. As far as possible green vegetation should be protected like the spouse of mankind. Mārishā represented the fruits of the vegetation useful for the mankind. It is just possible that people took it for granted from that day not to cut the green trees and it was included in the rules of religious law.

Further, it evolved a theory in the society of mankind that life of man and the life of vegetation are complementary to each other. The oxygen coming through plants and trees gives life to man. So economy of vegetation, where makes available directly consumable fruits and cereals etc. for the safety of life, it causes the supply of fresh air too, which is also a necessary element of life. A land without vegetation becomes rainless. The intervention of Brahmā to stop the disastrous activities initiated by Prachetās indicates such a viewpoint also. Had He not intervened, the territory of Prachetā s would have become a dessert.

Bhāgwatpurāṇa

A deep study of Shāstras brings to light that not only kings and householders took part in the developmental works, but sages too took up such works where ever occasions arouse. The name of sage Kardam in this regard may be taken with great honour. According to the Chapter twenty two of Book three of Bhāgwatpurā ṇa sage Kardam was married to the daughter of first king Swayāmbhuva Manu. Till his marriage he was an austere yogi. He had no house. One day his wife, the daughter of king Swayāmbhuva Manu, named Devahuti, expressed her desire to have a house for proper marital life. Accepting her request sage Kardam built a house by applying his yogic power which was like that of a plane capable to fly in the air. The onward story as narrated in the Bha¯gwatpurāṇa in this connections is as follows-

Seeking to oblige his beloved wife, the sage Kardam, O Vidur, exercised his wonderful yogic power and instantly produced an aerial mansion which could move at will. (3/23/12)

It was a wonderful structure, containing all sorts of jewel, adorned with pillars of precious stones, capable of yielding what one desired and was equipped with every form of wealth, which tended to multiply in the course of time. (3/23/13)

It was provided with divine articles of domestic use. It was comfortable in all the seasons and was decorated with bunting and flags of variegated colours. (3/23/14)

It was further embellished with wreaths of charming flowers that attracted the sweet humming of bees, as well as with tapestries of linen, silk and other fabrics of various kinds. (3/23/15)

The house looked charming with cushions, beds, fans and seats separately arranged in the several storys one above the other. (3/23/16)

The beauty was enhanced by the works of art, here and there and it was provided with pavements of emerald and coral daises. (3/23/17)

Its entrances shone with coral threshold and had doors of diamond. Its domes of sapphire were crowned with gold pinnacles. (3/23/18)

With the choicest of rubies set in its diamond walls, it appeared as though possessed of eyes; and it was furnished with wonderful canopies and highly valuable festoon of gold. (3/23/19)

It resounded with the cries of swarns and pigeons, which flew up to their likenesses, thinking them their own kind. (3/23/20)

With its pleasure –grounds, resting-chambers, bedrooms and inner and outer yards, designed with an eye to the comfort. It caused astonishment as it were to the sage himself. (3/23/21)

The quality of the house got built by the will power of the great sage Kardam as narrated in the above description appears to be imaginary and illusory. Yet there are reasons to believe that a person like sage Kardam who would have reached the zenith of his austerity and yogas could erect a building by exercising his inner powers or by will-power. Move over, it is not our problem here. Our problem is to establish here that the aseetics too were interested in the developmental works . By coming into action on the request of his wife sage Kardam placed an example before the sages for building a shelter rather than, living in the state of nature for austerity. It is, perhaps, from then the saints began to build her- mitage, such steps can be treated as marching ahead in the field of development in the study of economics of the past.

Brāhmapurāṇa

There was a king named Indradyumna, ruler of Avanti territory. He was a righteous man having his mind and activities in the performance of religious rites and sacrifices etc. for the cause and welfare of his state as well as the people. He was also interested to take up such public works and sacrifices which may facilitate the path of heaven to him and to his subjects in general. All the time he was giving a thought over his self created problem. In the mean time an idea cropped up in his mind that a temple of Lord Vishṇu be erected at the sea-coast of his state and that a horse-sacrifice be performed there. These works would surely facilitate the path of heaven. With this idea in mind he decided to take up those works. The onward story in this regard as described in the Brahmapurāṇas is as follows—

Brahmā said- O Brāhmaṇas ! Thinking so, that king (Indradymna) started to erect a Vishṇu (Hari) temple. (47/1)

He invited, in a happy mood, priests and astrologists well versed in the Shāstras and searched out good land (with their help for the said purpose). (47/2)

Then with the consultations of Brāhmaṇas and ministers versed in Vedas and Shāstras, having good knowledge, versed in architecture about good moment, time, day, positions of moon, stars and planets and finding them in suitable position he worshipped with the mutterings of good words, songs of musical instrument, voice of Vedas, songs, sweet words, and other material of worship like flowers rice-fried paddy, pertinences earthen pots and earthen lamps. (47/3 to 5)

Thereafter, he gave libation of water with devotion cautiously.

Being free these works that king told to the kings of Kalinga, Shur, Utkal and Koshal. (47/6-7)

You people go to bring rocks with care and cooperation. Go to Mount Vindhyāchal which has the beauty of many caves and spread long with the well skilled artisans, cut the rocks of its peak and bring them through boats soon. (47/8-9)

After giving orders to the kings so, the king (Indradyumna) then said his priests and the ministers. (47/10)

The emissaries should go to everywhere and convey my orders that all the Kings of the earth (i.e. of his empire) must come to Indradymna soon with their elephants, horses, chariots, soldiers, ministers and priests. (47/11-12)

Brahmā said — Thus getting orders of the king (Indradyumna) the emissaries went to the kings (of the other states of his empire) and conveyed them his (Indradyumna) orders. (47/13)

Listening the words of emissaries the kings proceeded with their soldiers soon. (47/14)

They had with them soldiers mounted on chariots, horses and also foot soldiers and ample wealth. (47/17 I part)

Becoming aware of the orders of Indradyumna a good number of Brāhmaṇas also reached. (47/17 II Part)

Looking at the Kings came with their priests and ministers Indradyumna began to tell the object of his work with honour and in a happy mood. (47/18)

He placed his object before them in these words — O kings! You people listen to my words which I am telling with full concentration. At this holy place which provides enjoyment and salvation, well-being, how I perform the great horse-sacrifice and build a Vishṇu temple, my mind is worried about it, O Kings! If you people extend your help then finding able associates like you people I can do all such things. (47/19 to 21)

Listening the words of learned king (Indradyumna) all the kings under his control became glad. (47/22)

They provided with all the different kinds of rural and forest products like cereals, cow products and ghee full of hundred thousand vessels, edible and coating material, which were to be used as oblations and offerings. (47/27-28)

King (Indradyumna) became glad to visit the huge amount of riches (properties) and the sacrificial material, priests, persons versed in Vedas and Shāstras as well experts in sacrificial performance, sages, seers, god sages, austeres, Brahmachāris, householders, Vanāsprasthis, ascetic, graduates, Brāhmaṇas performing sacrificial fire, preachers, teachers, engaged, in self study persons, Brāhmaṇas engaged in austerity, members skilled in Shāstras, and other holy persons and said to his state-priest. (47/29-33)

Brāhmaṇas versed in Vedas may go and inspect the place of sacrifices. (47/34)

Brahmā said — Listening to the words of king state Priest did so. He proceeded with the ministers gladly. (47/35)

Keeping the Brāhmaṇas having good skill in the sacrifice before all the learned priests got built the sacrificial place, lanes and pigeon places at the village named Dhivar, according to the rules by the skilled artisans. (47/36-37)

Beautified with good jewels, decorated with gold, good to mind and alike palace of Indra, they got built hundreds of palaces. (47/38)

They also got built palaces (for ladies) for the stay of kings of various states decorated with columns, arches golden sacrificial – place. (47/39-40)

Also got built residential buildings for the stay of Brāhmaṇas and businessmen in numbers. (47/41)

The kings and their queens came to attend the ceremony with stones and jewels as gifts to king Indradyumna. (47/22)

O Brāhmaṇa ! The king paid honour to all the Brāhmaṇas who visited to his sacrifice with their pupils and saw them off personally to their residence. (47/46-47)

That brilliant king gave leave to proud. The artisans after

building the structure stated to the king about the accomplishment of the same. The King became hearty glad with his ministers. (47/48-49)

The king then asked — The princes should bring the horses of good qualities and having good signs, and then let them to move on the earth. (47/75)

Learned and versed in religion began to offer offerings to the fire (sacrificial fire). The sacrifice be started by calling the Brāhmaṇas and bringing the black goats, black deer, herdsmen of ox, cow and other animals and that Vishṇu-temple be erected. (47/76-77)

The desired goods be given in donation to the Brāhmaṇas. Beggars be given women, precious stones, village, town, good fertile land, territory and good wealth. (47/78)

No beggar should be replied with the word 'No'. The sacrifices be kept continued till god does not appear at the sacrificial place. (47/79-80)

All the persons were healthy, austere, sage, having long life in that sacrificial ceremony of the King. (47/97)

No sacrifice was ever performed in the past as that of the same with huge quantity of wealth. O great able Brāhmaṇas! The king (Indradyumna) got accomplished, thus, the performance of horse-sacrifice and building of Vishṇu –temple. (47/98).

The above description regarding the building a Vishṇu-temple and performance of a horse-sacrifice by a southern India king of the past in his empire throws light on the issue of developmental work. In which all the kings of his empire took part, offered gifts of various kinds and shared in the expenses by way of offering wealth. Whether it would have been under the pressure of political power or by pleasant heart, it matters little. Anybody who participates in a ceremony politically organized and monetarily contributes in the same plays an important role. His participation and contribution had values in the ancient Indian empires. With the passage of time it became conventional to participate in such works or ceremonies, if invited.

The Brāhmaṇas, the subjects and the poors witnessed such functions as a token of their appreciation and good wishes to the organizer king. With the viewpoint of economic, it may be said that it was a kind of distribution of the wealth ceremony of a state among the subjects of various classes.

However, the building of glorious Vishṇu temple in his empire, may be treated as the beginning of its kind. It paced an example before the kings and wealthy persons to follow the suit. The people and the kings in ancient India did follow and began to take interest in such works thereafter.

■

Index